Columba

Ian Finlay

Richard Drew Publishing
Glasgow

First published 1979 Victor Gollancz Ltd.

This edition first published 1990 by
Richard Drew Publishing Ltd.,
6 Clairmont Gardens
Glasgow G3 7LW

© Ian Finlay 1979

The publisher acknowledges the financial assistance of the Scottish Arts
Council in the publication of this book

British Library Cataloguing in Publication Data
Finlay, Ian
Columba.
    1. Christian church. Columba, Saint of Iona
    I. Title
    270.2092

ISBN 0-86267-276-7

*Printed and bound in Great Britain by
Cox & Wyman Ltd., Reading*

EIRINN
AND
ALBA

Names underlined
indicate Columban
foundations

LEWIS

HARRIS

SKYE

NORTHERN PICTS

Inverness

MORAY FIRTH

Burghead

Applecross

Monymusk

Loch Ness

GREAT GLEN OF ALBA

Drumalbain

The Mounth

RÙM

SOUTHERN PICTS

Dunkeld

STRATHMORE

Brechin

COLL

L. Linnhe

Arbroath

F. OF TAY

TIREE

LORNE

Abernethy

MULL

DALRIADA

F. OF FORTH

IONA (Hy)

COLONSAY

ORONSAY

Dunadd

Dumbarton

LOTHIAN

JURA

Glasgow

Coldingham

KINTYRE

STRATHCLYDE

Lindisfarne

ISLAY

ARRAN

F. OF CLYDE

Melrose

NORTHUMBRIA

Swilly

Tory

GALLOWAY

Ruthwell

Foyle

Gartan

Coleraine

DALRIADA

Aran L.

Temple
Douglas

Derry

Drum Ceat

Whithorn

Kirkmadrine

Glencolumille

Raphoe

Moyola

MAN

Lough
Neagh

Bangor

Moville

Strangford
Lough

Emain
Macha

Armagh

IRISH SEA

CUMBRIA

Cul Dreimne

Sligo

Drumcliff

Kilmore

Louth

Kells

Teilte

Monasterboice

Ardagh

ANGLESEY

Clonard

Tara

Swords

Durrow

Dublin

Clonmacnoise

Kildare

Noone

Clonfert

Glendalough

WALES

N

E

W

S

Contents

List of Illustrations

Foreword

Not many visitors to Iona, Lindisfarne and the Irish foundations mentioned in this book go there in the spirit of the ancient pilgrims. Those places are on the tourist circuit. In the summer season, the castle of Lindisfarne is beleaguered by an army of parked cars as Bamburgh opposite once was by the pagan hordes of Penda of Mercia. Now Iona may be under a threat more lasting than the Viking forays. Before this book is published a car-ferry service, subsidised by "Euro-money", will be in operation between Fionnphort and the island, although we are assured it is for residents' convenience only. Difficulty of access was the main factor in the choice of such consecrated places. The fathers of the Celtic church were willing to suffer the "red martyrdom" for a cause which combined service to the community with the search for truth through contemplation in lonely spots. Columba, it is true, was a man in whom secular ambition often conflicted with the urge to preach the Word of God, yet he is not remembered as Wolsey and other princes of the church who were also statesmen are remembered. He was a king-maker, but he built no palaces nor owned any worldly riches. There is a great deal in him for our contemporary world to ponder on.

It was in an attempt to re-kindle fire in the long-cold ashes of a church which had perished in the face of worldliness and material power that the (then) Rev. George MacLeod founded the Iona Community in 1938, and the outward symbol of its efforts is the restored abbey-church. The abbey is medieval. It is therefore scarcely referred to in the pages which follow; but the spirit behind its restoration is a memorial to the saint who for half his life made his home on this island, and it is fitting that white doves now coo and flutter about its eaves, even if at times Columba could be hawk as well as dove.

Once, long ago, to my astonishment, the late T. S. Eliot invited me to write a book bearing on an aspect of church history, and I declined in some confusion since I knew I was not equipped to do such a thing. I am even less well equipped to write about a saint. I am doing so now only because I believe that Celtic art, both pagan and Christian, may be able to throw a little light into the darkness of the age of this particular saint. Consequently, this is a very personal interpretation of the life and times of Columba. Certainly no one else is involved in the conclusions drawn. One or two specialists have been consulted on particular points. Professor Charles Thomas, now Director of the Institute of Cornish Studies, has been good enough to comment on queries which I put to him. Dr Isabel Henderson has been most helpful on Pictish issues, and I am indebted to Dr Wendy Davies of University College, London, for many corrections and suggestions in Chapters II, X and XII. Professor Frend kindly allowed me to make a drawing from a photograph he gave me some years ago. I would also thank Mark Fiennes for the trouble he took in taking photographs specially in Ireland, and the Scottish Arts Council for a generous grant towards the cost of the Irish photographs.

I

The Pagan Heritage

The familiar St Columba, the Columba of the story-books, comes very close to being a myth. Many of the great figures of far-off times have had their images transformed or contorted through the centuries, but with Columba the process began almost as soon as he was dead, and the real man has been obscured—some would say beyond recall. The search for him is a search for evidence which, if it cannot be verified, at least has a certain ring of truth about it. From this it may be possible to piece together a convincing personality who fits into the picture of what is known about the age he lived in.

We have to go right back to the beginning, but what is the beginning? Some would say the place mainly associated with him in the popular mind: Iona. It is certainly a tempting place to begin, evocative. entrancing. Thirty miles or so of road winding through Mull on a summer afternoon culminate in a silvery seascape, and the sacred island floating darkly in a path of light. The road ends on the rocks of Fionnphort. A short wait for the ferry-boat gives time for the eye to grow accustomed to the incredible colours of rock and sand and water, especially the translucent, transmuting water. It seems to be the verge of another world. Impulsively one feels the story of the man who set the seal of fame on it should write itself. On the other side of the ferry this feeling becomes stronger. On a calm day the drowsy air, warmed by the sea current which brings with it the occasional exotic nut or even a loggerhead turtle from the Gulf of Mexico to these western shores, is made more seductive by the scents of the water-margin and the flower-flecked *machair*, the cropped turf behind the beaches. The Gaelic names of bay and creek are mostly linked with the saint. The ancient cross of St Martin, slim yet surviving a thousand years of winter gales, and the abbey, and the tombs of kings of Scotland, Ireland and Norway—all these things confirm one's belief in the rightness of this as a starting-place . . . until it is realised that perhaps not a single stone of them all, not even "Columba's pillow", has a direct link with the saint. This is where he lived for half his life, and there is a great deal to find out about him here when one knows what one is looking for, but Ionà is not the place to begin the search. There is certainly plenty of the baffling beauty in which so much of the Celtic world is misted over; but as for Columba, we are left with that familiar ghost-image of a man too insubstantial to have survived a year in the ruthless environment of the sixth century.

Is the search, then, to begin on the library shelves? The earliest book on the saint was written by Cuminius, or Cuimine, Abbot of Iona about half a century after Columba. The most celebrated *Life of St Columba* is by the slightly-later abbot, Adomnán, which has appeared in various translations, with learned commentaries. Then there are numerous chronicles of later times, such as the "Old Irish Life" contained in the *Leabhar Breac*, compiled towards the end of the fourteenth century, and the annals of an Abbot of Clonmacnoise who lived in the days of William the Conqueror, Tigernach O'Braein. Last but not least, there is the *Ecclesiastical History* of the Venerable Bede who, about two centuries after Columba, collected an astonishing amount of information on the history of the British peoples without stirring beyond the walls of his monastery at Wearmouth and Jarrow.

Of those books Adomnán's is by far the most important for a study of Columba, and yet it is a curious, bewildering work. The Duke of Argyll, in his little volume on Iona published in 1884, confesses to an early inclination to throw Adomnán across the room, so exasperating did he find the book. The ducal reaction is understandable. At first glance the *Life* reads like a rather rambling fairy-tale. Although its title seems to promise a consecutive account of the saint's birth and career and death, it provides nothing of the sort. Strange, sometimes enthralling, only in its final, moving episode does it cease to be frustrating. There are three sections to it. The first deals with Columba's prophecies, the second with his miracles, the third with his visions of angels. Even within those categories there is not much sense of order and, as the duke protests, many of the happenings are so childish that it is astonishing they were acceptable even to the age for which the book was written. It has had many critics in modern times. In *The Early Scottish Church*, the Rev. Thomas M'Lauchlan went far further than the duke and said of Adomnán that "a greater congeries of absurdity and pure fable does not exist within the range of literature, civil or sacred, than his life of Columba".

Cuimine the Fair, from whom Adomnán drew much of his material, is no more factual, although he must have met and spoken with people who had known the saint. The "Old Irish Life", a discourse which Professor W. F. Skene printed conveniently in translation as an appendix to Volume II of his monumental and invaluable *Celtic Scotland*, is in similar vein. Bede is another matter: his account alone aims at being a true chronicle of events, but what he has set down is hearsay, and with him, too, history slips easily into hagiology, although he was not a fey Celt but an Angle. Together those works build up an idealised picture of the saint, and in the last century or two they have given rise to the sentimental tales and the equally sentimental paintings which are accepted as though based on proven facts.

Yet we have to be wary. It is easy to sway back too far the other way, as M'Lauchlan and other writers have done, disbelieving almost everything. Those ancient hagiologies were set down as paeans of praise, sometimes deliberate "writing-up" for political ends, but they are not to be swept aside as unfounded. The man they are all about was real enough, and much that looks as if it must be true can be sifted from them, but it is not so much a question of study as of what is now commonly called gut-reaction. There is a world of difference between trying to discern Columba in those early writings and trying to get a picture of the historical Christ from the gospels. The Columban hagiologists copied one another, the gospels provide four separate narratives, four versions of their subject. And the gospels can be placed in a setting of Roman and Jewish history which is in many things verifiable: we know beyond doubt that Pilate was prefect of Judaea at the time of Christ's death, and that one Jesus of Nazareth was executed for "sorcery" on the eve of the Passover. But there is no framework of contemporary chronicles against which to check Cuimine or Adomnán. So as far as those books on the library shelves are concerned, we seem baffled by a smoke-screen of pious praise. Columba is still a ghost, and there is nothing yet which feels real to the touch.

Biblical exegesis is being helped by archaeology. Is it possible, then, to find any pointers to the truth about Columba by digging for them? Biblical history was made among peoples who were builders and engineers, so that excavations can reveal much. The Celt built in perishable materials. We know from Adomnán and Bede that the structures of Columba's day were of wattle and daub or of timber, and were modest at that. Material evidence of habitations or places of worship in the age of Columba, therefore, consist mainly of a few small stone structures scattered in remote places, and even those are subsequent replacements of the timber cells and oratories which the saint and his brethren knew. However, Professor Charles Thomas in his *Early Christian Archaeology of North Britain* firmly holds the view that it is possible to construct a framework for Christian events of the fifth to the eighth centuries using only archaeological, artistic and architectural data. This brings a gleam of hope, if it does not promise any direct light on the personality of Columba.

I am not an archaeologist. My own field lies in certain areas of art history, and there are no obvious clues here because in Columba's lifetime Irish Christianity had shown few signs of the wonderful contribution to the arts which was to come. I had in fact decided there could be nothing worth following up when there came to mind a gloomy winter day during a period of some weeks, long years ago, when my duties led me to the National Museum of Antiquities of Scotland. On that particular day I handled for the first time an object which is among the museum's most precious possessions: the Monymusk reliquary. I spent some hours with it, making notes and drawings—drawings because some of the detail is too delicate for a camera to do it justice.

I was not looking for anything new, because the reliquary has been described and discussed by scholars over many generations, but I recall the excitement of discovering for myself the beauty of this little box, and also a sense of privilege in being able to handle it. In the middle ages many must have looked on it as the Palladium of Scotland. Is the other name for it not the Brec-bennoch of St Columba? There was an ancient tradition that if it be carried thrice, sunwise, around the army of the clan of Columba himself, the Cinel Conaill Gulban, victory must follow.

Reliquaries were made to contain relics. The repute and potency of this one were supposed to derive from its being the receptacle of a celebrated relic, the *Cathach* or "Battler", a psalter reputedly penned by Columba. The *Cathach* survives and is preserved in the Royal Irish Academy in Dublin, but is rather too large to have been contained in the Monymusk reliquary. This awkward fact does not rule out the possibility that the reliquary held some other equally precious relic of the saint. Whether there is or is not any real connection with Columba, the reliquary certainly belonged to the Columban church and must reflect the essential spirit of that church. It is one of a very small group of similar reliquaries to have survived, and is perhaps the finest of them. They are widely scattered. Some—the two fragments at St Germain-en-Laye, for example—may mark the routes of forgotten Irish missions; others, whole or in fragments salved from Viking graves, are in Scandinavian museums, memorials to unknown monks martyred by the Northmen on Irish or Scottish shores. They are all witnesses to the nature, aims and influence of the church which Columba served, although after his time, and in their way are as solidly significant as the Basilica of St Peter's. And this reliquary was made by an unknown craftsman at approximately the time, give or take twenty years or so, when Adomnán sat in his cell on Iona writing the *Vita Sancti Columbae*.

The reliquary is quite tiny, about $4\frac{1}{2}$ inches long, a wooden box carved from the solid, clad in thin sheet bronze and silver plates, with areas of enamel. It resembles a house of hip-roofed type—a roof, that is, with sloping ends and sides—and here we come to the first and most obvious glimpse of the age which produced it, for it is modelled on one of those stone oratories already referred to, among the best examples of which are the Gallarus oratory in Co. Kerry and the building known as St Columba's House at Kells, Co. Meath. Translate stone back into wood and we have a rough idea of the primitive chapels with which Columba and monks of his time were content. The ridge-member of the reliquary represents the roof-tree of the oratory. But there is much more to learn from this little piece, from its materials and technique and from its ornament. The sophisticated and tasteful handling of metals betrays a very ancient Celtic tradition reaching back into the Iron Age culture which the Celts brought from central Europe to Gaul and Britain. The use of enamels points to the same tradition. The most important evidence, however, is to be read from the decorative patterns, especially those lightly pricked on the silver surfaces, which take the form of zoomorphs, fantastic animals borrowed by the Celts from the pagan eastern neighbours. Nowhere on this holy object is there anything recognisable as a Christian symbol:

Monymusk reliquary: detail of silver panel

neither cross, nor image of Christ, nor even the *Chi-Rho* sign denoting the name of Christ which appears on some of the early stones.

It seems strange that the pious abbot, Adomnán, was describing miracles and visions of angels for a community dedicated to spreading the gospels while blessed relics were being preserved in boxes entirely pagan in their decoration. Nor is this feature confined to reliquaries: the magnificent Ardagh chalice in Dublin, only surviving chalice of the early Irish church, could be the wine-cup of a pagan king but for a band inscribed with the names of the Apostles. Why this should be is wide open to speculation, but it would seem that ancient ways and perhaps ancient beliefs were still alive in the minds of those who made and used those pieces, consecrated though they must have been.

So the Columban church was employing, or tolerating, pagan imagery and symbolism a hundred years after the Age of Saints, the sixth century. . . . This might be a chink of light through the mists. It is not enough to illuminate the figure of Columba himself, but perhaps enough to help us read more than seemed evident at first in the pages of Adomnán and the others. One difficulty is that we examine those pages with our twentieth-century eyes which distort, possibly grotesquely, the outlook of early Christians, and particularly early Irish Christians. With the reliquary as pointer, we can go back to Adomnán and maybe discover new significance in much of what he says. Adomnán himself might be bewildered if he knew what the modern world had made of his saint. Columba's love of place, of his people, and above all of trees, birds and animals, have touched off a response in us which makes us picture him as something between St Francis of Assisi and the Vicar of Selborne; but the briefest scrutiny of what we know of sixth-century Ireland should make it clear that this notion is as wide of the mark as it could be.

A century or more ago eminent scholars such as Skene and Bishop Reeves certainly saw him as a commanding spiritual figure, but they knew far too much about the period and about Columba's own background to picture him as the conventional idea of a saint. He was a man of the earth he trod, who shared in the instincts and emotions of his people. The reliquary also proves that the church did not regard the pagan heritage as the antithesis of its own faith, did not require that it be thrust out as of the Devil. We know there was a practice of patient replacement of pagan meanings by Christian ones, and that old tales were re-interpreted, which may explain the Irish crozier found at Ekerö in Sweden on which a plainly pagan monster swallowing a man is to be read as the whale consuming Jonah; but the reliquary suggests not so much reinterpretation as actual duality of belief, keeping the options open.

I may be reading too much into some zoomorphic decoration; but it has to be remembered that in those times decoration was never meaningless, as it has become today, and the idea of keeping the options open is a perfectly natural and understandable one in a world where superstitious terror was universal. It seems at least there was no simple antagonism between new beliefs and old. Perhaps in Columba's day the ancient teaching was looked upon not as false, but as night preceding day. There is a common belief that St Patrick converted Ireland to Christianity in the fifth century. If he had made it a clean sweep we should expect Ireland to be familiar with Christian iconography a hundred years after Patrick's death. True enough, after Patrick much of the country lapsed into apostasy; but by the time Columba came much ground seems to have been recovered. That reliquaries and other sacred objects take this curiously equivocal form long after Columba's lifetime would imply that the people still wanted the best of both worlds, pagan and Christian, and that in some sort of fashion the church went along with them, if only to keep its hold on them. St Patrick, with his episcopal hierarchy, may have been more uncompromising: he was not an Irishman, but a Roman provincial. In Ireland, where the legions had never set foot, much of what he stood for must have been alien. Tribal society in Ireland was not structured to support a church on the Roman model, however successful initially Patrick's mission may have been. Ireland still belonged in the Iron Age. This is what the anomaly of the reliquary means. To get at the real Columba, then, surely first we have to look into his pagan heritage.

However, it would be wrong and misleading to think the Irish were "uncivilised" by comparison with the Christian Britons over the water. Superficially they might have seemed so; but despite the long Roman occupation, in Britain itself an Iron Age mentality and outlook lurked very close below the surface of society. In towns and on the estates of the big villas people may have lived much as they did in other parts of the Empire, and, when Christianity replaced the old gods as the official religion, the ruling class at least conformed. After the legions withdrew, the framework of civil institutions and of military establishments enabled the faith to survive indefinitely in its established form, although barbarian hordes had cut communications with Imperial Rome herself. Yet there are signs in plenty that in the country districts, at least among peasantry and slaves, the old paganism was very much alive and needed only a weakening of authority to show itself. There is no lack of artistic evidence for this. Crudely-sculpted stone heads have turned up in numbers showing features which reveal a hoary ancestry reaching back into Gaul and Germany and as far as Bohemia. In Ireland of course the ancient beliefs and superstitions were overt, for the *tuatha* or tribes were living in conditions more like those in Gaul before the time of Caesar, or in Boudicca's Britain. They were ruled by petty kings who lived as their ancestors had done, fighting among themselves, eating and drinking hugely, worshipping nature spirits and believing in a fantasy world of gods and heroes sung by bards whose honour and prosperity depended upon the eloquence with which they gave pleasure to their patrons. How missions like Patrick's—and his was not the first—escaped martyrdom in such a country is astonishing, but it is a matter for careful thought.

If it is surprising that the church could come to terms with such paganism and tolerate its symbolism, it is even more so that the pagans did not at once obliterate Patrick and in due course Columba and other saints. Just how primitive were those pagan beliefs? Mercy and love played no part in them. Tradition and legend make this obvious, and indirectly so do some surviving art objects. Take that odd-looking stone monument in Co. Galway, the Turoe stone. It is a four-foot monolith with domed top, carved in low relief in the style known as La Tène, originating in the early Iron Age. What rites it may have been involved in no

one can say, but it probably has phallic significance. The important thing is that it points back to other comparable stones, the Kermaria stone from Brittany now in the National Museum of Antiquities at St Germain-en-Laye, the Pfalzfeld pillar in the Landesmuseum at Bonn, monuments to a cult universal among the Celts. The Pfalzfeld pillar reveals a little more of what lay behind those stones, because the sinister head with lobed horns carved on it appears to involve it in the grisly head-cult of the Celts, the most explicit evidence of which is to be found in a museum on the waterfront in Marseilles, where there is a fragment of the temple from Roquepertuse with niches for

Turoe stone, Co. Galway. 2nd cent. BC

the skulls of slain enemies. Classical writers say heads were fixed on stakes at the doors of houses, heads which the Gauls dedicated to their gods. The early literature tells of Irish warriors doing the same, a practice which may well have persisted into Columba's day. What is certain is that the universal magma of primeval superstition in Ireland was not overlaid even by that thin crust of distaste for such things obviously existing in the Empire, where some at least thought murderous rituals beastly. It would hardly have been surprising if Columba's head had ended up on some chieftain's doorpost.

There were several reasons why he and his brother-saints went unharmed in Ireland, but perhaps the main one is that they thought and felt like the people they converted in such numbers. The reliquary is a good symbol of their attitude, their virtual dualism. Hints that this is true can be deduced from a careful reading of Adomnán. Look, for example, at Columba's pre-occupation with birds. All accounts of the Irish saints record their love of birds, and of the bond between the saints and the birds. In Huyshe's edition of Adomnán's *Life* the editor remarks that Adomnán was right not to omit the "charming incident" of the visiting crane, "although of minor importance". This celebrated incident is not of minor importance, nor does "charming" describe it. In that dark, dangerous age there were no bird-watchers or bird-lovers in the sense in which those words are now used, and if Columba did indeed rescue the crane stranded on Iona—and there is no reason to doubt he did—then I think this is some kind of symbolic allusion. This bird had been sacred

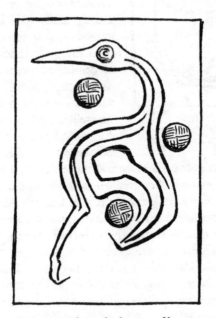

Crane or stork on cheek-piece of bronze helmet. Eastern Celts, Yugoslavia, 2nd cent. BC

among his ancestors for a thousand years or more. In a later chapter it will be mentioned that he was contemptuously referred to as "the crane-cleric", and that in his anger he changed his tormentor and her maid into cranes. The truth is buried deep in a tangle of legends, and we may be sure it is stranger than the charming fiction which has grown around it. Why was the saint so incensed at being associated with this bird? Had the antagonism between his beliefs tortured him?

Many things point to his awareness of his pagan heritage. The struggle within him is expressed in some of the verses attributed to him, such as the often-quoted lines:

> I adore not the voice of birds,
> Nor the *sreod*, nor a destiny on the earthly world,
> Nor a son, nor chance, nor woman:
> My *drui* is Christ the son of God.

Skene considers the struggle is between him and the pagan system he opposed among the Picts, but this view ignores the references to "son" and "woman". Surely the meaning of it is that he is trying to renounce his own desires and temptations, and those include the urge of pagan beliefs such as bird-lore. Of course there is no way of proving he ever wrote those lines or others like them, but whoever did was aware of this struggle within.

Ornithomancy was a powerful force in Ireland and in western Scotland, and persisted into recent times. The early art of the region is crowded with bird images, all of them significant. Even more is the literature filled with them. Devotion to poetry is so often stressed in the old accounts of Columba that we may take it to be true. He must therefore have loved the legends of how Cuchulainn harnessed swans to his chariot and of the swans linked by silver chains in the Dream of Angus. More, he cannot have been impervious to the bird superstitions of his race, and must have shared in their fear of the dreaded raven goddess, the Morrígan, dark prophet of doom; however, he may have preached to them that the Word of God drives out such weakness. There was not a day when the croak of ravens did not filter through the mists cloaking Benbulban or the Mourne Mountains, or the slaty shoulder of Ben More opposite Iona, a sound better able to deafen its hearers to the Word, if they were Celts, than any image of the gods was able to make an apostate of a Christian Roman.

References to animals as well as birds in Adomnán must be weighed for their possible cult significance, and this does not exclude the saint's friend, the old white horse. The tale of its fore-knowledge of his death and of his sad farewell to it has been told over and over again, and paintings of it like John Duncan's have been used to illustrate books about the saint. I would not discount the incident as another romantic legend, any more than I would discount the crane incident, but I do suggest there is more to it than at first appears. Some may say I am looking into simple stories for a significance which is just not there, but I am sure none of those ancient stories is as simple as it seems, although one may well make the wrong deductions. I am not alone in this suspicion. Dr Ross singles out the white horse legend, and puts it in the category of what might be called the hero-and-horse association. There is a parallel in the gift to Cuchulainn of horses foaled at the moment of his own birth. Throughout Celtic history there was an association between the warrior-aristocrat and his horse, and in the princely burials of the Rhineland the remains of horses and chariots and rich horse-furniture are emblematic of the status of the dead. On Celtic coins the horse appears as a weird, abstract symbol of power and authority. Does our concept of chivalry not derive from the ideal of the gentle knight raised above lesser men on his horse's back? Columba was a prince of the blood-royal, a chevalier, in Roman parlance a member of the *Equites*, and the annalists may have felt a deep impulse to try somehow to associate his passing with a horse—his horse. This notion sounds grotesque: the old horse was no charger, but the animal which drew the milk-cart from the byre to the monastery. Well, the horses on the coinage might have been drawn by Walt Disney. It was the symbol that mattered. It is possible the lesson of this story is that Columba was looked upon not only as a Christian saint but as a Celtic hero.

Adomnán repeatedly describes the saint's power over animals, and nobody familiar with Celtic mythology would take those

stories at their face value. Some at least symbolise his struggle with
the old beliefs. A good example is his confrontation with a dreaded
wild boar on the Isle of Skye, which will come into a later

Gold coin of the Parisii. 1st cent. BC

chapter. The boar was a common animal in the forests of Britain,
and of Ireland too, but it is one of the principal cult animals of
the pagan Celts everywhere. Representations of it are numerous
in early Celtic art. They range from the curious, stylised emblem
on the Witham Abbey shield in the British Museum to the
exquisitely carved creature on the breast of the boar-god from
Euffigneix at St Germain-en-Laye, and there are good Scottish
examples like the boar of Knocknagael, near Inverness. There
were ritual boar-hunts, and it was a boar-hunt which Columba
witnessed on Skye. I am confident Adomnán saw this encounter
as a pagan-Christian one.

This close understanding of, and even sympathy with, the old
beliefs is part of the reason why the Saints of Ireland were not
martyred for their faith; but there is more to it than that, for
there was one element in their beliefs which, in a way, Irish
pagans and Christians held in common: the belief in a life after
death, preached by the druids. How Christians could have anything in common with a pagan religion presided over by a body

with such an unsavoury reputation as the druids must be hard to envisage, so perhaps the first step is to look a little more closely at the druids.

They are not a priesthood about which a great deal is known for certain. Adomnán is rather uninformative on the subject. He refers to them as Magi, in the sense of sorcerers, but tells us nothing except that they were the core of the opposition to Columba. There is not any specific archaeological evidence about them anywhere at any time, although anything we may infer from the Roquepertuse temple or from objects like the Gundestrup cauldron in Copenhagen suggests a sinister rôle. To make things more difficult, there has been in the last two or three centuries an accumulation of romantic nonsense which has obscured what little we know with an entirely fictional image, and this has excited such impatience in some scholars that they may have underestimated the druids. Their attitude may be summed up in the verdict that because we have little or no hard evidence of druidic achievement or wisdom the druids may be dismissed as the shamans or witch-doctors of the Celtic barbarians. Classical authors provide the foundation for this idea. Caesar, Strabo, Tacitus and others describe ritual sacrifices, including human sacrifices, and Tacitus specifically implicates the druids of Britain, declaring that they covered their altars with the blood of captives and used their entrails for divination. Here we have to remember that crushing the druids was central to Roman policy in the subjection of Britain, and it was carried out mercilessly, as in the massacre on Anglesey in AD 61; so that Tacitus' emphasis on the bloody groves and howling priests could have been to justify Paulinus and his soldiers. No doubt cruelties were perpetrated by those priests: mercy was not a common virtue in the ancient world, and the abominations in Roman arenas were obnoxious to Augustus himself. The real reason for exterminating the druids is that the Romans saw them as repositories of power. Celtic peoples were scattered over the countryside, without administrative centres. It is difficult to defeat conclusively such peoples or to hold them down, and if the druids had a strong spiritual or superstitious hold on the community an invader naturally would try to eliminate them. It is in the druids, as Professor Piggott has said, that the "essentially un-Roman Celtic tradition was concentrated". The attack by Rome on druidism is perhaps the most solid evidence we have of the supreme status and power of the druids.

What we cannot know—and this is of prime importance in looking at the transition to Christianity in Ireland—is about the quality of druidic thought. Were they philosophers and theologians, or just controllers of the sacred rituals? The comment of a modern writer that their ritual and beliefs "were banality itself" is sheer speculation *in vacuo*, since we know little for sure about their ritual, and not much more about their beliefs. Oddly enough, some classical writers put their intellectual and spiritual standing very high indeed, and equate their achievement in moral philosophy with that of other ancient peoples. One thing which does seem certain is that they believed in life after death, for it was with a promise of this that they exhorted warriors to show courage in battle. It was not mere *quid pro quo* for self-sacrifice.

Gibbon records in a footnote that the Gauls entrusted not merely their lives but their money to the security of another world. He is referring to the amusement of Valerius Maximus over the willingness of Gauls to lend money on the assurance it would be paid back in the next life. Diodorus Siculus says that at funerals letters were thrown on the funeral pyre so the dead might read them. The druids certainly preached immortality. For the Celt, the place of the dead was no gloomy underworld but a paradise, a paradise somewhere in the setting sun. Procopius of Byzantium, roughly contemporary with Columba, tells of the northern Gauls' belief in the Happy Isles, to which the souls of the dead were ferried. This is the Gaelic Tir nan Og, the Brythonic Lyonesse, the Arthurian Avilon

> Where fall not hail or rain, or any snow,
> Nor ever wind blows loudly; but it lies
> Deep-meadowed, happy, fair with orchard lawns
> And bowery hollows crowned with summer sea.

Descriptions of this abode are countless in the ancient legends:

"Jewels and gold there are in abundance, and honey and wine; the trees bear fruit and blossoms and green leaves all the year round. Fine swords and rich robes, steeds and hounds, countless herds, maidens without number; and above all, neither decline, nor death, nor decay." These things were offered to Ossian by Niam of the Golden Hair. It is an unsubtle sort of heaven. It cannot be translated into metaphysical terms or justified in terms of morals—morals, that is, as we might use the word, for to the Celts it was a reward for behaving as a warrior should.

It is not even easy to know whether those visions of an after-life represent what the druids and bards really taught, as they were committed to the written word by Christian scribes whose own notions may have influenced the transcriptions. Were the souls of the dead kinds of angels, or ghosts wandering in a paradise? How does one differentiate them from other spirits, from the *side*, ghosts of ancestors supposed to tenant the great prehistoric barrows? The otherworld seems a confused and rambling concept, but there is no doubt that from earliest times the Celts did believe in the survival of the soul. Is it possible Columba's own heaven was coloured by those legends?

This belief in an immortal soul, however far removed from the Christian belief, must have made the process of conversion to Christianity less difficult. For a Roman to become Christian was a much more traumatic experience, surely. He had to accept a doctrine emanating from the province of Judaea proclaiming that some inexplicable part of him, which he could not feel or know, would go on living after his death. It contradicted everything the wisdom of the world's greatest civilisation had to say on the subject of death. In the *De Senectute*, Cicero sums up Graeco-Roman thought about death: it brings an end to the troubles and suffering of this life, and if we no longer suffer we no longer exist. Long before, Plato had made Socrates assure those who vainly voted for his acquittal that death is no evil—either it is a long, untroubled sleep or a world in which there are no unjust judges; but this is hardly a promise of immortality. Roman society probably thought about the problem as Lucretius did: "The end is a sound slumber, and a long good night." Whatever peasants thought, the leaders and intellectuals had long ago seen through the mythology which served as a state religion, with its amoral deities and unpredictable rewards and punishments, and those who still offered sacrifices on the splendid altars in the temples did so in hope of gain in this world, not in another. Even poets dreamed of nothing more encouraging than a dark existence beyond the Styx, and Achilles' ghost tells Ulysses he would rather be a pauper's hireling on earth than a king of all the dead. Caesar himself in the Senate declared his disbelief in an after-life. The Christian promise of entry into heaven may have been grasped eagerly by the downtrodden, but for the average Roman citizen, born to an empire founded on material power and possessions, there was a high price to pay for eternal life, whatever that might mean.

Classical writers who said favourable things about the druids, like Posidonius, may have seen them through rosy spectacles for their own purposes, but a priesthood which managed to survive from a primeval age must have dispensed more than accumulated superstitions. There was, surely, a considerable store of wisdom in their teaching. Druidical thinking has been virtually obliterated from the pages of history because, as Professor Proinsias MacCana has put it, "the monastic redactors did in fact suppress elements of druidic teaching and practice which they could not record without seeming to compromise the doctrines of the universal Church". Something we do know is that the druids were largely responsible for education among the Celts, and this was not limited to ritual. The fragmented Calendar of Coligny, of the first century, reflects mathematical capacity of a high order. We have no way of knowing the full scope of their learning; but the ancient Celts, if they were devious and ambiguous—as Celts still are!—were nimble in mind and brilliantly imaginative, so those who taught their young people must have been proficient. How Irish Celts of the sixth century stood in such matters can only be guessed at; but there may be an indication in the remarkable learning of some of the early monks, who were able exponents of Latin, sometimes of Greek, possibly even of Hebrew, because ability of this order implies a certain background of intellectual attainment. That druidical schools had considerable pedagogical standards is indicated by the fact that the earliest monastic schools sometimes took them over.

There is one element of druidical worship which keeps covertly creeping into the pages of Adomnán, recognisable if one is alert to it. It is the sacred wood. This has played a strange, an obsessive part in the history of western beliefs and superstitions from prehistoric times, and Columba seems to have been influenced by it. The sacred grove is of course part of the very fabric of Frazer's great book, *The Golden Bough*, beginning with its unforgettable picture of Lake Nemi and its grove. His evidence shows how worship of the oak, the tree of Zeus, is deeply implicated in the Aryan religions and how sinister were some of its mysteries. The name of Nemi, a Latin word meaning a grove, or a grove with a clearing in it, is perpetuated in the Celtic *nemeton*, and this occurs in place-names scattered from Galatia in Asia Minor right across Europe as far as Scotland. Creag Neimidh in Glen Urquhart, the Rock of the Sanctuary, is an example. The depths of such groves, especially oak groves, were typical sites of druid sanctuaries. Lucan's *Pharsalia* describes them and their dark rituals, and when Caesar felled the trees of such a sanctuary in the Marseilles neighbourhood the men who were ordered to do it, perhaps as a calculated part of the humiliation of the priesthood, were terrified of the task. Ireland had such groves, called in Old Irish *fidnemed*. Eventually wooden temples were built in the clearings, but it is the oaks themselves which were sacred. Oaks and wisdom are identified. And the mistletoe, to which the oak is host, is a vital element in the mystery, the druid cutting it with a golden sickle. Mistletoe seems to have been the repository of the secret of life and death among several ancient peoples. It was, in fact, the Golden Bough. Divinity was invisible, intangible, beyond man's apprehension, but somehow was embodied in the oak. We have to keep this in mind, I think, when we read in Adomnán those apparently casual references to the oak, those nostalgic memories of Derry . . .

My Derry, my little Oak Grove.

There were no oak groves on Iona. Columba's feelings were no mere sentiment; they went to the roots of his being.

So in the years of Ireland's conversion to the Christian faith there were no martyrdoms, whereas the arenas of Rome had been drenched in Christian blood. Not only did the old belief live on beside the new in Ireland: the faith of the church in Ireland in one respect at least seems fundamentally different from the Christianity of the Roman Empire. From the start the Saints of Ireland are like strangers to the world which centred on the Eternal City. They believed in the same gospels as their Roman contemporaries, they were able to converse in the same tongue, yet Celt and Roman were no more reconciled than their ancestors had been when they watched one another warily across the barrier of the Alps. The deep difference between them is clearly seen in their art. Before they accepted Christ the Celts had tended to avert their eyes from what was sacred to them and took refuge in symbolism. The new faith took centuries to change this. The Romans had seen their gods in the likeness of men, and before long so did they see God. The Judaic prohibition of images could not prevail against the heritage of Hellenism, and the cult of the holy icon was to grow until in the end it dominated Christendom. Adomnán by the time he wrote the *Vita Sancti Columbae* had surrendered to pressure and adopted Roman ritual, and in his First Preface he apologises for the "barbarous Irish tongue", so harsh by comparison with foreign speech; but his natural instincts are unchanged, and he seizes upon the first opportunity the Scriptures offer him to communicate in symbols. He introduces the man of blessed memory he is writing of with a play on words which almost sets his subject beside Christ, when he reminds us the Holy Ghost "descended on the Only Begotten of the Eternal Father in the form of that little bird which is called columba". This is the kind of symbolism which any of his countrymen could understand. It belonged in the dream-world of their pagan heritage.

II

The Coming of Christianity

The active presence of paganism in Ireland in the Age of Saints is more easily recognised than the routes by which the new faith was introduced. Nor is it at once obvious whether one can extend the theory that, in Ireland, the new faith somehow differed from Christian practices on the continent of Europe, making it less hard for the Lamb of God to lie down among the lions of a notoriously fierce and quarrelsome pagan people. Here again the early literary sources are not of great help. There is, however, some surviving evidence, visual evidence, mainly from the sixth century which will help to throw light on those problems.

We must turn to a group of rather crude monuments in the south-west corner of Scotland, which reaches out towards Ireland. Rough-hewn they may be, but they are extraordinarily moving. They are like flickering tapers promising a new dawn in a very dark age indeed, and to see and touch them now, fifteen centuries after they were chiselled, is to experience a kind of awe which major monuments do not always inspire. The oldest of the stones is in the Priory Museum at Whithorn, in Kirkcudbrightshire. It is called the Latinus stone, because the inscription, in not very good Latin, records it was erected in memory of one Latinus and his daughter by his grandson Barrovadus, and the date ascribed to it is about AD 450. The inscription begins with "We praise thee, O Lord". The other stones in the little museum are considerably later in date; but across Luce Bay, at Kirkmadrine Kirk in the Rhinns of Galloway, are several more stones, two of them sixth century, carrying the symbol we have been looking for, signally absent from the Monymusk reliquary: the cross. It is in the form so often used in the ancient, persecuted church, the *Chi-Rho* monogram, XP, representing the first two letters of the Greek rendering of the name of Christ. The *Chi* is in the shape of a dominant cross, the *Rho* a small appendage of one of its arms, and the whole is bounded by a circle which may stand for a halo. We are apt to forget how inspiring symbols of this sort must have been to those who risked their lives for what they stood for. Once, during the war, I showed a visiting party of the Maquis, the French freedom-fighters, around the Palace of Holyroodhouse in Edinburgh. Suddenly one of them pointed and shouted "Le Croix de Lorraine!" He had spied the double-armed cross, the Maquis symbol, in the arms of Mary, Queen of Scots, high on the west wall of the palace, and the effect was dramatic. The *Chi-Rho* was scratched on walls by Christians taking refuge in the catacombs as witness to their faith, just as here well north of the security of Hadrian's Wall.

The little *Rho* part of the symbol is not drawn as P but as P, the loop is incomplete, a form known as an open *Rho*. This occurs widely in southern Gaul, and has been said to have its origin in the East. Certainly these crosses stand at the end of a long road which leads back right across Europe, and from them we can read much about the church of Columba.

This road begins, as we would expect, in Palestine, but unlike the route which first brought Christianity to Britain it was not the direct road which had carried the legions. We know from the Bible it was the practice of holy men to withdraw into the wilderness, to lead a contemplative life, to exist on what they might find—the "locusts and wild honey". This began before the time of Christ, for the Jewish sect of the Essenes by the Dead Sea led what sounds like a monastic existence, and the finding of ancient manuscripts in caves near Qumran is material proof of such communities. As we know, Jesus too "lodged with the beasts" in the wilderness. But it was the persecutions of Nero and some emperors of the second and third centuries which drove large numbers not of Christians only but also of Jews into desert places; and it appears that fear of persecution was not the only motive, for the Empire had become corrupt and distasteful to men and women of principle, while, as Peter F. Anson has noted, even taxation and the cost-of-living were factors in the decision to flee to a simpler, purer life. Thousands made their way into the Egyptian desert where it was possible to exist in caves within reach of the fertile Delta and the Nile valley, which supplied them with food.

Behind this self-imposed exile, however, was a deep urge to seek the pure spirituality of the founding fathers of the church, by fasting and self-chastening to rid the flesh of all subjection to temptation. It was a primal longing the memory of which even the centuries and vast distances could not kill, if we read correctly the scene carved on the south side of the base of the great North Cross at Ahenny, Co. Tipperary, with its lone figure sitting under a palm tree surrounded by beasts. He could be St Anthony. St Anthony personalises the solitaries for most people. He has been dramatised by writers like Anatole France, who gloried in painting the temptations, reviled by others such as Gibbon, who called him an emaciated maniac; but communities of ascetics like him in the early fourth century made an enormous impact, and it was not their self-deprivation which carried the new spirit far and wide, so much as that return to a life of simplicity and love for their fellows, the teaching of their Master. Palladius in his *Historia Monachorum* tells of the joy with which the brethren came out to meet strangers, lavishing upon them what they had, and of their gentleness and humility and never-failing kindness. He also describes how their communities were self-supporting, in food and the weaving of linen. They were, of course, the founders of the monastic ideal.

Those big communities did not satisfy the extreme eremitical spirit. Visitors interrupted the life of contemplation, the meditation upon Holy Writ, the self-imposed discipline. Those hermits in desert places—and this perhaps is important to our understanding of the Celtic religious practices presently—were individualists. This in itself led to temptations, the urge to cast doubts on what they contemplated; and at the beginning of the fourth century the doubts of Arius of Alexandria about the divinity of Christ led to a wide schism in Lower Egypt, the Council of Nicaea denouncing Arianism in 325. More disputes disturbed the communities of solitaries. Seeking peace of mind, those men moved further and further west along the north African coast, for ever searching for a wilderness innocent of the world and its ways. And it was one of those who refused to accept the Arian heresy and was driven from Egypt who spread the idea of the solitaries across the sea to the western Church. In 336 Athanasius of Alexandria was banished to Trèves (Trier), and a few years later found his way to Rome. Here, although Pope Julius I restored him to his see of Alexandria, his doctrine of asceticism was looked upon with disgust. After Julian the Apostate's avowal of paganism, the Romans had reverted to the outward trappings of the past and saw in the ascetics a threat to their society, especially if the ascetic happened to be a patrician. So the eremitical exodus entered a new phase. The solitaries, denounced by Julian for turning their backs on the restored gods as well as on society, sought exile again, this time on lonely islands off the coast. And in the mid-fourth century we discover our last link between the East and the stones of Kirkmadrine. A legionary convert to Christ called Martin was expelled from Milan by its Arian bishop and travelled west by way of the Ligurian coast into the ancient Celtic province there, from which he crossed to the island of Gallenara. There for a while he lived alone.

Presently word came to him of the wide repute of Hilary, orthodox Bishop of Poitiers, and Martin left his island to go north into Gaul. At a place called Ligugé, near Poitiers, he built up a community of hermits. He brought with him many of the attitudes of the Eastern monks. In 372 he was created Bishop of Tours, and at Marmoutier, a mile or two from this town, he collected another community of hermits living in caves or other rough dwellings, a settlement to which the bishop could retire periodically to live by himself like the other solitaries.

There is a strong tradition, amounting at least to a probability, that the Briton, Ninian, who is recorded by the Venerable Bede as having been "regularly instructed at Rome in the faith and mysteries of the truth", returned home by way of Tours. There he would certainly absorb the ideas of Martin as regards the contemplative life. The tradition continues that he carried his mission beyond the Solway with the intention of taking the faith to the Picts, and that he built his church at Whithorn—Whitherne, as it used to be called—in the year of Martin's death, 397, dedicating it to that saint. Bede refers to it as a "stately church" of stone, called Candida Casa, the White House. Archaeology here throws in some question-marks. A little Celtic chapel has been excavated at Whithorn, its walls with vestiges of whitish plaster, but this seems to date from the second quarter of the fifth century. Is Ninian's mission later than was thought, or is this the work of a successor? Whatever the truth, there was certainly a Christian settlement here. And the *Chi-Rho* stones of Whithorn and Kirkmadrine are a culmination of a route of returning Christianity, marked by similar stones in Wales and Cornwall, thus pointing back to Gaul. A western route was inevitable, as the pagan Saxons had the east of Britain under threat.

Before turning to the link between Whithorn and Ireland, which had such an influence on Columba's church, we must look at the mission of Ninian to the Picts. The Picts bulk so large in Columba's story that claims for a prior Ninianic church in Pictland have to be explored.

There is no Life of Ninian extant. Consequently the evidence for his mission is so thin that we have to rely on one or two passing references. Bede mentions that the southern Picts, by the preaching of "Ninias", had "forsaken the errors of idolatry" long before Columba's mission. This is his only reference. Douglas Simpson in *The Celtic Church in Scotland* made out a lengthy and one might almost say impassioned case for the penetration of Ninian's mission far beyond the territory of the southern Picts and, although he is careful to admit we have to be wary of the Ninianic place-names because of later dedications to the saint, nevertheless he traces a route confidently through Glasgow right up to Strathmore, then into the far north-east. Much of his claim has been discounted since he wrote. Glasgow is a possibility, but the association with St Ninian's near Stirling has no foundation, since here the name is linked to a medieval name, Eggles or Eccles, derived from the British word for church, while the Arbirlot attribution rests on the Maltese cross carved on the

Pictish symbol-stone in the manse garden which Simpson traces back to Candida Casa, a stone certainly much later in date than the saint. Indeed the very fact that stones of the Whithorn type, with their Low Latin inscriptions, do not occur anywhere along this supposed penetration route is in itself at least negative evidence. Dr Isabel Henderson has referred to the effort of some scholars to press for Ninian's achievement at the expense of Columba's because Ninian is assumed to have been a protagonist of the orthodox Roman and not the Irish church. There are certainly times when Simpson's arguments, for all their scholarship, read like an extension of the seventh-century controversy which came to a head at the Synod of Whitby. Charles Thomas goes so far as to say he sees no evidence that Ninian ever engaged at all in a personal mission to the Picts.

That there were Christian converts among the Picts before Columba, however, does seem likely. St Patrick in his *Confessions* launches an attack on the "apostate Picts", thus implying there were Christian Picts some time in the first half of the fifth century. Where those apostates were located is impossible to say. The Whithorn area was populated by Strathclyde Britons, at that time ruled by Coroticus from Dumbarton, and it seems to have been Coroticus' Pictish mercenaries who were the targets for Patrick's wrath. This does nothing to suggest there was any massive number of conversions among the Picts as a whole, and if there were any communities of Christians it is surely likely they were confined to the southern Picts of what is now Perthshire and Strathmore.

Whatever the truth about a Ninianic mission and the extent of its influence, a Christian settlement at Whithorn existed. If there is no indication of an actual monastic centre here at the time when the stones were erected, the stones themselves seem to point towards Ireland if we accept the evidence in the paragraph which follows. Bede would have it that the influence of St Martin presided here, although there is no recognisable evidence of this. Whithorn was a very isolated settlement, even if in touch with the continental churches, and must have come to generate a type of faith increasingly different from the distant centre of

Christendom, from which it was almost cut off by the pressure of the pagans from the east. For encouragement it must have depended more and more on the Irish Christians across the water. Its Welsh counterpart, in a very similar situation though at a rather later date, was St David's. Whithorn did not really forge any strong link with Rome until perhaps the eighth century, when it came under the domination of Northumbria and therefore Canterbury, an event vividly illustrated by the St Peter stone on which the name of the saint appears to be scratched very crudely below an elegant cross which looks to be of earlier date. A short journey eastwards to the little church of Ruthwell by the Solway sets the seal on the change to orthodoxy in the shape of the beautiful cross re-erected in the well of the kirk, which combines Anglian ornament with classical iconography in a way which lifts it right out of the world of the Celtic west.

Emerging from the little museum at Whithorn to face a sou'wester coming in across the wide waters of Luce Bay, we are struck forcibly by the Celts' familiarity with the sea and ships. The line of succession to the monuments we have been looking at lies out of sight below the horizon, in Ireland. When candidates for the priesthood began to come here from Ulster to learn the rule of St Martin we have no way of knowing, but the passage of the stormy crossing was braved regularly. That the spiritual traffic was from east to west, whether from Whithorn or from St David's in Wales, is emphasised by the fact that stones bearing the *Chi-Rho* symbol are, in Ireland, of a slightly later date. The symbol on the St Peter stone is commonly dated as seventh century, because of the inscription, but surely it so manifestly

The St Peter Stone, Whithorn

pre-dates the roughly scrawled lettering that we may push it
back a hundred years or more, even if not perhaps to the fifth
century as Professor Hannah did. The dedication may be an
affirmation of orthodoxy after the Synod of Whitby, as Françoise
Henry suggests. Comparable symbols in Ireland, as for example
on the stone pillar from Aglish, Co. Kerry, now in the National
Museum in Dublin, may well be derived from Whithorn. Some
carry ogham characters instead of Latin. The stone at Reask, also
in Kerry, flowers into curvilinear decoration, and here the
inscription is in early Irish characters; the stone is probably
seventh century. The instinct to change the symbol from a
geometrical figure to an organic art-form pagan in its parentage
is an interesting reflection of the different Irish background, and
by this time Columba and his brother saints were long dead.

We do have some documentary records from later times of
this link between Whithorn and Ireland. In the *Chronicles of the
Picts and Scots* it is said that Cairnech, abbot of the house of
Martin—the Whithorn community—went to Erin and was
created first bishop of the clan Niall and of Tara. Other Irish
bishops, including Tighernac of Clones, were trained by
"Nennio", otherwise Ninian or a successor of the same name, in
a monastery called "white". The same monastery trained Enda,
who founded the community on one of the Aran islands, off the
Connacht coast, where a very severe discipline was imposed.
Naturally this link with Whithorn is mainly with Ulster. It must
have continued over a long period. It was from Wales in the
sixth century that the monk Gildas went to Ireland. Clonard in
Meath grew into a monastery of enormous proportions, its size
matched by its renown. Other foundations followed, all over
Ireland: Bangor, Clonmacnoise, Glendalough, Durrow. But it is
from the "three thousand saints" of Clonard that the "Twelve
Apostles of Ireland" came, one of whom was Columba. St
Patrick's mission by now can have been little more than a
memory. The new teaching may or may not have deviated from
Patrick's—there is evidence that it did not—but its emphasis on
the teaching of the founding father, gathering his "family"
around him, each community distinct from the others and

growing independently of them, and each linked to the existing tribal system, suited the Irish character, struck real roots into the soil, and prospered.

It is sad, in a way, that a movement of this kind by its very nature could leave few traces in a physical sense. As Hannah wrote, if the original Candida Casa had survived we should have had a church almost as old as the one at Bethlehem. But in Ireland virtually nothing remains to commemorate the phenomenon of the Age of Saints, not even a stick or a stone of Clonard itself. We can reconstitute the picture only from the early literature and from the surviving stone structures, both of which post-date the stirring time of the "Apostles", and then set out what we can visualise in the green fields of Meath or, perhaps better, in some sheltered valley like Glendalough in Wicklow where, even if the ruins are later they can at least create the mood. The framework of the Patrician episcopal system remained, and it would be wrong to think of a church existing on an entirely unworldly plane, for some foundations even drew great wealth to themselves; but the environments in which communities dwelt were of the simplest. We know the holy men lived in cells or bothies built of wood or wattles very much in the native manner. The bothies would be grouped around an oratory, no doubt of wooden construction shaped like the little reliquaries, but still not much more than a hut. The idea of doing honour to a deity by lavishing work upon a place of worship may not have been positively rejected, but emphasis was wholly on the contemplative life; and in any case, as we saw in the last chapter, among the Celtic peoples the holy place was usually a grove of oaks.

In the monastic communities worship included the declaiming of psalms and prayers, which must have resembled bardic recitations of praise. Mortification of the flesh also had its place in worship. Here again there was a carry-over from the past, for lengthy penances performed standing in streams must have been a familiar ritual to people for whom water had always had a sacred significance—sacrificial deposits have been found in marshes and lakes from Lake Neuchâtel in Switzerland to Gundestrup in Denmark, and in Ireland itself. And the movement had its anchorites, as in Egypt. Those the quest for truth drove forth from their communities, even in the face of their abbot's command, to seek solitude in wild and lonely places, involving intense self-discipline. Enda and the Aran isles have been mentioned; harsher still is the site of the huts perched on the crag of the Great Skellig, off Kerry, lashed by Atlantic storms. The faith of those monks required example, not proselytising. There were no rewards in this life. Indeed, with a diet of the simplest kind, and with long fasts and vigils, it must have been hard to survive the damp and chills of the seaboard climate. Yet by the end of the sixth century the movement had penetrated to the furthest corners of Ireland, and was already spreading back to other western areas of Britain.

The Age of Saints is an almost incomprehensible phenomenon in European history. Irish Christianity, says John Richard Green, "flung itself with a fiery zeal into battle with the mass of heathenism which was rolling in upon the Christian world". But I remember sitting on a mossy stone at Glendalough, amazed at the thought of this once being a power-house of embattled Christendom. It is easy to look up at the Colosseum and hear the tramp of the legions and the trumpets through six lanes of traffic; but here at Glendalough there is only the twittering of birds, and fourteen centuries ago there was nothing more martial to add to it than the monks singing their psalms. Fortress Ireland began the battle with no weapons other than faith and zeal.

When one thinks of the fierce rivalries among the clans of Ireland, rivalries which persisted through the centuries to come, an evangelisation covering a period of perhaps a century and a half must be considered relatively rapid. The chief factor in the wholesale conversions is, surely, the teaching by example to which I have referred. Bede, despite his orthodoxy, has nothing but admiration for the devoutness of the Celtic monks. Of St Aidan he writes: "he taught no otherwise than he and his followers had lived." Perhaps never in the history of Christian missions have so many men come among the heathen refusing to compromise between the way of the world and the teaching of their Master. But I have small doubt that the nature of the pagan beliefs outlined in the previous chapter was a factor too. The very locations sought by the solitaries must have had special meaning in the eyes of that Iron Age society. I have referred to Tir nan Og, the Isles of the Blest, the heaven beyond the sunset. It is not to be thought the men who went to settle on the Aran islands or the Skellig gave thought to such things, but their choice of dwelling-place must have struck a chord in the minds of the men and women of Ireland, even before they began to grasp the meaning of Christianity. We may feel ourselves guilty of escapist dreams when we are fascinated by an afterglow behind the Blaskets or the black outline of Rhum, but we have to remember that for a sixth-century Celt such scenes were pointers to the life to come, and as real in that sense as heaven to an early Christian. Therefore a new religion whose priests made sanctuaries on the crags and skerries which made stepping-stones along the golden causeways leading to the Blessed Isles was half way to converting that Celt.

The same sort of painless transition seems to have happened with some of the old deities. St Brigid of Kildare is a case in point. Whether or no she ever existed, her famous nunnery and monastery were founded in the sixth century, apparently on the site of a druidical cult-centre. Brigid, daughter of the Daghda, in Irish legend the father of the gods, was a goddess of first importance among the Celts, in Gaul and Britain as well as Ireland. She presided over learning and literature, and in Ireland she was worshipped as goddess of craftsmen and of the healing arts. She was veritably a mother-goddess, a fertility figure. Historically, St Brigid, or St Bride, is a vague personage. Like Columba, her father was of the royal blood of Ulster, and she seems to have lived from about 452 to 523. She built her cell under an oak tree— again, the oak—and the meaning of Kildare is "church of the oak". Both Dr Anne Ross and Professor McCana have said that, unlike slightly later saints, she was neither missionary nor evangelist, yet her cult sprang up all over Ireland and in neighbouring Britain, blowing into life embers of a cult that was very ancient. At Kildare her sanctuary is described in terms which make it sound like a pagan sanctuary, for no man might pass through the hedge which surrounded it, within which her sacred fire burned continuously tended by her virgins. Giraldus Cambrensis adds that the heap of ashes never grows: that each of the nineteen nuns keeps vigil for a night, and on the twentieth night the saint is invoked with the words, "Brigid, take care of your own fire, for this night is yours." It is said this fire burned for a thousand years, ending only with Henry VIII's dissolution of the monasteries. Her name is still potent in some parts, and identified with the Virgin Mary. If a belief, originally pagan, can survive into our own times, it helps us to understand what happened in the Age of Saints.

The emphasis I have put at times on pagan practices and tribal strife may have left the impression that Ireland was inhabited by savages, an impression with which most provincial Roman Britons would have agreed. If this had been so, early Christian Ireland would never have made the mark it did on European history. Civilisation is equated with an "advanced society", whatever that means; I should prefer to define it as a state of society subject to law and order and capable of sustaining a high degree of intellectual attainment. Law and order were no doubt flouted in Ireland every day of the week, but they existed, and I doubt if they were ever cynically ignored in Ireland quite as they were in Rome by Nero, Caligula and some other heads of state. As to intellectual attainment, there were Irish scholars who re-lit the torch of learning in the west and kept it burning until the early middle ages.

We need to know a little about the pattern of this Irish society. The tribe or *tuath* has been mentioned. Each *tuath* comprised a group of families, and kinship ties were basic to the system. A *tuath* was ruled by the *ri*, or king, and groups of *tuatha* owed allegiance to over-kings. Sovereignty had a certain divine sanction, and this continued into Christian times, in which it was no different from the rest of Europe. The class system must also have persisted. The *tuath* was in fact a little world of its own, and into this the monastic community grooved perfectly. Each community was known as a "family", as mentioned earlier; and the family received its lands as a gift from the king, so that the monks were not an invading spiritual sect owing allegiance to far-off Rome, but were rather an element in the web of loyalties which held society together. As the De Paors have pointed out in *Early Christian Ireland*, so much was the monk still part of the family group that if he exiled himself as a penance it was a penance indeed. The Christian "take-over" could hardly have been smoother. The king's druidical advisers merged gradually into monastic ones.

There have been references to the teaching function of the druids being taken over by the monks, also to the achievement of Irish scholarship. Attachment to learning and teaching is one of the two main ways in which the Irish monks differed in their aims from the anchorites of the desert. Adomnán in his preface comments with scorn upon "the barbarous Irish tongue", although it was his own native speech; but generally speaking the more scholarly monks used both Irish and Latin. Their Latin was by no means only a formal accomplishment, to be used as the vehicle of religion, but brought them widely in touch with classical literature, so that some of them were able to express themselves with elegance in the tongue of Cicero and Virgil. But at the same time they were steeped in the lore and legend of their pagan Celtic past, hitherto passed on by word of mouth, and so for the first time those rich stores of imaginative poetry were rendered into a written literature, the medium not Latin but Irish. It is to the scribes in those early monasteries, therefore, that we owe most of our knowledge of the sagas and superstitions of the Celts. Sometimes the scribe would have a twinge of conscience, or was afraid of the abbot looking over his shoulder, when he would add a footnote or a postscript disclaiming his own belief in such imaginings; but it is impossible to doubt his pleasure in what he had written, or that this heritage had a profound influence upon him and his fellows. The bardic tradition persisted.

The stimulus of writing Irish produced a new wave of creative literature, and initially the monasteries fostered this. So their function was by no means confined to training ecclesiastics and teaching laymen. They were the stewards of Irish culture, and brought about a renaissance in it, both literary and artistic. Among a people who exalted poets and artists, this must have greatly speeded the conversion to Christianity. Skene claims the process took only a single generation. On the evidence of the arts, I myself cannot believe it was such an open-and-shut case; I believe there were too many pockets of reservation not only in the country but in the minds of men, even in a man such as Columba. Yet if we remember that the big monasteries numbered their students in thousands, and that even the tiny communities perched on the crags of the Aran isles and the Skellig had their schools, there is no conversion in history more impressive.

The other main point of difference between the Irish monasteries and the desert communities lay in their commitment to missionary activity. The hermits of Egypt were refugees from persecution and moral degradation. The exodus of missionaries from Ireland, continuing for centuries, began with a personal urge. In the first instance it seems to have been an urge not so much to evangelise but to do penance, and to do it by exiling themselves from the land and the people they loved. Traditionally, Columba is represented as sadly banishing himself from sight of his homeland. This is not the place to discuss his motives for leaving Ireland: that will be done in due course. But self-imposed exile from the safety of the close-knit ties of family was a strong element in the spirit of Irish monasticism. The monks called it the "white martyrdom". They looked on themselves as *peregrini*, pilgrims, wanderers upon the face of the earth, whom God's will alone would direct. It should be kept in mind, I think, that Columba's pilgrimage in some respects differed from the pattern of such pilgrimages. Mostly, they went much further afield. The monks braved long voyages to the Faeroes, even Iceland. The settlement on Lindisfarne was an extension of the works of the abbots of Iona, and will be dealt with in its place; but there were many other missions to England, now largely heathen again, and foundations such as Glastonbury prospered. As early as Columba's own time Irish monks were crossing Gaul in numbers, and reached the Rhine and the Alps. Everywhere they went they won converts or rallied a laggard Christianity, never by the stern righteousness of a church militant, always by their example, their meekness and their dedication. St Gall in Switzerland became a great monastery and famous under the Benedictines, but the Irish monk whose name it carries dwelt in a cell among the mountains. The most celebrated of all those pilgrims is St Columbanus, founder of the monastery of Bobbio in Italy, and a great scholar who carried the arguments for Irish monasticism to the very gates of Rome, arguments which no doubt he plied with Irish persuasiveness and charm.

I have sometimes wondered if an underlying motive with the *peregrini*, those who sought the continent, was not to tear themselves free of those pagan roots which are so constantly showing themselves, as in the decoration of the reliquaries. Some, perhaps the most devout, may have felt a certain uneasiness about the transfer of allegiance to the new faith. Without suggesting this as a motive for pilgrimage Skene does raise the point when he says the rapid conversion of the Irish excites our wonder, "if not our suspicion". He writes: "We know how readily a rude and primitive people invest with superstitious and supernatural power those claiming superior sanctity." He goes on to show how converted pagans may merely substitute Christian sanctions for pagan, how the missionary may have been invested with precisely the intercessionary powers of the druid. The new faith could be seen in the light of the old superstition. He finds his suspicion reflected in the Brehon Laws, with their insistence on tithes and first-fruits and alms as the price of avoidance of "the worthlessness of the world". In short, he means the church had taken over the system of rewards and penalties—blessings or maledictions—which existed earlier.

Undoubtedly Skene is right in seeing here one reason for the swift progress of the conversion. A *quid pro quo* relationship does seem to have existed between church and tribe, a contract in which the church had its "rights" and the tribe reciprocal ones. But this was not peculiar to sixth-century Ireland. The equilibrium of medieval society was maintained by a similar system of rewards and sanctions in which the church maintained its power by threats of excommunication and hellfire which had little to do with the teaching of its Founder. This is not necessarily to condemn the church: it may be argued that the well-being of society needs such a system, and that our problems today in part stem from our inability to impose it. But such a compromise with the realities of the situation must have troubled many of those truly saintly men who in the seclusion of their cells had sought nothing but the will of God, and it is not difficult to see here a motive for their self-chosen exile.

This chapter began with a description of the little groups of monuments at Whithorn and Kirkmadrine, crude monoliths on which the symbol of Christ is chipped almost furtively though defiantly, as it had been in the catacombs. In Ireland itself there are not a great many monuments to mark the beginnings of the new faith. But the scholarship and dedication of the *peregrini* in Europe are commemorated in the rich heritage of manuscripts left like a tidemark of Celtic culture towards the furthest points reached by the missionaries. Although these sacred books date from a century and more after Columba's time, indeed to the period of the chapter which will be devoted to the Golden Age, I shall say a few words about them here because they embody so splendidly the spirit of the movement which created them. Gospels and psalters were in circulation in sixth-century Europe, but in the hands of the Irish monks who copied and elaborated them they were to become rare and precious works of art. Thousands must have been lost, but enough remain to inspire us with awe at the industry and artistry which went into them

I have mentioned Columbanus and the monastery of Bobbio. Some of the surviving Bobbio manuscripts have found their way elsewhere, for example to the Ambrosian Library in nearby Milan and even back to the Library of Trinity College, Dublin. There are continental elements in the scripts, but the Irish character is unmistakable to palaeographers, and one does not have to be a skilled student to recognise the developing Celtic style of decoration. How deeply dependent the scribes were upon the art of the pagan past may be seen in the detail from ancient brooches or from fragments of enamelled metalwork. Sometimes there is a poignant touch. Françoise Henry has drawn attention to a detail of the Dublin manuscript attributed to the Bobbio scriptorium, the Codex Usserianus Primus, a *Chi-Rho* symbol with Alpha and Omega tucked under its arms closely resembling the symbol cut on a stone at Loher, Co. Kerry. Was this mere chance? It is certainly ironic that the source of most of what we know about Columba himself, the copy of Adomnán's *Vita Sancti Columbae* probably made by one Dorbbene on Iona and carried off to save it from the Vikings, found its way to the monastery of Reichenau and is now preserved in the Town Library at Schaffhausen.

III

The Coming of Columba

Adomnán, at the beginning of the third book of the *Life*, describes the signs and wonders which foretold the coming of Columba. The account given by Cuimine the Fair is similar; so also the story in the "Old Irish Life", compiled possibly in the tenth century as a tribute to the saint on the occasion of his festival. An angel, we are told, appeared to Columba's mother in a dream, presenting her with a mantle of exquisite beauty, glowing with the hues of all the flowers in creation, according to Adomnán, and in the words of the "Old Irish Life" stretching from Innsi-Mod to Caer-nam-Broce, which is to say from Clew Bay in Co. Mayo to Burghead on the Moray Firth. Adomnán, following Cuimine, says the angel was a man of "venerable mien", the "Old Irish Life" that he was a young man in splendid raiment, but they agree that he took the mantle back and sent it whirling away high into the air. When she protested at its loss the angel—Adomnán has it simply "a voice"—answered that she was not to be perturbed or sorrowful, and the mantle seems to have dwindled into the distance and at the same time spread until it covered mountains, valleys and plains, a characteristically Celtic phenomenon. This reassured the woman, Eithne. She would bear a son of great beauty who would be remembered among the prophets of the Lord. It is said a woman in attendance also saw a vision, in which the fowls of earth and sky bore "the bowels of Eithne" all across Erin (Ireland) and Alba (Scotland). And again, it is recorded that the abbot Buite, son of Bronach and founder of Monasterboice, as he died declared: "A child illustrious before God and men will be born in the night tonight, and he shall come here before thirty years from this night. Twelve men, moreover, will be his company; and he it is that will discover my grave, and measure my cemetery; and our union shall be in heaven and in earth." These last incidents appear in the "Old Irish Life".

This annunciation legend, this prelude to the birth, at once invites comparison with the gospels. There is no suggestion that Eithne's child was conceived miraculously, but otherwise the signs and wonders have much in common with the "Christmas story" in Matthew and Luke. The build-up implies a near-divinity in Columba. It is interesting to turn to the commentary of Dr C. H. Dodd on the Christmas story in the two gospels mentioned, for he demonstrates how the authors found this "structure of imagery" necessary to illustrate "that the ob-scure birth of a child to a carpenter's wife was . . . a decisive moment in history, when something genuinely new began". It is not fantasy, but a tremendous fact emphasised by the use of poetic symbolism. The writers on Columba of course had the examples of the gospels before them, and clearly imitated them, and being Celts they did so with much recourse to their own imaginations; but we must keep in mind Dr Dodd's advice, which is that only a bold man should "presume to draw a firm line between fact and symbol". The fact here is that Columba made a resounding impact on his own and succeeding generations, and that the chroniclers are recording this in their traditional way. But they are very careful to make clear that the son to be born is the true son of Eithne and her lawful husband. It is as important a part of the legend of Columba to proclaim his blood and ancestry as to proclaim his spiritual mission. They would have you know the saint was no humble subject. To the ancient Irish, not even God's appointed purpose for a man could be allowed to obscure the fact that he was kin to him who occupied the throne of Tara of the Kings.

Adomnán briefly states the saint's noble parentage in his Second Preface, in what might be called a prose run-up to his epic narrative. Eithne his mother was eleventh in descent from a King of Leinster, Cathair Mor. His father, Fedhlimidh (Phelim) by name, was a son of Fergus, son of Conaill Gulban, whose father was Niall Nóigiallach, the famed Niall of the Nine Hostages. Niall's rule is generally dated from 379 to 405, although it may have lasted longer. He seems to have been half Saxon, as the bard refers to his mother as Cairenn, "curly black-haired daughter of Sachell Balb", a captive from Britain. Niall is a shadowy figure, lauded by the poets as a mighty warrior, but from the dim background of legend he does emerge as an historical figure. Raids such as the one which captured Cairenn were common, and there are hoards of Roman provincial silver loot to witness to them. What we do know of Niall is that he built up the power of his clan, the Uí Néill, until it dominated the north from Tara, and this was accomplished in part at least by means of an extraordinary accumulation of myth and legend contrived by the poets. In early Ireland the poets had probably more power to make or break public figures than the media have in the modern world. Columba himself seems to have been well aware of this power, as will be seen.

Spiritual and cultural power were every bit as important to the Celt as political power, indeed they were bound up with it. This sort of power the Uí Néill achieved by seizing Eamhain Macha (Navan), an ancient centre close to Armagh, a name which is really Ard Macha—Hill of Macha. Eamhain Macha means Twins of Macha, Macha being probably a pagan goddess connected with a horse cult. It had been a sacred place since the Bronze Age. Its deep significance and influence were recognised by St Patrick, who built his church at Armagh on what was evidently a druid sanctuary, and relics still preserved in Armagh cathedral include typical ritual stone heads which tradition now associates with the name of Patrick himself. Since Patrick was the presiding saint of the people they had defeated in order to seize Eamhain Macha, the Uí Néill had possessed themselves of a keypoint comparable to Tara. Both places had roots reaching deep into pre-history, as archaeological digs have proved. Preoccupation with such objectives was not just a move to win the priesthood or the church to their side, for there was a strong tradition in this tribal society that their kings should take Macha, the earth-goddess, as their ritual bride, so to ensure the fruitfulness of their realm. The forces of the age into which Columba emerged were dark and complex, and his task was far from being a straightforward crusade.

Columba was born on Thursday, 7 December, in the year 521. The place was Gartan, meaning "a little field", in Co. Donegal, situated on a hillside overlooking some lakes, sheltered by mountains to west and north, and a few miles west of Lough Swilly. Nothing is told of his infancy. Miraculous happenings are limited to a reference by Adomnán to the priest into whose care the child had been placed, who, on returning from church, found his house bathed in bright light, and discovered a ball of fire hovering over the face of his sleeping charge. The priest shook with fear and prostrated himself in amazement, recognising it as a sign of the grace of the Holy Spirit. This has the feel of a Nativity story, but it was probably borrowed from pagan lore, for a countenance lit by an unearthly light suggests legends of heroes such as Lugd of the Long Arm, the "Shining One", who was father of Cuchulainn. Sometimes one has the impression the chroniclers used their legendary past almost as the gospel-writers did the Old Testament, filling in a detail "that it might be fulfilled which was spoken by the prophets".

The priest who saw this vision was Cruithnechan, son of Cellachan. The Cruithni or Cruithentuath is the Irish name for Picts, but whether there is a connection between this and the priest's name is impossible to say. Cruithnechan the presbyter had been given the child to baptise and to foster. He baptised him Colum, which in Latin becomes Columba, the dove; but later writers say he was also called Crimthann, the fox, which Reeves thinks may have been a secular name. According to the *Leabhar Breac*, his constant visits to the little church of Tulach-Dubhglaise (Temple Douglas), close to his birth-place, to read his psalms, brought the local children to nickname him Columcille, Colum of the church, and it is as Columcille he became known all over Ireland. The practice of putting out a small child for fosterage may seem to us strange, but it was not unusual in the ancient world and in pagan Ireland it was normal procedure, especially among the ruling classes. A chief might send his son to the family of a sub-chief, who would be entitled to a fee of 30 *sets*. Fees varied according to rank, all such things being regulated by the Brehon Laws. Whether the fosterage were paid for or undertaken for love, resulting ties were as close as blood-ties, and in later life the child would have obligations to his foster-parent. Both sons and daughters were fostered. Boys of the upper classes were instructed in manly sports and the use of arms, girls were taught domestic accomplishments such as embroidery. That Colum was given into the charge of a priest implies that he was intended for the priesthood from the start, for presumably Cruithnechan could not have passed on to him the martial accomplishments of a boy of noble birth.

The few things recorded in the "Old Irish Life" about Columba's stay with Cruithnechan belong to the category of signs and wonders, although some no doubt had a factual basis. It is told that the cleric consulted a certain prophet about the right time for the boy to begin his lessons. After observing the heavens, the prophet advised Cruithnechan to write an alphabet for his pupil there and then. It was written on a cake, and Columba ate half of it east of the water and half west of it; which, according to one version of the text, the prophet interpreted as meaning the boy's land would lie half to the east of the sea, and half to the west, which is to say in Alba and in Erin. It is wisdom after the event, of course, but the implication is that the precocious boy discerned his future. On the other hand it is likely enough that the priest did in fact bake him a cake with characters on it to make learning fun, as parents still do, and that the child hopped across a small burn while eating it.

Another tale relates how Columba and his guardian visited Bishop Bruga at the rath, or hill-fort, of Magh-enaig in Co. Donegal, and that Cruithnechan, when asked to officiate at a holy festival, found he was unable to recite a certain psalm, the 100th. His pupil recited it in his place, although he had only just mastered his alphabet. This could have been true. Memory-training was a part of bardic tradition, and it is likely enough that Columba was a prodigy.

The third incident is rather more dramatic. Tutor and pupil went to visit a sick man, and Cruithnechan's foot slipped on a rock in the path through a wood, so that he fell and—so it is said—died. Columba put his cloak under the old man's head, believing him to be asleep, and began to rehearse his lessons aloud, so that some nuns in a nearby church heard him and came. They told Columba to "awake" his tutor, which he did, afterwards giving thanks to God and begging to be given the gifts of chastity, wisdom and pilgrimage. It is a peculiar tale.

For a family of the blood-royal to commit their son to the church from birth seems a surprising decision, but none of the early writers discusses the issue or betrays any doubts about the way things went. An alternative does not seem to have been considered. Sometimes one reads versions of his story which imply, or even assert, that Columba himself made the choice of the church when the throne of Ireland was his for the asking, had in fact been offered to him. It may be so: it is hard to prove a negative. But the belief that the High-Kingship was ever offered him seems to arise from the short paragraph in the "Old Irish Life" which runs: "He was eligible to the kingship of Eriu according to family, and it was offered to him, if he himself had not abandoned it for God." Skene's footnote to this reads: "The text should probably be *taircfid*, 'would be offered'." The sense then becomes that, because of his family, he would have been eligible for the kingship if it had been offered him, but it was not, because he had entered the church. And the chronicler at once sets about affirming Columba was fated to be an elect son of God, thus fulfilling the words of the prophets, as Mochta of Lugbad when he prayed:

> A youth shall be born out of the north
> With the rising of the nations;
> Ireland shall be made fruitful by the great flame,
> And Alba, friendly to him.

I think there is no doubt his parents intended Columba for the church, but this in itself is interesting.

We have to remember how spiritual and temporal power complemented each other in tribal thinking, and that the sixth century saw a revolution in the first. The church belonged not to the world, but to the tribe. The tribe needed the church as the

church needed the tribe. If the dreams of the royal princes of the
Uí Néill were to come true, and they were to rule Ireland and
expand their foothold across the sea in Alba, they would need
the favour of God as well as the sharp edges of their swords.
Fedhlimidh and Eithne may have seen in their son the vehicle of
this favour. Or is it possible the choice was not theirs, but determined by the law? . . . It is laid down in the Brehon Laws that
every firstling, every first-born, may be claimed by the church
as a tithe, to render the service of a "free monk" to the church,
which in return will teach him learning. We know nothing of
whether Columba was a first-born son; but what we do know is
that a churchman was a loyal member of his tribe, his *tuath*,
could share in its ambitions, and could promote them. This is
not the church as we think of it today; it is not the medieval
church whose leaders could cynically behave like temporal
leaders when they chose. It is the church of that reliquary:
an oratory adorned with pagan myths and yearning, a symbol
of piety and at the same time of ancient loyalties. Perhaps only
in Ireland could this sort of compromise have been made to
work for long. As it seems to me, we have to remember that
although Columba's parents were Christians, Christianity was
still a strange and untried faith; and, when they gave him to
Cruithnechan to foster, they gave him as a few generations
earlier they would have given him to a high druid or to an
ollam fili, a chief poet, honoured vocations devoted to serving
the highest interests of the tribe.

One gropes for fragments of tangible evidence about the
sort of world Columba was born into, for glimpses of something more substantial than Adomnán and the other writers
supply.

The importance of Tara, as the chief centre of Columba's own
people, makes it a natural location in which to look. At first
sight, it is disappointing. Colourful publications have so familiar-
ised people with Baalbek and Persepolis, the shrines of India and
the temples of the Aztecs that they expect to find lost civilisations
marked by impressive ruins. Tara is situated in a rolling midland
plain of rich pastures, with contented herds of cattle and vast

skies above. An experienced environmentalist might read a lot from this: that the health of the green grass and the beasts grazing it is not just the product of eighteenth-century "improvers", that those are ancient pastures. The land on which some of the cities of the Near East were built has died for want of the wells or aqueducts which men built to serve them; but here at Tara there is natural wealth and prosperity for those who know how to win them. This was a favoured place. At some dim time before history Tara became a centre of the cult of that formidable deity Medb, insatiable goddess of war and of fecundity, with consorts beyond number; and the weird contest between her and the hero Cuchulainn in the *Táin Bó Cuailgne* saga over possession of a great brown bull is quite plainly a contest for the means of survival and growth. Tara was rich land in an age when bogs and forests covered much of the country. So there were temples at Tara, and fortifications, and a palace.

On the Hill of Tara are the only obvious remains, two sets of concentric circles, comprising ditches and ramparts, raths which would have been completed by stout wooden stockades surrounding timber buildings. Although the hill is not high, it commands a wide view of the plain. One of the earthworks, the Rath of the Synods, has yielded evidence of trade with Roman sources; but the nearby Mound of the Hostages covers a very early burial site, showing the hill must have been a sacred place from far-off times, certainly the Bronze Age. Here stood the Stone of Fál, a phallic monument which vented a shriek in the presence of a rightful king. The choosing and consecration of the king were conducted at the Feast of Tara, and as this was the very focus of druidical power Tara naturally became the scene of a major confrontation with the new faith. Here at Tara the rite of the Bull-Dream took place. A bull was slaughtered and a druid fed on its flesh and broth, and when he fell insensible, spells were chanted over him, and on waking he was able to point to the rightful successor to the kingship. Whether this and other unpleasant rituals connected with the inauguration of kings were still practised in the sixth century does not seem to be recorded, but druidical control is not in doubt. While royal blood was a

prerequisite, a new king had to prove his fitness, and here is
where the priesthood wielded its power.

As for the temples and the palace which have left no trace at
Tara, they would be built of timber. There is a tendency to
think Celtic buildings in all ages were simple to the point of
crudity, and that life in them was primitive. Remarks of some
classical writers may suggest this, but I know of no evidence to
prove it; and I find it difficult to understand how a people who
appreciated such delicacy of workmanship in their metalwork
could be content with crudity in their buildings. The royal halls
at Tara may have been simple in construction, perhaps a framework of stout timbers joined by boarding or wickerwork
partitions, but there must have been areas of intricate carving
such as one looks for in timber-using areas, for example Scandinavia. There is little point in elaborating on what is mere
guesswork, but a traditionally aristocratic society with a taste for
personal splendour must have seen to it that this was reflected in
their dwellings, if only in the embellishments. Usually Celtic
communities were small. Tara may have covered a greater area,
for it was the meeting-place of five "great roads", and as wheeled
vehicles were in common use those roads must have been more
than mere tracks.

We have a fair idea of what people looked like in Columba's
lifetime. Since Iron Age class distinctions were still the rule, both
men's and women's status was recognisable by the garb they
wore. Both sexes wore a half-length tunic of wool (*leine*) and a
cloak of the same material, the weight and size of which seem to
have increased with the importance of the wearer. Folds were
fastened by brooches, probably of penannular type, of bronze,
silver or in some cases of gold, precursors of those masterpieces
of jewellery of a century or two later which included the superb
Tara brooch. Much of the evidence comes from works of art of
a rather later period, but it is doubtful if there was much change
in fashions. For example, the "Arrest of Christ" scene on
Muiredach's cross at Monasterboice, Co. Louth, shows soldiers
wearing short trousers. Trousers had been a characteristic Celtic
garb from early times, and long trousers are depicted in manu-

scripts. What the sculptures cannot tell us about, of course, is the colours and patterns of the woollen fabrics. Classical authors indicate that bright colours were popular among the Celts. So

Arrest of Christ, Muiredach's cross,
Monasterboice, Co. Louth. Early
10th cent.

do descriptions in the myths and legends. Texts suggest that the under-tunic may have been white or the natural colour, but that the cloak was dyed in a wide range of hues, which is what we should expect among a people highly conscious of the effect they made on others. Both sexes wore the hair long, and the later sculptures record men as either moustached or with full, pointed beards. Bracelets, combs of bone and other personal ornaments were much worn; but there were strict regulations which laid down what size and type of ornament each class of society might wear. Ecclesiastics had long habits probably of the natural colour of the wool. Often they are shown as clean-shaven, but sometimes with pointed beards. The tonsure involved shaving not the crown of the head but the fore-part, from ear to ear. This is of considerable significance, for it is a reversion to the druidical tonsure—plainly a deliberate reversion from the coronal tonsure

which Patrick must have introduced from Britain. Why did the
Saints of Ireland choose to be different in this, and cling to it so
tenaciously for so long?

Priests of Columban church with sceptre or
flabellum. Cross-slab, St Vigean's No. 11.
8th cent.

Adomnán describes the second stage of Columba's upbringing
at the beginning of Book II. We are told that, while yet a youth,
he stayed with St Finnian or Findbar, "learning the wisdom of
Holy Writ". The Finnian here referred to in 540 founded an
ecclesiastical school at Moville at the head of Strangford Lough,
a deep inlet of the sea in Co. Down now popular with yachtsmen.
Columba must have been one of the first pupils here, and he was
made a deacon. Here too we have an early reference to his
miraculous powers. It is said he heard the priests complaining
that the wine for ministration of the Holy Eucharist could not
be found. He took the cruet and went to a spring, where he
blessed the water and called upon the name of Christ, asking that
the miracle performed at the marriage at Cana in Galilee be

performed again. Adomnán tells how the water duly became wine which Columba brought to the altar, saying, "Here is wine for you, which the Lord Jesus has sent for the celebration of His Mysteries." Columba disclaimed his powers, giving the credit to "the holy bishop Vinnian". We are told nothing more of Columba's stay at Moville. Finnian's *familia* there must have been a small one, probably housed in a cluster of wooden huts or bothies.

Still a deacon, Columba left Moville to be tutored by an aged man called Gemman in Leinster, a man described by St Finnian of Clonard (not to be confused with Finnian of Moville) as a "Christian bard". This is interesting, for it seems to imply a time of study of Irish literature and rhetoric, a very sensible preparation for preaching, as we should think. Neither Adomnán nor the "Old Irish Life" has anything to say of his studies with Gemman, but both record an extraordinary incident which happened there. When Columba and Gemman were reading in the plain of Meath a man approached, "a cruel persecutor of the innocent", chasing a young girl. It seems Gemman and his pupil were at a distance from one another, and the girl ran for protection to Gemman, who called to Columba to help him. The two managed to throw their cloaks about the girl, but with a spear the man killed her at their feet. Gemman called upon God to avenge the crime; but Columba exclaimed that in the same hour the girl's soul went up to heaven the soul of her slayer would go down to hell. At once the murderer fell dead. News of this vengeance spread across Ireland, and the fame of the young deacon with it.

The importance of this story, surely, is not so much whether it is fact or fiction, but that it is related at all. It involves the first of many curses attributed to the saint. In the swiftness of his anger and the merciless exercise of his powers, this is not one of the meek saints who won the praise of Bede, but rather an Old Testament prophet—"Behold, the day of the Lord cometh, cruel both with wrath and fierce anger." It is the ancient law of an eye for an eye and a tooth for a tooth, and a life for a life. I do not think Adomnán would have included this tale if he had not been persuaded that it was at least in character, in fact, that Columba was capable of striking a man dead in his righteous wrath.

The complexity of the saint's character becomes apparent in the pages of Adomnán. The period with Gemman, a bard, signifies more than a love of a traditional art in the young deacon. Obviously, he had become aware of the dawning renaissance of his country's literary heritage mentioned in the last chapter, a movement so strong that as late as the twelfth century the Irish was the greatest of Europe's vernacular literatures. But Columba knew also that the bard's was not only an honoured craft: bards and poets had the power to influence events, for they were masters of satire, and the emotional Celts dreaded satire more perhaps than the sharpest weapons of war. Professor Byrne goes so far as to say that in some ways they "wielded more power than did the kings", that they were moulders of public opinion in the sense they were mentioned earlier in this chapter. With the industrious recording in written texts of the oral literature at this time there must have been contagious excitement and a new awareness of the strength of its custodians, the *filidh*, the bards. That Columba never forgot the importance of bardic power among his countrymen is seen long after he left Erin for Alba, since there is a tradition it formed one of the items for discussion at the Convention of Drum Ceatt.

Now came the move which completed Columba's training for his vocation. He went to Cluain-Erard, otherwise Clonard in Co. Meath, where the more celebated of the two St Finnians had founded a great monastic school about the year 520. Finnian had considered going on a pilgrimage to Rome, but an angel is said to have come to him saying: "What would be given to thee at Rome shall be given to thee here. Arise and renew sound faith in Ireland after Patrick." So at Clonard he gathered about him his 3,000 students. This enormous gathering of young men would be accommodated within a rath, an area enclosed within a protective ditch, possibly with a stockade as at Tara, and on this "campus" each student would have his own cell of wood or wattle construction daubed with clay. The students seem to have built huts for themselves. Columba is believed to have asked Finnian where he should set up his cell and was told to do so at the church door, but he built it a short distance away. Asked by Finnian why his instruction had been disobeyed, Columba replied that eventually the church door would be beside the site he had chosen. And, of course, this happened: as the monastery expanded, so did the church. Students looked after themselves as the Fathers in the desert settlements did, ploughing and sowing the fields outside the stockade, and maintaining herds of cattle.

The church or oratory, although a larger building than the others, in Columba's day would be a wooden structure, probably of riven oak planks supported by posts. Other buildings larger than the cells would be a refectory and a house for guests. Much of the instruction must have taken place in the open air, for the church could not have accommodated more than a small proportion of the students. In spite of Columba's prognostication about the growing size of the church, there is reason to think needs were met by adding more small buildings. It may be that addresses or sermons were not a feature of religious observance in the early church, which laid more stress on prayer and on the penances mentioned earlier. Study of the scriptures and copying the gospels were done in the brothers' own cells. At this time there was no symbolic monument corresponding to the beautiful high cross of later centuries, but there might be a smaller monolith, inscribed with a cross or perhaps a *Chi-Rho* symbol. No such stone, however, and no vestige of the great school or even traces of its rath have been discovered on the site of Clonard. Columba, according to the "Old Irish Life", referred to Clonard as a "city", and said his bothy was beside where its gate would be. Perhaps those big monastic settlements were the nearest thing to a town in an Ireland of small communities and farmsteads.

Adomnán has nothing to say about Columba's stay at Clonard, apart from the incident of the siting of his cell. Skene warns against accepting the tales of later writers if they are not to be found either in Cuimine or in Adomnán. The golden curtain of the miraculous had already fallen over the saint's life and veiled it before the "Old Irish Life" was compiled, so the incidents it associates with Clonard are of interest mainly because they are typical of the curious artlessness of so many of the legends which grew round Columba's name. We are told that at the time of the "night-feast" (supper) each of the apostles (Finnian's disciples) used to grind his corn in his quern to provide the food for the meal, but that an angel of the Lord used to grind Columba's for him, as a mark of honour, "because of his nobility above all". The chronicler may have considered it beneath a prince of the blood to do the usual menial tasks. Then again, Finnian himself is said to have seen two moons, one golden to the north illumining both Erin and Alba, one silver over the Shannon to the south. The golden moon represented Columba, the silver denoted Ciaran of Clonmacnoise. Oddly, Adomnán's *Life* has nothing to say about the one occurrence at Clonard which appears to be factual: that he seems to have completed his training there, and was ordained priest by Bishop Etchen of Clonfad. Columba, there-fore, derived his training from two main sources of instruction: in the first place from Finnian of Moville and ultimately from Finnian of Clonard.

Thus ordained—although Angus the Culdee seems to be our only authority for it—Columba set out from Clonard with three friends to travel to Glasnevin, now a suburb of Dublin. The friends were Comgall of Bangor, Ciaran mac Antsair, and Cainnech. Here, on the banks of the Tolka river, St Berchan Cláirainech, usually called Mobhi, also from Clonard, had set up a monastery and school east of the river, with the bothies of the 50 pupils or monks on the opposite bank. There is nothing, again, to indicate the site. Apparently there was a ford, but in spate the river became dangerous, for Mobhi praised Columba for crossing fully clothed when he heard the bell for matins. The church is described as a large one. A curious discussion is said to have occurred among the friends about what each would like to see it filled with. Ciaran's preference was for sons of the church who frequent the canonical hours, Cainnech's for books to be used by "sons of life"; but Comgall asked only that his body be afflicted by sickness and diseases to his "subjugation and chastisement". Columba's wish, on the other hand, was that the church be filled with gold and silver for the making of reliquaries and monasteries. Probably this is another apocryphal tale; but again there is a hint that memories of Columba are of a man different in temper from his fellows, a man of less simplicity and more forceful views. Individually the hints are fleeting, but they add up gradually to produce a quite firm impression.

The stay at Glasnevin was not lengthy. Mobhi warned his monks and followers to disperse because there was a threat of plague. He called it the *Buidhe Chonnaill*, the Yellow Plague, which took its name from the colour of the skins of its victims. Among the insubstantial material of the "Old Irish Life" one grasps at this sort of allusion as something possibly firmly factual. Gibbon relates that pestilence was rife throughout all Europe in those years (about 543–4). One of his authorities is Procopius, another Gregory of Tours. He is quite specific about the symptoms, among them the appearance of buboes, showing it to be what we know as bubonic plague; and the disease passed from the Middle East and Byzantium along the African coast, and then through Europe. Procopius indicates that it spread from the coasts inland, which means that ships brought it to the ports. There was a surprising amount of trade with Ireland, so that Ireland was not safe. The Yellow Plague may not have been bubonic—the Black Death was so—but then again we do know there was widespread pestilence in the reign of Justinian, and that the plague began in Egypt in 542, decimated Italy in 543. The very gospel-books which were so eagerly sought in Ireland could have been bearers of the disease, and the tale of Mobhi's warning to his people does seem to have a link with history.

Columba took his leave of Mobhi, whose parting instruction was that he should not receive land until he had sought his, Mobhi's, permission to do so. Columba went to "Cenel-Conaill", which is to say he returned to the lands of his people in Ulster. His journey took him across a river called Buir, which Dr Reeves identified with the Moyola in Tyrone, flowing into Lough Neagh. Here he prayed that the plague might come no further than this point, and went on his way to Derry.

This is the start of Columba's career as a leader of the church, as a founder of monasteries and a missionary, and we shall be concerned with his doings virtually to the exclusion of the other Saints of Ireland; but we have to remember he was only one of twelve apparently selected for the task of completing the conversion of their country. Finnian of Clonard is the dim presence behind them all. Finnian it was who, probably under the influence of Gildas of Wales, established the nature of the church in Ireland, reinforcing the tottering Patrician episcopal system by a type of monasticism peculiar to the country, and effective. The Martyrology of Donegal likens him to the Apostle Paul. Himself an abbot-presbyter, he sent out his twelve apostles to serve in the same capacity. Already when Columba made his way to Derry, Ciaran had founded Clonmacnoise, and within a few years Brendan would set up Clonfert. So with the rest. Emphases varied with the abbot and with the situation: Bangor, for example, became celebrated for scholarly achievement. But by the end of the sixth century Christianity was the recognised religion of the greater part of Ireland, and its pilgrims had streamed out in their hundreds across the seas to found new monasteries in Europe. The chroniclers might well scorn facts and write in terms of miracles.

IV

The Cursing of Tara

Columba must have been a man of no more than 24 when he turned his face to the north, filled with missionary zeal. He was exceptionally well equipped for the task. As we have seen, through Finnian of Clonard he may have had the fruits of the teaching of Gildas and the Welsh school, through Finnian of Moville perhaps the influence of Whithorn. His studies with the two Finnians might be interpreted as giving him, in terms of our own day, the equivalent of courses at two universities. Fully as important is the period with Gemman, because it confirmed him in his love for his national heritage through the myths and literature, and there too he may have developed his inborn powers of expression and rhetoric. His task was to establish centres through which the new faith could be spread. He knew his ability and had confidence in it. He may have been so confident as to have been impatient. As I have said, we have only Angus the Culdee's evidence for his ordination by Bishop Etchen, but it is a strange story that he tells. When Columba came for his ordination, Etchen was pointed out to him as a man ploughing a field. Columba remarked, "It is not meet for us that a plough-man should confer orders on us; but let us test him." Apparently satisfied, Columba went with Etchen to the church. But Etchen ordained him priest, "although it was the order of a bishop he wished to have conferred upon him". It is likely enough there is no substance to this story, but has it been fabricated from a lingering tradition that Columba was a man of a proud temper?

In going north into Ulster and among his own people, he must have been well aware of the advantages of his royal blood. Niall of the Nine Hostages was already a legend, and Columba was of his race. The king, Aedh, son of Ainmire, was his cousin-german, and Columba must have sought him as soon as he arrived in the north, for Aedh offered him as a place to build his church the royal *dun* or hill-fort at Derry, the name of which then was Daire Calgach, the oak wood of Calgach. Columba did not at once accept: he remembered Mobhi's injunction that he should not take land without his permission. But as he came down from the *dun*, so we are told in the "Old Irish Life", he met two messengers carrying Mobhi's girdle and the necessary permission to accept land. Mobhi had died. Was he perhaps a victim of the plague he had foretold? Columba took up Aedh's offer and proceeded with his plans. The hill on which the fort was built seems to have been clothed in oaks. If this be true, and it is firmly part of the ancient tradition, it would appear possible that the king had made over not merely a royal stronghold but a sacred grove, a *nemeton*, and if so he must have done it for a special reason. It may have been a mark of recognition of Columba's kinship, as Skene suggests, to give him a royal fort; but the gift may have been significant for other reasons, perhaps because it set Columba's first foundation firmly on a traditional base, lending it added validity in a time of transition.

Columba's own attitude to the place is very interesting. One version of the "Old Irish Life" relates that he burned the fort and its contents. Reproved by the king for destroying much food and drink, Columba answered rather cryptically: "No one shall be a night feasting there against his will." The fire, however, spread to the oak wood itself and looked like consuming it. To protect the wood Columba uttered a *rann*, an incantation, the words of which are obscure and apparently untranslatable; but it is recorded that this *rann* has been "sung" against fire, thunder and lightning ever since. Douglas Simpson cites another story, to the effect that Columba was unwilling to fell the oaks because of his love for the place. At least everything suggests the saint had a special attachment for the oaks, and I do not believe simple sentiment can be accepted as the explanation. His zeal to found monasteries was great, and to credit a Dark Age zealot with the environmentalist compunction of our own urban age is surely unrealistic. We are forced to look for other motives. We recall the terror of those druids forced by Caesar to destroy their oak groves. To quote old poems, as Simpson does, to make it look as if an early Irish monk must share our feelings about nature is, I am sure, a misinterpretation of those very poems. The belief that "Heaven's angels" were in every leaf of those trees, the warning "Woe to him who violates it!" have an ancient significance; and as for the lines:

> Though I am affrighted truly
> By death and by Hell;
> I am more affrighted, frankly,
> By the sound of an axe in Derry of the west

they are much too strongly phrased to mean anything less than the stirring of a primeval fear of the consequences of destroying a sacred tree, whether the fear was Columba's or in the man who wrote the verse. "Affrighted" is not the word of someone merely concerned about the loss of a beautiful tree.

This first of Columba's many foundations took place in 546. The site is in what is now called Long Tower Street in Londonderry, and is occupied by St Columba's Church. Naturally enough, nothing is left to mark the original settlement, or even later structures of what became the premier monastery of the north, but the present name of the street implies there was a characteristic round tower here, erected perhaps in the ninth or tenth century. Exposed as it was to easy access from the sea, the Vikings inevitably sacked the place. By their day it must have been a rich settlement. Unlike remoter sixth-century foundations, Derry lay among good pastures and the monastic communities soon settled down to work the land. Sheltered by hills and with excellent sea communications, the monastery would not only become prosperous but would attract clerics and scholars from far places. It may be indicative of the shelter and good husbandry that it was at Derry the first of the recorded miracle harvests took place, according to the "Old Irish Life". Columba had sent his monks to a wood to cut wattles to build a church, which they did without permission from the young man who owned the wood. He complained, and Columba told his people to take him the value of the timber in the equivalent amount of barley grain, telling him to sow it, although midsummer was already past. The young man did as they instructed him, and the barley ripened about Lammas, six weeks from sowing to harvest.

We are told Columba loved the "city" of Derry very much. His feeling is put into his mouth in a well-known verse:

> The reason why I love Derry is
> For its quietness, for its purity;
> For 'tis full of angels white
> from one end to the other.

The Celt's undoubted attachment to place has never curbed his restlessness, and Columba in his later twenties seems to have done much travelling. At Derry he is believed to have contemplated a pilgrimage to Rome and to Jerusalem. The *peregrini* were already on the move, and their urge must have been infectious. There is no proof that he made any such pilgrimage, but the "Old Irish Life" has it that he did go to "Tor-inis of Martin", which is to say the Tours of St Martin, whose teaching must have been ever-present in his mind when he studied at Moville and Clonard. It is perhaps surprising that Adomnán makes no mention of such a journey, or of any miracle or vision evoked by it. Yet there may have been vessels from as far off as Brittany coming into Derry, so that a pilgrimage to Tours would have been no exceptional feat. The tale goes so far as to say he "brought away the gospel that had been on Martin's bosom one hundred years in the earth". It was nearer a century and a half since Martin's death, and the book's survival in legible condition would itself seem to be a miracle, but such books were often invulnerable to damp and rot, if the legends are to be believed. Columba, like all his brother-saints, was avid for gospel-books to copy, and to possess as precious relics. He is thought to have left St Martin's gospel in Derry. However, one must set against this tale the fact that Tor-Inis, literally "towery island", is also the name of Tory Island off the north coast of Donegal, which has firm associations with the saint.

This collecting and copying of precious books raises the rather baffling question as to how the primitive cells of the monks could have been fit places to keep manuscripts in. They must have been more skilfully built than accounts of them suggest, but those men were practical as well as intelligent and zealous. I recall Professor Baldwin Brown in one of his lectures quoting the comment of a countryman-builder: "Give cob good boots and a hat and he will last for ever." As cob is nothing more than clay and straw, his dictum would apply to wattle-and-daub huts, so we can assume the monks knew all about firm stone foundations and how to lay thatch. Probably the cells contained stone aumbries or cupboards, like the stone cells on the Skellig. Churches also were perhaps just a little more solid and sophisticated than they sound. In the first chapter I compared the Monymusk reliquary with an early oratory. By the date of Derry's founding the church may have developed from wattle construction to a building of hewn oak. The Gallarus oratory in Co. Kerry is, after all, a stone structure put together with much skill, and is not so very much later than Derry in date. The damp-proofing of those buildings was probably much more effective than we imagine. Recently I helped excavate the gable-end of a 200-year-old cottage on one of the islands off the west coast of Scotland in the belief that soil piled against it must cause damp, only to unearth a carefully-devised drainage system which, after two centuries of neglect, instantly disposed of as many pails of water as we cared to pour into it. The Gallarus building and its fellows are, as the De Paors say, of petrified wooden construction.

We can only guess at how far joiners and wood-workers had carried their skills into the realms of art, as mentioned in discussing the buildings at Tara, but the caste of artificers had certainly survived; and literary evidence—again to quote the De Paors—shows timber oratories were built of jointed planks with shingles as an alternative to reed thatch, so that secure wooden aumbries too may have been available in the new monasteries. Cogitosus' description of St Brigid's church at Kildare goes so far as to mention windows and screens, paintings and linen hangings, as well as an ornate door. As at Tara, it would be interesting to know more about the decoration, and especially the use of sacred symbolism, but nothing of the kind is mentioned. Nor is there mention of what sacred vessels there may have been, or of what form they took, but it will be remembered that at Glasnevin Columba wished for gold and silver to make reliquaries. Mass-chalices there must have been, but we do not know what they were like. The only other feature beginning to appear was a stone monument, a monolith, usually marking the founder's grave, but surviving examples are a little later in date than this.

It was a challenging time to be alive in, and Columba knew it. He was *miles Christi*, a soldier of Christ, and like any good general he had studied the terrain and had tried to read the minds of his enemies. Iron Age society, ruled by heroic chieftains warring in their chariots like Boudicca or the Rhineland princes of earlier times, was rapidly giving way to more settled communities based on cultivation of the land. Local fighting and cattle-reiving of course continued, and would do for centuries; but there was a tendency for the *tuatha* to come together in alliances or associations, and for Ireland to divide into two broad feudal sectors, the north under the kings of Tara, the south under the kings of Cashel. The web of ancient myths which explained everything in creation back to the beginning of time and enabled everyone to know the part he or she had to play was by no means pulled asunder by new happenings; but there were new myths in the making, the myths of the Age of Saints.

Magic and miracles had always been part of the Celtic way of life, sometimes trivial, sometimes splendid, setting ideals which were interwoven with exaltation of the warrior caste. Now new myths were in the making, doing for the *milites Christi* what the old myths had done for the warrior-chiefs, and often as not the new myths were borrowed from the scriptures. There is water turned to wine, there are tempests calmed. At Derry itself there is the tale of the child brought for baptism, when, because there was no water near, Columba made the sign of the cross over a rock from which immediately a fountain gushed. Ireland is not Sinai, and one is apt to be impatient at the thought of a saint who works a miracle of this kind in a countryside filled with springs and rivulets; yet the important point is not the miracles, often childish, but the attempt to substitute new myths for old. Perhaps it should be said to marry new myths to old, for the old heroic myths survived until the eighteenth century, and in the Scottish Highlands seized upon such a figure as Charles Edward Stuart. The cult of the saints did not drive out the cult of heroes. The kings kept a good edge on their swords. The Uí Néill scented the sovereignty of Ireland. And Columba had not forgotten he was a prince of the Uí Néill.

The door to the expansion of the power of the Uí Néill opened upon Alba. The fighting-men of the Dal Riatá of Antrim had crossed the sea to what is now Argyllshire, probably in the second half of the fifth century. It could have been part of the inflow to the vacuum following the retreat of the legions from Britain, part of the general closing in of the "barbarian" peoples on the fringes of the Empire. From southern Ireland there had been an exodus to Wales, although the desperate Britons contained this and prevented deeper penetration. The Dal Riatá, on the other hand, may have found a weak point where the frontiers of several peoples met, the Picts and the Britons of Strathclyde particularly. The Picts were powerful adversaries. The Dal Riatá, the Scots of Dalriada, could however expand in no other direction but across the sea to Alba, and they hung on rather precariously to their new Dalriada there. Their king, Fergus Mór mac Erc, with his brothers Loarn and Aengus, had brought with them a force of only 150 men, according to an account of three centuries later. It is not stated what opposition they met with and Bede is in two minds as to whether they were received as friends or enemies, but they seem to have annexed a considerable region of the south-west Highlands and islands.

Aengus settled on Islay. Loarn took over what is now consequently known as Lorne, centred upon Dunolly, just north of Oban. The family of Fergus himself occupied Knapdale and the peninsula of Kintyre, and their capital on the rock of Dunadd became the capital of Scottish Dalriada as a whole. Until those invaders came there were no Scots in what is now Scotland, for Scotti was the name given to the Irish by the Romans, and this was the first massive penetration of the Gaels who were to contribute so much to Scotland's history. The first king of all Scottish Dalriada was Gabrain, grandson of Fergus, and his tribe, the Cinel Gabrain, dominated the kingdom; but they were coming under heavier and heavier pressure from the Picts just when Columba rose to prominence. In 557 the Picts under their king, Brude MacMaelcon, slew Gabrain in a battle. Gabrain's crown went to his cousin, Conaill. Now that the Uí Néill had sway over northern Ireland the cause of Dalriada had become their cause too, or at least their opportunity.

If Ireland had had the makings of a nation at this time, Conaill's position would have been stronger. We have to remember, however, that Christianity had not cured the chronic state of division there. Power had been consolidated in the hands of the Uí Néill in the north and in those of the Eóganacht at Cashel in the south, for a start, but within those areas tribal jealousy was slow to die. Indeed, it has been doubted if there was any real advance in "civilisation" in Ireland from the time of Niall Nóigiallach to the Anglo-Norman invasion. It is true Niall's descendants were over-kings until the year 1002, but the history of those times is a bewildering confusion of battles and assassinations among tribal chieftains of north and south. It might be asked if Christianity had done nothing to unify them, since it had spread so early and so rapidly. Like later and more powerful rulers elsewhere, they seem to have used their religion as a convenience; but unlike those other rulers they sometimes changed their faith quite openly to paganism and back again as it suited them, making for further confusion. One such over-king of Tara later prominent in the story of Columba, Diarmaid mac Cerbaill, was an open polygamist and had recourse to druids' services in a great battle central to the Columban issue. As Professor Byrne says, even the regnal lists give a false image of stability and dynastic continuity. The annals were of course compiled in a later age. And the scribes were subject to a system of patronage in which credit or blame were apportioned as it suited the patron. But whatever we are to believe of those chroniclers even sections of sixth-century Ireland were incapable of sustained, concerted efforts along the line of a predetermined policy, so that the Pictish threat to the existence of Alban Dalriada was very real.

One man who perhaps did have a predetermined policy is Columba. After the founding of Derry he spent fifteen or sixteen years industriously establishing churches and monasteries all over the north.

> Three hundred he measured, without fault,
> Of churches fair, 'tis true;
> And three hundred splendid, lasting books
> Noble-bright he wrote.

There is no authority whatever for thinking that during this period he was motivated by anything but missionary zeal; yet if we look back on it with hindsight from the vantage of events preceding his leaving Ireland we have to wonder about the full implication of his plan. Certainly he hoped by the evangelisation of the tribes to bring about a stable Ireland: a glance at the distribution of his foundations on a map shows they were carefully located to cover the area. Conscious as he was of his kinship with the king, and proud of his heritage, it must have been part of his purpose to strengthen his people and make them more effective in the face of a threatening world. We have grown so accustomed to the image of Jesus as one transcending the bounds of Judaism, as one who loved the Gentiles as he did the Jews, that we think of the saints as necessarily following in Jesus' footsteps; but if we ponder the loyalties between church and state throughout the centuries right down to our own, are we justified in believing Columba did not put the interests of his people first?

At the same time it is now we begin to glimpse the stature of Columba, a stature of which the popular image of a plaster saint does not admit. The number of his foundations is great and proves his immense organising and executive ability, his unbending will. He must have been a man of great courage, worthy of the Cinel Conaill; because in spite of the absence of a show of violent pagan hostility to the early missionaries it was a different matter when the cleric opposed the will of a strong man—St Patrick himself was nearly murdered by Coirpre mac Néill at Tailtiu, and the saint used his only effective weapon and cursed Coirpre's descendants. As I have said before, those men were not stained-glass window saints. Columba too could curse. He was a man of his times. He was both shrewd and wise. He knew too much about the myths and mysteries ministered to by the druids to despise them as empty superstition. There is an old text quoted by Proinsias MacCana which tells how one of the spirits of the otherworld paid Columba a visit. The saint took the being aside out of hearing of the monks who were around them "in order to converse with him and to question him about the heavenly and earthly mysteries". The discussion went on for 24 hours, the monks watching from a distance. Suddenly the stranger vanished. The monks begged Columba to tell them about the conversation, but Columba replied he could tell them nothing and "that it was proper for them not to be told". As Professor MacCana comments, the tale is of course apocryphal but not invented from nothing.

Columba, I think, not only respected the knowledge of the druids but, in a sense, believed in it: believed that the ancient lore such as we see in the symbolism on the reliquary was part of the very fabric of the race, to destroy which would render his people helpless in the face of evil. If this seems to credit Columba with the insights of a twentieth-century psychiatrist, it should be remembered that Carl Gustav Jung had to reach back across the centuries to discern the importance of linking by myth with "the world of the ancestors" and point to the havoc which may be wrought by loss of this mythic world. Columba lived on the very edge of this world. It is not extraordinary if its reality was obvious to him. Jung sees in detachment from the race-myth the source of neuroticism in certain people in our times, but such a race-myth was basic to life in sixth-century Ireland.

If the verse quoted above exaggerates the number of Columba's foundations, nevertheless they were many. The "Old Irish Life" points to 100 "on the margin of the sea alone", with a mass-chalice in every one of them. Some of his monasteries are named.

About 553 he went to preach to the King of Tethba—Teffia, a locality embracing part of King's County and Westmeath—and the king, Aed, son of Brenand, gave him ground at Dair Magh, now Durrow, where the monastery was destined to become one of his greatest. The name, one is tempted to say inevitably, means the plain of the oaks. Did those chroniclers even as late as the tenth century still feel the need to underpin the Christian faith by demonstrating that its magic was as powerful as the old magic done in those druidic strongholds? Durrow had been such a pagan sanctuary, and not only the "Old Irish Life" but Adomnán himself in Book II describes the apple tree there bearing bitter fruit which "injured more than delighted" local folk, but became sweet when commanded in the name of God to change its nature. Miracles in the gospels are always significant; but this kind of miracle is not worthy of the saint, and I can only explain it as a rather perfunctory piece of symbol-making, an utterance of exorcism to reassure the superstitious.

Durrow, however, became one of the famed scholastic establishments, known everywhere for the manuscripts it produced. More and more, copying of the gospel-books was one of the main preoccupations of the holy men, filling in their time when they were not otherwise committed. The earlier anchorites had penned their books in "secret little huts in the wilderness", the song of birds in their ears, but in big centres like Durrow the multiplication of books grew into something like an industry. Yet books never ceased to be rare and precious possessions, objects in which holy power resided, and indeed the commitment of thoughts to permanent visual form must still have been a matter for wonder to men whose grandfathers, maybe, had known no other way of passing them on except memory and the spoken word. From now on the scriptorium of the monastery was a place of first importance. Gradually the book became the chief medium for the renaissance of Celtic art, with the new faith as its driving force, and something will be said in the next chapter about this. Columba's own passion for books had a part in it. For a long time it was believed the saint actually was the author or scribe of the celebrated Book of Durrow, now in the Library of Trinity

College, Dublin, which lay in the Abbey of Durrow until the sixteenth century, after which it came into the hands of a local man who tried to cure his cattle by giving them water in which he had dipped the sacred book. The association with Columba is due to his name appearing in a late addition to the text which, coupled with the book's having come from a Columban foundation, seemed conclusive; but it belongs to a later century and will be mentioned again in the appropriate place.

The kings and chieftains and warriors whose patronage had sustained the Celtic artist through many centuries were increasingly to be ousted in this function by the monasteries. The poets too devoted much of their verse to the holy men; but it was perhaps the artists principally who congregated round the monasteries, as they needed protection and stable conditions for their workshops. The metalworkers especially would be welcomed by the abbot. But books were the means of learning and were crucial to the spread of the faith, and for a long time reading and writing must have been an accomplishment of the monks alone. It seems unlikely that the kings and the chief men of the *tuatha* at first would feel the need for those skills, and would rely on clerics or "clerks" as the leading men of other countries were to do. The importance of making records for posterity was quickly recognised. Writing such records became of prime importance in the monasteries, and in the course of time the Scribe of the Annals seems to have been elevated to the mastership of the scriptorium.

The *paruchia Columbae* covered, more or less, the northern half of Ireland, from Durrow to Derry, the territory dominated by the Uí Néill. Among his other foundations in the area were Clonmore in Co. Louth, in Co. Dublin Swords and Lambay (on an island off the coast), Drumcliffe and Drumcolumb in Co. Sligo, Moone in Co. Kildare. Dr Reeves fully listed the rest. Of course, Columba was not alone in this work. Bangor (Bennchar) in Co. Down came into being in 558 under Comgall, one of the three companions with whom Columba had set out from Clonard. Possibly the most celebrated of Columba's own foundations was at Kells in Co. Meath, the "Middle County" created by his

kinsmen. Another royal gift of land made this possible. The site
was a *dun* of the high-king mentioned earlier in the chapter,
Diarmaid mac Cerbaill, of the southern branch of the Uí Néill,
the man with a foot in both pagan and Christian camps. It seems
Columba was held up at the door of the *dun*—the Irish is variously
rendered as "tarried" and "delayed"—and one is left with the
impression he must have been impatient, even angry at having
his entry barred. The "royal prophet" of the king was present,
Becc mac Dead by name This presumably means a chief bard.
Columba is recorded as saying to him:

> "Tell me, O Becc—
> Broad, bright-grassed Cenandas [Kells]—
> What clerics shall possess it,
> What young men shall abandon it?"

And to this Becc answered:

> "The clerics who are on its floor
> Sing the praises of a king's son;
> Its young men depart from its threshold;
> A time will come when 'twill be sure."

This oracular exchange is rather obscure. The "king's son" is
Diarmaid's son, Aedh Slane. The "clerics" singing his praises
appear to have been druids, for Columba's question implies the
clerics in the *dun* were not his own followers, and the "young
men" then are warriors, probably the garrison of the fort.
Columba therefore was asking when the fort was going to be
handed over to him, and Becc replying the garrison would leave
just as soon as the druids completed their praise of Aedh Slane.
When he had taken possession, the saint proceeded to mark out
the monastery and to bless it, foretelling it would be the most
important of his foundations; and at the same time he turned
towards the south-west, and began to laugh heartily. Asked by
the monk Boithan why he laughed, he gave a cryptic reply,
apparently announcing the birth of a saint at that very moment
at some place in the direction he was looking.

At Kells too there is a story about an oak. We are told a great tree under which he stood, possibly sheltering, lived for "long ages" after, until thrown down by a storm; and when a man used some of its bark to tan his shoes no sooner had he put them on than leprosy seized him from head to foot. Many of those tales about Columba make him seem more like a magician than a holy man: they seem to do nothing to promote his reputation for sanctity, and foster dread rather than admiration. In this category is his warning to Aedh Slane, the king's son. This prince sounds like a typical, hot-blooded Celtic bravo, careless of the injuries he did, for Columba admonished him, although Professor Byrne calls it a friendly warning. The saint assured him of a long life if he avoided being a parricide, for if he committed this crime "there would not be but four years of his age", meaning he would only have four years left to live. To protect the young man he blessed a cloak for him, telling him he could not be wounded while he wore it. Eventually Aedh Slane slew the son of his brother, Colman Bec. Under the law this *fingal* or kin-slaying came under the crime he had been warned against; and when four years later he set out on an expedition and forgot his cloak, the same day he was killed. The compiler of the "Old Irish Life" evidently saw nothing odd in a saint condoning the behaviour of a bully, short of kin-slaying, and for this reason if no other the report of the incident is significant.

The multiplication of miracles and wonders at this time is bewildering. It will be recalled that on the day of Columba's birth the dying Buite, founder of Monasterboice, predicted the new saint would find his (Buite's) grave and "measure his cemetery". This prophecy was fulfilled when Columba went to Monasterboice, for his *bachuil*, his staff or crozier, struck the glass ladder by which Buite had ascended to heaven, the sound of it reverberating through the church. It is a quaint way of indicating that the means of ascent was invisible. The numerous books written by Columba, too, had miraculous powers, for they survived immersion in water without so much as a letter being "drowned", as the text puts it. And when he went to Lambay island with his two old companions, Comgall and Cainnech, to visit the monastery, both saw a fiery column appear above his head when he made the offering of the body and blood of Christ.

But the myths and miracles which bulk so large in the early accounts of the saint should not be allowed to obscure his solid educational achievement. The teaching function of the monastic system has been mentioned (Chapter II); the thought and energy which must have gone into realising it in practical terms make the Columban educational achievement a more remarkable one by far than John Knox's famed contribution to Scottish schooling. Monasteries seem to spring up and bloom like flowers in the footsteps of Columba, as though he created them with a wave of his *bachuil*; but we know that in the first place he had to negotiate with the king of the tribe for the grant of land on which to build his "city", then for endowments with which to launch and maintain it. We have seen that the monks sometimes took over the druidical schools, but those would provide nothing which could be called capital equipment, whereas the monastic schools involved the provision of books and writing materials in quantities and, by implication, accommodation for their safe keeping. Such things were given free to the students, who were also granted free food and clothing. This system was maintained only by an elaborate farming programme carried out by the monks, and the numbers of students in all Ireland must have amounted to tens of thousands, many of them from other lands, because in Ireland almost alone could such establishments of learning be found. Even staffing problems must have been considerable, because however willing in spirit the brethren might be it has to be remembered Latin was now the second language of instruction and the teachers must have had to be taught. To set up a comparable chain of establishments in the modern world would require the creation of a civil-service hierarchy and a complex system of committees, yet we are left with the impression Columba and his brother-saints created everything much as God created the world in the first chapter of Genesis. It is quite wrong to think that in simpler times it is a simpler matter to achieve such objects, even though Parkinson's Law did not apply.

Something has been said about Tara as a location, and about its significance as the scene of the choosing and consecration of the king, which took place at the Feast of Tara. The Celtic concept of kingship was a strange one. The king was part divine, and there can be no doubt it is because this belief was so deeply held by Celts that the Stuart kings' doctrine of the Divine Right found such response among the Highland clans. In ancient times the king was the spouse of the country, and his consecration was the ritual marriage of the two. This sacral union was a time of extreme vulnerability, and Professor Byrne has pointed out that mythological references make the still-visible ramparts at Tara "a defence against a hostile Otherworld". Certainly the bank round the inner enclosure here, as at other royal sites, is not devised as a defence against flesh-and-blood enemies since, as Bernard Wailes showed, the ditch is inside not outside the rampart. At this critical event, therefore, Tara was compassed about by magic and had to be protected by powerful spells, so that at this of all times it was the druids came into their own.

The sanctity of Tara may have been primeval, but the particular myth binding it to the Uí Néill kingship began with Niall of the Nine Hostages, whom the priesthood, the seers, the bards had elevated to a legendary personage who, consenting to a union with a repulsive hag guarding a well from which he wished to drink, suddenly finds the woman he has embraced is more lovely than the sun. She it is who foretells the centuries of rule of his descendants, the Uí Néill. She is in fact the personification of Ireland. The mortal king—Niall was of course an historical figure—has to impose his will upon this divine being, and the union symbolised the gift of fecundity to the kingdom, transforming it from a barren waste to productiveness and beauty. Obviously, it is a world-wide myth. What the ritual was at Tara is obscure. It may have been too repugnant for later chroniclers to describe, but Giraldus Cambrensis claims the custom was for the king to mate with a white mare, which was slaughtered, sliced up and boiled, the king then eating the flesh while sitting in a bath of broth made from the blood. The king, says Giraldus, is no prince but a brute. Giraldus naturally was seeking to discredit pagan tradition in every way he knew, but such rites are not unknown elsewhere in the world. Inauguration of rulers is the very cornerstone of state religions, and the druids would devise ceremonial to dramatise their power. A confrontation between them and the new faith at Tara was inevitable.

The last man to hold the Feast of Tara is the king we have met with, Diarmaid mac Cerbaill, in the year 560. That he held the Feast is conclusive proof that he had not forsaken pagan superstitions, whether or no he professed Christianity, as Adomnán implies he did. It was a challenge to the church, a gauntlet thrown down demanding a duel for spiritual sovereignty. But Diarmaid himself, not the druids, made the challenge. Twice he broke one of the fundamental rights of the monasteries—the right of sanctuary. The *Annals of Tigernach* relate that he slew at Tara a son of the King of Connacht, Prince Curnán, who had accidentally killed a playfellow at the sports which were part of the Feast, although Curnán was under the protection of Columba. Diarmaid also slew another prince of Connacht, Aed Guaine, although he had sought sanctuary with St Ruadán of Lorrha. Ruadán was of the Eóganacht of Cashel. Diarmaid at the same time seized someone who had taken refuge with Ruadán, and refused to give him up. One legend has it that Ruadán brought together "the saints of Ireland" to fast against Diarmaid and "the four kindreds of Tara", and that they went to Tara and cursed it, saying there would not be a house there, foretelling the ridge-beam would fall on Diarmaid, in fear of which the king had it pulled down and taken out to sea. No doubt the Cursing of Tara is a myth of later fabrication, perhaps to help strengthen faith in the power of sanctuary and the vengeance of the church, but it is symbolic of a real and vital conflict in which the church emerged as victor. Columba had a major part in it, although the legend does not mention him as present at the Cursing, and his confrontation with the king, as we shall see, was real enough and probably a turning-point in his career. Also real is the breaking of the power which Tara symbolised, for the grass seems to have begun to grow over it thereafter. The title of King of Tara continued proudly, at least until the coming of Brian Boru, but Tara of the Kings was no more.

V

The Battle of Cul Dreimne

We are approaching a point in Columba's life when he appears to have reached a crisis. On the interpretation of what happened at this point hangs much of the evidence for an assessment of his character, yet accounts are contradictory and baffling and there is no consensus of views among modern commentators. A guilty-or-innocent issue arises on which verdicts tend to be decided subjectively, on a basis of circumstance with no fragment of fact to go upon. One grasps at straws as pointers to the truth, and the only wisp is the celebrated *Cathach* referred to near the beginning of this book.

The *Cathach*, it will be remembered, is too big to have lain in the Monymusk reliquary. What originally preserved it for us is not known: perhaps one of the leathern book-satchels mentioned by Adomnán, a type depicted on the Great Cross at Clonmacnoise. Towards the end of the eleventh century, and already in bad condition, it was put in a closely-fitting box of wood covered with metal and, to judge by the decoration, made at Kells. The man who had this done was the then chief of Columba's own tribe, the northern Uí Néill, more familiar by this time as the O'Donnells, and the chief's name was Cathbarr O'Donnell. In 1497 the *Cathach* was carried by its hereditary keeper before the army of the O'Donnells, without conspicuous success. Shortly after, one Manus O'Donnell wrote a life of Columba in which the *Cathach* is referred to as "the chief relic of St Columba in the territory of the Cinel Conaill Gulban. It is in a silver-gilt box which must not be opened. And each time it has been carried three times, turning towards the right, around the army before a battle, the army came back victorious." After the Treaty of Limerick in 1691 the Jacobite army fled to France, an O'Donnell among them carrying the *Cathach*. A silver casket was made to contain it. In 1802 Sir Neal O'Donel brought it back to Ireland, and Sir William Betham, working on the papers of the O'Donnell family, managed to open the box and found the book in a sad state because of damp. He contrived to separate the pages. The beginning and the end leaves had gone, and only about half of the original psalter had survived.

What is left is of intense interest. In Book II of Adomnán, the eighth and ninth chapters describe the miraculous power of books "written by the dear and holy fingers of Columba" to survive immersion in water, even when other books with them are found to be decayed and rotten. One, a book of hymns for the week, is said to have lain in a river "from the Feast of the Nativity of the Lord to the end of the Paschal Season", and was found on the bank as clean and dry as if it had lain in a desk. The tradition associating the *Cathach* with Columba's hand makes attribution of age of the first importance. The script is a very early, indeed archaic type of Irish majuscule, and palaeographers accept that it may date from the sixth century. More than that, to all appearance it seems to have been written by one person. The book has not exactly revealed the miraculous properties of damp-resistance indicated by Adomnán, but, that apart, is there any good reason why the tradition of Columba's authorship should be dismissed? Probably there is none. We can go no further than this; but on the other hand we have to guard against allowing our natural scepticism to condemn all such myths and legends, perhaps especially in Ireland where these have a way of proving not quite so improbably founded as they seem. After all, this book was firmly in O'Donnell hands in the eleventh century, and we know its history from then on.

Anyone who has spent a lifetime in a museum, as I have, grows wary of family traditions, but the false attributions we meet with are proved to be so usually because the manifest age of the heirloom in question conflicts with the tradition—it is just not old enough. The *Cathach* has been dated by Carl Nordenfalk at about 625, but only a very few years need to be lopped off this to bring it into the saint's lifetime. It is therefore possibly old enough to be Columba's work. H. J. Lawlor insisted it was his. Françoise

Henry is tempted to believe that the story "holds some truth", because the text from which the book is copied, the "gallican" translation of the psalter by St Jerome, had probably been unknown in Ireland up to that time, so that anyone as eager as Columba to make copies of such documents would exert every effort to include this.

The *Cathach* in the first place yields confirmation, clear visual confirmation, of events we have been discussing. If anyone is inclined to doubt the debt owed by the Saints of Ireland to the Desert Fathers, and the implied longing to seek basic gospel truths in lonely places, there is something significant here. It is to be looked for in the decoration. The art of illumination which was to attain such magnificence in the Celtic monasteries within a century or two is not even promised on the pages of the *Cathach*, which are not very exciting to the layman's eye; but the great gospel-books of later times such as Kells are so complex, so eclectic, so sophisticated, that they bewilder and at first sight obscure the evidence.

Two pointers to be singled out in the decoration of the *Cathach* are the colours employed and the little dots used to fringe the capital letters, normally in red. Both reflect the Coptic manuscripts of Egyptian monasteries. If it seems a long way for a slight feature to travel in dark, dangerous times, nevertheless there it is. Dr Henry has speculated on the effects of traffic between the Near East and Ireland, and if there were only an occasional boat it might well have brought Eastern monks seeking refuge from the Arabs, and their gospel-books would be their most precious possessions. Pottery from the Near East, after all, has turned up in quantities on south Irish sites such as Garranes, near Cork. In the second place the *Cathach* confirms the early scribes' awareness of their pagan heritage. Initial letters have a free, swirling quality and tend to curl off into details plainly influenced by patterns on contemporary jewellery such as penannular brooches and those long pins with little ornamental heads known as hand-pins, found both in Ireland and Scotland. As Nordenfalk remarks, it is the lingering tradition of La Tène art. The grand freedom of line is not yet there.

Strokes are still rather tentative, but the feeling is already present.

Then in the third place something is to be learned from the script itself. Most "barbarian" peoples who had been without a written literature would have copied precisely, or as well as they were able, the style of lettering of the books they used as models. The Irish borrowed the uncial lettering of the Romans, as indeed they had to as they learned to write in Latin; but rapidly they devised a "Celtic" script, quite distinct from the scripts used on the continent, and by the time the *Cathach* was written this script had acquired a marked character of its own, with the clarity and assurance of some maturity. The Latin of the *Cathach* is more easily read than the Latin of many a manuscript of the middle ages, or later. There is nothing laboured about this script. It has a deftness, a liveliness, a fluency of outline which somehow confronts one with the scribe himself, and prompts speculation about what sort of a man he was, and what were the circumstances in which he penned those lines. . . .

Is there anything in the records to help us with such speculation? There are numerous references to Columba as a scribe, for example in Book I of Adomnán. It is the book of the prophecies, and contains some of the material which may have irritated the Duke of Argyll, because the prophecies described are, as prophecies, derisory. There is No. 24, for example, in which Columba, sitting by the hearth, spies one Mugbe, "of the tribe Mocumin", reading a book. "Take care, son," says Columba, "take care, for I think that the book which thou readest is about to fall into a vessel full of water." And when the young man gets up with the book tucked carelessly under his arm it falls into a jar of water. Then again the following chapter describes the saint sitting in his hut, presumably at his desk, when he hears someone shouting across the strait at Fionnphort. Columba remarks: "The man who is shouting is not a man of refined sentiment, for today he will upset and spill my ink-horn." Presently the man arrives and in his eagerness to kiss the saint he duly upsets the ink-horn. It is all a little reminiscent of Ernest Bramah's delightful *Kai Lung's Golden Hours.* Yet ridiculous though they may be as "prophecies", I wonder if as stories those are not perhaps among the true records in Adomnán's book. They do nothing for the glory of the saint, but quite a lot for his credibility. Here are the water-borne voices of a still day in the Hebrides, the smell of a turf fire and of kelp on the foreshore, maybe a twinkle in the grey eye of the saint. We can visualise the ink-horn itself: such a horn appears in an Irish manuscript at St Gall. Here at least are the sort of conditions in which books like the *Cathach* were copied.

Then again, if we are to accept the most interesting story associated with the *Cathach*, the conditions were not quite the same. It is said that Columba's master, Abbot Finnian of Moville, had been on a pilgrimage to Rome and had returned with an especially beautiful book of psalms, which he placed in his church. Some time in the year 560 Columba is thought to have gone into this church and to have copied the book secretly over a number of nights, although he had not asked Finnian's permission. The abbot discovered what had happened, and insisted the copy must belong to him: an incident which Douglas Simpson refers to as an early example of action on copyright. Columba refused to give up the copy he had made. Eventually he and Finnian referred the dispute to the king for his decision, and he of course was Diarmaid mac Cerbaill, who had already incurred Columba's anger by his slaying of Curnán when the saint had given sanctuary to the youth. Diarmaid's judgment, somewhat Delphic, was the famous one: "To every cow belongeth her calf, to every book its little book," meaning that a copy must belong with the original. Columba had to give his copy back to Finnian, but he could not control his indignation and cried: "This is an unjust decision, O Diarmaid, and I will be avenged!"

Are we to believe this story, so crucial to an assessment of the personality of Columba? There is no mention of it in the pages of Adomnán—it would be surprising if there were. It is rejected by Skene, who declares it inconsistent with the affection and respect which, on the evidence of Adomnán, existed between Finnian and Columba. Skene does say in a footnote: "This transcript appears to have been the book termed the *Cathach*, which remained among the relics of St Columba, and the tradition seems to be connected with it." No doubt he meant to say "alleged transcript": this matters little. But why should such a tradition be connected with such an important relic? There is something here which has been hidden from us by the hagiographers. It is hinted at by Adomnán in Book III, chapter iii, where, without mention of the *Cathach* or of anything definite, he admits that Columba had incurred blame "for some venial and quite excusable causes", and apparently at just about this time. Reeves comments there is no means of knowing what Columba had done. Skene's refusal to believe him capable of doing anything arising out of resentment or indignation simply because of what Adomnán said of the friendship between him and Finnian is, to my mind, wholly unrealistic and nearly amounts to suppression of evidence.

Reading between the lines, then, we seem to discern a crisis in Columba's life. Indeed, it is a major crisis. Whatever it is about, it involves the king, Diarmaid. Tradition has it that Columba, following his threat to avenge himself on Diarmaid, brought pressure on his tribe, the Uí Néill of the north, to make war on the king, and that he enlisted his cousins of the Cinel Conaill and also the King of Connacht to rally to his cause. His grievances were two: the judgment on the *Cathach*, and the slaying of Curnán in sanctuary. The *Annals of Tigernach* emphasise the second, although they omit the first. The northern Uí Néill did in fact make war on Diarmaid in 561. The armies met at a place called Cul Dreimne (Culdrevny or Cooladrummon) a little north of Sligo on the lower ground at the base of Benbulban, where Columba had founded a church. The ancient church is gone, but it may have been close to the present church of Drumcliffe, with its beautiful tenth-century wheel-cross. This is the church of which William Butler Yeats' grandfather was vicar, and the poet at his own request is buried here. He wrote his own epitaph, those strange lines:

> Cast a cold eye
> On life, on death.
> Horseman, pass by!

There is a theory that Yeats' horsemen were visionary beings which a Sligo servant girl used to say she saw in this place. I recall my wife and I talking with a priest a few miles along the road south of here, he stubbornly insisting Yeats was no true Irishman; but the curious haunting quality of the place comes through with every word.

> That pale, long-visaged company
> That air in immortality
> Completeness of their passions won;
> Now they ride the wintry dawn
> Where Ben Bulben sets the scene.

Maybe it was the spectres of the hundreds slain at Cul Dreimne the girl saw, for it is believed to have been a bloody conflict. Neither Adomnán nor the "Old Irish Life" have anything to say of what happened, and references in later sources are doubtless inventions, so that any description of the battle must rely mainly on imagination. There is a tendency to look on it as a trial of strength between the new faith and the old paganism, the miraculous outcome being 3,000 dead on the heathen side against a solitary casualty among the Christian warriors, but probably we are not justified in making such a clear-cut issue of it. Diarmaid, despite his behaviour, was not an open enemy of the church—he has a place on the Cross of the Scriptures at Clonmacnoise—and on the other hand the northern Uí Néill were not solely interested in the triumph of Christianity. Diarmaid almost certainly called upon the druids to perform their battle ritual and cast spells to render the enemy impotent, but most Dark Age commanders in such situations would hedge their bets when it came to magic; and while the *Annals of Ulster* claim the battle was won "by the prayers of Columcille" it would seem likely that in the eyes of the fighting-men this was merely a substitution of Christian for pagan magic, and it would be surprising if they too did not mutter a few pagan incantations.

Where we can perhaps fill in detail with more assurance is in the military aspect. It must be concluded that the sixth-century Irish equipped themselves and fought on a well-established pattern, for it is doubtful if this had changed much since the Celts of Gaul and Britain fought the legions. Bardic descriptions are not of much help, for Irish legendary descriptions of battles are full of supernatural interventions and of heroes who change their shapes outrageously or have multi-coloured hair and other fantastic attributes, so the basis of reconstruction has to be the records of classical writers which, because of Ireland's isolation, may not be so far from the truth.

The strength of both armies probably lay in the horsemen, for first chariots then cavalry spearheaded the Celtic attack, and so impressed were the Romans by their horsemanship and tactics

War-chariots, base of Cross of the Scriptures, Clonmacnoise.
10th cent.

that they recruited Celts in large numbers for their own cavalry. Ireland must always have been a good country for horse-breeding, with the best of pastures, so there is no reason to think the *Equites* tradition of the Celtic aristocracy had declined. The horse, which figures so frequently on the ancient Celtic coinage, was very much a cult in Ireland—warrior-heroes such as "Fergus, Son of Great Horse" have a sort of Red Indian ring about them. Garb and weapons of warriors at Cul Dreimne were also perhaps not so different from those worn in the days of Boudicca. There is not much evidence from finds of the period, but chiefs and their bodyguards must have had accoutrements of considerable splendour, for it was not the Celtic way to go into battle modestly caparisoned. In the *Táin Bó Cuailgne* heroes bore shields with animal devices wrought in gold or silver, which suggests their helmets too may have carried Iron Age blazonry. If so, were their swords sheathed in splendid bronze scabbards like those found in a bog at Lisnacrogher, Co. Antrim? If those finds are much earlier, the smiths of Tara may have been every bit as skilled as their forebears. The Lisnacrogher scabbards had apparently been deposited as a votive offering, or they too might not have survived.

Great noise and shouting were traditional, so the two sides must have joined battle with thunderous clamour. The huge

Carnyx (war-trumpet) on Gundestrup cauldron, 1st cent. BC. National Museum, Copenhagen

war-horns, the *carnyxes*, would bellow like bulls or growl like an avalanche as the Viking *lurs* do as recorded in the National

Museum in Copenhagen. The very din of iron meeting iron when thousands of armoured men hurled themselves upon one another is something which does not fully enter our minds when thinking of ancient battles, and the echoes rebounding from the crags of Benbulban must have been terrifying. Fury in the first onslaught was always the Celtic way. The armies may have been reinforced by Feniañ bands, fierce mercenaries who hired themselves out to other tribes. One must not underestimate the part played by the druids on Diarmaid's side, for they formed not only a dreaded magical barrier but also a kind of psychological warfare unit whose gestures and curses and taunts had a daunting effect, even on the Roman legions attacking their holy place on Anglesey.

Adomnán evades the direct implication of Columba in the battle and says nothing of any part he played, and later writers usually follow his example, but Skene points out that Adomnán's narrative does not rule out Columba's having been the cause of it. Nor, then, does it rule out his presence on the battlefield. He may not have borne arms, as some histories have suggested; but I have difficulty in believing that a Celtic prince with Columba's background would have hesitated to use the weapon he knew well how to wield, or that he avoided the challenge of the druids. No: surely he rose up against them and called down the wrath of heaven upon the enemies of the Cinel Conaill Gulban. Indeed, he had a duty to do so. If he built his monasteries on lands granted by his king and his tribe, he had an obligation to intercede with heaven on their behalf in time of danger, and part of it involved marching with the warriors if need be to smite the foe with mighty swords and miracles—and perhaps to carry a holy book thrice sunwise around the army. And why not? It is unhistorical to judge him by the behaviour of clerics in later times, kneeling at their altars to pray for victory for distant armies, even more unhistorical to think of him as one who would never do otherwise than follow the Sermon on the Mount. The man who is reputed to have struck dead a murderer with his curse may be credited with exulting in his great voice, drowning druid imprecations with the *orationes Coluim Chille*. Diarmaid left the field of Cul

Dreimne a defeated man, knowing that his days as king were numbered, and also knowing which man had brought him low.

King Diarmaid lingered for a few more years before his fate caught up with him. He struck one last blow at Columba, which will be described presently; but his progress towards his doom has become a part of Irish mythology, and is worth recounting here if only because it complements the success of his sainted adversary. It will be remembered St Ruadán foretold that the ridge-beam of Tara would fall on the king, who therefore prudently had it thrown into the sea. But Diarmaid remained uneasy. He therefore called his druids to him and demanded of them how he would die. As might be expected, they replied in riddles. The first said he would be slain while clad in a shirt made from the material grown from a single flax-seed and a mantle from the wool of a single sheep. The second said he would be drowned in a vat of ale brewed from a single grain of corn. The third said he would be burned while he sat before a dish of bacon from a pig that was never farrowed. Not surprisingly Diarmaid felt reassured: all the prophecies seemed impossible of fulfilment. So in due course he went on a progress round his kingdom. In Antrim he was invited to a feast. His wife, Mugain, warned him against invitations, but Diarmaid agreed to enter a house at Rathbeg, and his host offered him not a meal only, but his beautiful daughter for the night, an offer which mightily pleased the king. The girl brought with her a shirt and mantle for him, and her father extolled their qualities—was not the shirt made from a single seed of flax, the mantle from the wool of one sheep? Then came the meat and drink. "This," said his host, "is good bacon, the bacon of a pig that was never farrowed." Diarmaid, perhaps alerted at last, demanded how such a thing could be and was told the piglets had been cut live from the sow with knives, then fattened. And as to the ale, the host boasted, it was brewed from one grain of corn, for the grain was found in the crop of a dove, and when sown it yielded a "sickle-full" of corn, the grain from which, when sown, produced the corn to brew the ale. By this time dread must have gripped the king.

He looked about him, possibly for the means to escape his fate. He saw that although the house was new, the roof seemed old, and he asked how this could be. His host explained that when he and his people were fishing at sea they saw the ridge-beam of a house floating, and they brought it ashore and built this house, on which they placed it. Now Diarmaid saw the end had come, and attempted to fly. But Aedh the Black blocked the doorway and thrust a spear through his breast. Diarmaid realised the house was surrounded by his foes, the Ulstermen, and fell back, but they burned the house over him. To escape the flames he climbed into the ale-vat, but the roof-tree fell in and struck him on the head, so killing him.

Professor Byrne links this story with the legend of Macbeth, also lured to his death by a series of contradictory prophecies. The Three-fold Death is familiar in Celtic mythology. Also, Diarmaid's death took place on the Feast of Samhain, the first day of November, a very special day in the Celtic calendar, when the dead rise from the otherworld and come among men. Professor MacCana points out that not only Diarmaid but Cuchulainn himself is supposed to have died on this day, so the legend seems to reflect a certain ritualistic element, reminiscent again of *The Golden Bough*. But the aspect of the story most relevant to the subject of this book is Adomnán's attitude to it. In chapter xxxvi of Book I he records a prophecy about Aedh the Black, described as a priest irregularly ordained, but "a bloodthirsty man and a murderer of many" who had even slain Diarmaid, "ordained by God's will ruler of all Ireland". Columba, Adomnán maintains, had prophesied that the hand which ordained Aedh would rot and go before its owner into the earth for burial "after great tortures of pain", and that Aedh would "return as a dog to his vomit, and be again a bloody murderer; and at last his throat shall be pierced by a lance and falling from wood into water, he will die by drowning". Here again is "the Three-fold Death" of legend, subscribed to by an abbot of Iona. Nowhere does Adomnán make criticism of Diarmaid who, as far as he is concerned, was a good Christian king. He actually makes Columba revile and damn the man who slew him whose defeat in battle, according to the *Annals of Ulster*, was due to "the prayers of Columcille". Of course, it is not wholly inconsistent: murder of a king was a sacrilegious offence. Are we then to discount the *Annals* entirely? Have we got the battle of Cul Dreimne wrong? We can never be sure of what happened; but for my part I am sure Adomnán has left out something which is not to his liking here, and that the "blame" which Columba incurred and which he, Adomnán, dismisses as "excusable" refers to the *Cathach* and Cul Dreimne events.

The sequel to the battle gets us yet deeper into what I am tempted to call the whitewash—a temptation which I hasten to say must be resisted, because I do not think Adomnán is any more culpable for omitting things he did not like than is any artist for omitting details which interfere with his statement of what he believes to be the essential truth. Adomnán was primarily concerned with promoting the Christian faith. On the subject of battles he is understandably oblique in his references. In the Second Preface he merely uses Cul Dreimne to date Columba's departure from Ireland. The heading to chapter vii of Book I is maybe significant: "Prophecy of the Blessed Man concerning the Din of Battles fought at a distance." There is a web of evasion cast over everything, a truly Celtic web; but if we return to Book III, chapter iii, the web drops momentarily, just long enough to reveal that Columba was "excommunicated by a certain synod", hastily corrected by the comment "not rightly, as afterwards in the end became clear". He describes the synod as an assembly convened against Columba, and later he says the place was Teilte, which is Teltown, Co. Meath. Apparently it was a synod of the Saints of Ireland brought together expressly to judge Columba, and it would seem they tried him in his absence and excommunicated him, for Adomnán says that when they saw Columba approach, St Brendan of Birr rose and reverently kissed him, for which some members of the synod chided him, since Columba had been excommunicated. Brendan's excuse for his action was that he had had a vision that day, in which God had spoken, saying Columba should not have been punished but exalted. This did not convince the others. Brendan had to go on to declare he had seen a "bright pillar" going before Columba, and angels accompanying him, and that he, Brendan, dared not slight a man who had been "fore-ordained by God to be a leader of nations unto life". This Adomnán insists convinced them and persuaded them to withdraw the excommunication. Nothing is mentioned of who called the synod, nor of the charges brought. It may well have been instigated by King Diarmaid. Teilte was a royal seat, and monarchs were sometimes known as Kings of Teilte. As to the charges, it is difficult to avoid the conclusion they were connected with the carnage of Cul Dreimne, for which the prophecy of St Berchan openly admits he was responsible. What is more I am convinced Adomnán knew what those charges were, for his account of the proceedings at Teilte is unconvincing and takes refuge in miraculous intervention. The traditional verdict of the synod is well known. Columba was enjoined to convert as many pagan souls as the number slain in the battle, and St Laisren, his confessor, laid upon him the penance of perpetual exile from Ireland, on which he was never to set foot or look again.

Is the departure of Columba from Ireland, then, the result of the exile imposed on him? It seems to me highly improbable. My first reason for doubting it is that as much as two years elapsed between the holding of the synod and the saint's departure. To gather a few companions and take ship for a lonely island would have occupied some days, or perhaps weeks at most. Columba had plans, and needed time. What was in his mind?

Whatever Columba's part in it, there was more to Cul Dreimne than an act of revenge or punishment for broken sanctuary. It had practical results. First, the evangelisation of Ireland; score upon score of monasteries and churches founded by Columba and other saints were given increased security against the threat of druid retaliation. Events like the Cursing of Tara and hostility to sanctuary-breakers show a growing militancy in the church. Its priests are bolder and are wielding their powers. This may seem to cut across the gentle virtues of the Fathers from whom the monastic movement drew its inspiration, but I am sure those virtues were practised still by the vast majority, since generations later they were being praised by outside observers such as Bede. The leaders, the abbots, on the other hand, could not afford to be indecisive or to exhibit weakness. Practice of the Christian virtues would win, and did win converts by the thousand, but perhaps mainly among the ordinary people; and, although kings and the privileged were also converted, expediency must have weighed heavily against them, as it did with King Diarmaid; and an abbot who was not both shrewd and firm, and when necessary commanding, would have small chance of reaching the goals he set himself. The notion that in the sixth century sweetness and light drove out the ferocious rivalries always present in Irish tribal society is an absurdity which does not need to be stressed.

Something which will perhaps bear repeating, however, is that relationship between monastery and *tuath*, that bond of mutual service, which committed the abbots to politics and at times brought them into opposition. Whether St Finnian took his stand with Diarmaid at Cul Dreimne, when Columba prayed for the army of the Uí Néill, one does not know; but some have maintained he did, and it is logical enough if the story of the copying of the *Cathach* is to be accepted. What I think we must accept at this point is that Columba has emerged as a man of strong views, proud, ambitious in the sense that he knew what he wanted and would not hesitate to give offence in pressing his cause. One gains the impression that in his strength and forcefulness he is of a greater stature than the other apostles of Ireland, and that at times they gave him a respect which is almost deference, if there is truth in Adomnán's version of the synod of Teilte, although of course this may have been coloured by the language of the hagiologists.

The "Old Irish Life" gives the simple explanation for Columba's wish to leave Ireland at this time as the spirit of pilgrimage, so basic to the Celtic church. He had been determined to go "from the beginning of his life". That he had this urge can hardly be doubted. Yet there is a difference in kind between the territory he had set his eyes on and the territories to which most of the other *peregrini* travelled. Europe, as we have seen, was the field to which so many turned their attention, others set out for far-off islands such as the Faeroes or Iceland. Columba had first concentrated on his homeland, consolidating his work there over many years; and when he decided to leave Ireland it was for Dalriada, virtually a colony on the doorstep of the homeland. Not that there was anything less bold or less courageous in this decision— no one could accuse Columba of lack of boldness or courage—but in Dalriada the problem was quite different. The community there was an Irish Christian one, but under military threat. His mission there, in a very real sense, was to be, in Adomnán's phrase, a soldier of the church, but his church was also a tribal church.

This brings us to the second practical result of the battle of Cul Dreimne. It was not fought solely for the purpose of discrediting the druids; nor yet, although the crime of breaking sanctuary may have been the most heinous of sins against the church, is a cleric who had been wronged likely to have been able to persuade his people to make war against the king to punish it. No: the battle was fought, surely, to destroy the power of Diarmaid himself in face of the rapidly growing strength of the Uí Néill. Professor Byrne makes this motive for the battle very clear when he writes: "Through the mists of oblivion and calculated obfuscation we may discern a large-handed partition of the newly won midlands among the sons of Niall, which was disrupted by the ambitions of Diarmaid, whose family dwelt around Slane and who also claimed descent from Niall." Cul Dreimne lay in a critical area. There had been two recent battles in the area, at Sligo and at Cul Conaine, both waged against the power of Connacht to the south; and although the King of Connacht was on the side of Columba's people at Cul Dreimne, the Uí Néill needed to consolidate their victories by dealing a blow at the High-King of Tara, counterpart to Cashel in the south. It can always be argued that the Uí Néill themselves were determined on this battle, that they called in Columba simply to reinforce their arms with his spiritual might. But why then was Columba arraigned before the synod of

Teilte? Were prayers for the victory of his people in themselves enough to justify his excommunication? We must, I believe, conclude that both as a churchman and as a prince of the blood-royal he was deeply involved in the councils of his people, and that his loyalty to them was a matter of high honour to him as to any other Celtic aristocrat.

I have already said it is unhistorical to judge him as one might judge a cleric of later times. I have said before how necessary it is to keep before us the Iron Age background and have emphasised, some may think over-emphasised, how it survived into the Christian era. Adomnán with his constant references to "the holy man" is so apt to make us think of Columba as a haloed disciple of the Lord walking by some Galilee in Ireland that it does not enter our thoughts that he may have been more like Moses leading the Children of Israel out of the wilderness, where necessary bringing about the destruction of the Egyptians. To an Iron Age people, that a man of God could also be a man of war would involve no contradiction. The Saints of Ireland themselves, for all their loving care in transcribing the gospels, must have found much reassurance in the Old Testament. Were not the Midianites struck down by the Sword of the Lord and of Gideon? And where did the Angel of the Lord appear to the mighty man of valour but sitting under an oak? When Columba looked across the sea to Dalriada in Alba, then, it must have been with a strong urge of responsibility for his people in danger there.

If Adomnán and the "Old Irish Life" agree that pilgrimage was his motive in going, tradition persists there was an element of penance: penance imposed by the synod, by St Laisren, or by himself. The notion of exile has been written deep into the story of his going. The later poems attributed to the saint himself contribute to this impression, for they are heavily loaded with nostalgia for Erin, and with sadness that "the soft grey eye" will never see its shores again. Nostalgia and sadness are natural enough in the circumstances: Columba would not be the last Irishman to weep for the green hills, without necessarily hasting home again. Whatever the verdict at Teilte, however, there is certainly no evidence of an imposed exile, and the lag of two years makes it seem unlikely. Not only was there no ban on his returning to Ireland if he wanted to, but Adomnán mentions no fewer than ten occasions when he actually revisited his native land. We must accept, therefore, that his going to Alba was a matter of his own choice.

His primary objective was to take the gospels to the Picts. This implies the northern Picts. Whithorn and its missions probably had done much to evangelise the southern Picts, although apostasy may have done a good deal to undo the work of Ninian and his fellows, but in spite of claims that have been put forward it is, I think, safe to say all the country north of Drumalban remained pagan. The colony of the Dal Riatá in Alba had taken its Christian faith with it from its homeland in the glens of Antrim, or so we must assume; but it had not been touched by the new wave of evangelisation, and its priesthood, perhaps even its faith, may have been weak. This Dalriada was an enclave driven into hostile territory, on its western side broken up into isolated and vulnerable island communities. The long glens behind them and the long sea channels dividing them must have held menace for the Dalriadans, since the Picts were both intrepid fighting men and skilled seamen. Alban Dalriada was at one and the same time Ireland's only salient into the outside world, and a hostage to pagandom. Its king, as we know, had been slain by the Pictish king. It needed a very strong man to hold it together. To turn it from a beleaguered defensive position into a springboard for a counter-attack against the pagan threat demanded not merely a strong man but a leader of bounding vision and supreme confidence. The reigning king, Conaill, son of Comgall, seems to have held sway over a shrunken province centred on Knapdale, or roughly where the Crinan Canal now is, and he had abandoned the old pretentious title of King of Alba for the more realistic Dalriada, if Tigernach is right.

With Dalriada in such a critical situation, Columba must have been deeply influenced by its needs. Conaill was a relative. Prince of the blood and, in a sense, prince of the church, at 42 the most revered of the Saints of Ireland, one who had humbled the High-King of Tara, did Columba not see in himself the man

who could save his people across the sea? A true Celt, it is hard
to believe he was never seduced by dreams of bardic epics
chanted by the winter fires, epics of a Columcille who carried
forward the frontiers of Christendom into the pagan east, driving
the Picts into their fastnesses beyond Drumalban, the Angles
and the Saxons out of the once-Christian Britain they had raped.
It is no criticism of one born to a heritage of myth and legend
so real that his ancestors lived their daily lives by it, to say he
may well have seen himself as a sort of Christian Cuchulainn
come out of the west to do the will of God.

VI

Passage to Iona

In the year 563 Columba set sail from Derry with, it is said, twelve companions. The names of the twelve are set down in a fifteenth-century manuscript of Adomnán in the British Museum: *Duo filii Brenden, Baithene qui et Conin sancti successor Columbae; et Cobthach, frater eius; Ernaan sancti avunculus Columbae; Diormitius, eius ministrator; Rus et Fechno, duo filii Rodain; Scandal filius Bresail filii Neil; Luguid Mocuthemne; Echoid; Tochannu Mocufir-cetea; Cairnaan filius Branduib filii Meilgi; Grillaan.* What the writer's source for the names was we do not know. Early annalists say nothing of the voyage itself. They treat what has become one of the most momentous and of course romantic journeys of its kind as though it had been a regular steamer crossing from Larne to Stranraer. Wonder at the achievement has perhaps been stimulated by the general belief that the crossing was made in some sort of small coastal curragh or coracle, a belief given apparent sanction by the name of the bay on Iona where the saint is said to have landed, Port-na-Churaich. An ancient poem associated with Columba's name refers to the delights of rowing "a little coracle", but it also refers to keeping watch "from the ample oaken planks", and Adomnán writes of "long boats of hewn pine and oak". One is inclined to opt for the more solid craft, yet curraghs could be quite large. They could have resembled the Eskimo *umiak*, which can be upwards of thirty feet long and six broad, and the covering of scraped hides, polished with butter until as smooth as glass, makes for minimal friction. Irish raids on Britain, carrying off slaves and cattle, may have been made in such curraghs across much wider waters than those between Derry and Dalriada. The seamanship of the crews should not be underestimated. Lethbridge recounts with relish encounters between the Picts, using such boats, and the war-galleys of the Romans. So Columba's voyage, adventurous as it seems to us, may in fact have been a regular-enough occurrence in his time. The vessel, whatever it was, must have been capable of carrying a complement of oarsmen and substantial supplies in addition to the saint and his companions. More speculations about the sea-going boats of the sixth century will be found in Chapter IX.

In a direct line, the distance from Derry to Iona is about 100 miles. The landfall for a long time has been in dispute, but tradition has it that Columba's passionate love of Ireland made him determined that his destination must be out of sight of her shores. He is said to have landed first on Oronsay, but found that from the highest point he could still see the Antrim coast. Neighbouring Colonsay seems a much more likely place for such a landing. Oronsay is a rugged, rocky islet where the great Atlantic bull-seals battle for the cows out on the skerries, and no part of it is much above the sea, whereas the highest hill on Colonsay rises to several hundred feet and on a clear day I have seen from it easily the blue outline of Ireland. Columba is then supposed to have proceeded to Iona and to have climbed the little hill behind the bay where his vessel put in to satisfy himself that his homeland was at last below the horizon, after which he had his curragh buried on the beach.

At the least, this tradition is a drastic over-simplification of what must have happened. The *Annals of Tigernach* have it that Conaill, King of the Scots in Dalriada, made a grant of the island to Columba. Bede credits the gift to the Picts. To reconcile the contradictory accounts and fit them into the framework of tradition, some historians have suggested that Columba did find Iona unoccupied, that Conaill confirmed him in his right to be there, and that when the Picts eventually were converted to Christianity their king confirmed the saint's possession of an island which originally had belonged to the Picts. This solution seems to me quite unacceptable. If Columba's motives in making the journey were, as I have argued, to consolidate the Irish bridgehead in Alba as well as to spread the gospels in the pagan hinterland, he must have had a plan of campaign, and it is unthinkable that he did not acquaint Conaill with what he proposed to do. Indeed his first objective surely would be to discuss with his royal cousin his purpose in settling within his territories. Moreover, Adomnán records that in the year he left Ireland Columba was living in "Britain" and speaking with Conaill. "Britain" surely means the mainland. It is a reasonable assumption, then, that Columba went first to the king, who granted him Iona. Dalriada, after all, at this time was closely invested by the Picts, who were probably patrolling the seaways and the firths, and it is unrealistic to imagine that Columba would unnecessarily imperil his mission by landing on one potentially hostile island after another merely to find out whether he could or could not see Ireland from it. If a meeting with the king was his first aim, then his vessel would make straight from Derry across the North Channel to the shelter of Islay and the Sound of Jura, and landfall then would be made close to the heart of this small Irish kingdom in Alba.

But we are left with another puzzle: was Iona itself not vulnerable? It has been suggested the Pictish "frontier" lay across Mull, marked by two hills, Carn-cul-ri-Eirinn and Carn-cul-ri-Alabainn. We can assume Pictish warriors held Morvern and Ardnamurchan. Yet there is no record of any Pictish attack on the island after Columba had established himself there. This suggests some sort of accommodation with the Picts before he landed, and Dr Isabel Henderson points out that the date given by Bede for the conversion of the Picts is 565, and therefore Columba could have spent as much as two years on the mainland, that is, of Dalriada, before he went to Iona. With communications as they were, negotiations would be protracted. What was going on? How did Conaill stand in relation to Brude? Tigernach, as I have mentioned, writes of Conaill as merely *Ri Dalriada*, King of Dalriada, instead of *Ri Albann* like his predecessor; and Simpson makes a case, based partly on St Berchan's reference to "an Irishman living in the east under the Picts", that Conaill was no more than a chief, with Brude his overlord. It is possible Columba himself communicated with Brude and asked him for a guarantee of safety for a settlement on Iona. Skene concedes that both Mull and Iona must have been lost by the Dalriadans to the Picts after the defeat of 560, but he puts it "lost in actual possession", and Conaill's gift of Iona to Columba may have been part of some process of reoccupation. Skene goes on to say that Bede nowhere states Iona was given to Columba by the Pictish king himself but—and I insert Bede's own words—"had been long since given by the Picts, who inhabit those parts of Britain, to the Scottish monks, because they had received the faith of Christ through their preaching". Skene then concludes the donation of Iona came not from the Pictish nation, but from local tribes, and as in Ireland the gift of land from the *tuath* always preceded the founding of a monastery, the same procedure had been followed here. Finally he quotes from the *Amhra Choluimchille*, supposedly written just after the saint's death, which refers to Columba as "a noble one who sought seven *tuaths* and definite for indefinite in it, or five *tuaths* of Erin and two *tuaths* in Alban", which curious wording seems to mean he sought definite titles from those tribes. All this could be interpreted as signifying that Columba spent some part at least of those first two years in converting to Christianity the Pictish tribes closest to Iona (the "two *tuaths* in Alban"), possibly in Morvern and Ardnamurchan, and that only when this had been done did he feel himself in a position to take up Conaill's gift of Iona.

His landing on the island raises yet another problem. The "Old Irish Life"—which maintains Columba went direct to Iona —records that "two bishops that were in the place came to receive his submission from him. But God manifested to Colum Cille that they were not in truth bishops; wherefore it was they left the island to him, when he exposed their real history and career". Skene contents himself with the comment they must have been "the remains of that anomalous church of seven bishops which here, as elsewhere, preceded the monastic church; and Columba appears to have refused to recognise them as legitimately entitled to the character of bishops, and the island was abandoned to him". This does not necessarily cut across the theory of an arrangement with local tribes. The tribes may have tolerated a few surviving and perhaps ineffective priests. What is the meaning of God's revelation to Columba that those men who met him were "not true bishops"? It could be that as an abbot of the monastery to be, he looked on as irrelevant the episcopal system of the Patrician church; but on the other hand the words "their real history and career" may imply they had become apostates and had ceased to witness to their faith and only resumed their religion when they saw Columba's ship approach. Manus O'Donnell has another explanation, supposing them to be druids in disguise. Skene considers there is no warrant for this; yet if Iona had fallen into Pictish hands it is just possible druids might have tried to trick him out of his purpose. Speculation is profitless. All we can conclude is that within two years of sailing from Derry Columba took possession of Iona, and that if there was some show of local opposition he firmly brushed it aside.

Montalembert, in his *Moines d'Occident*, paints a gloomy picture of this island which became Columba's base for the rest of his life, a picture of desolate rocks in a dark sea, with the mountains across the strait hid in mist and cloud. The Frenchman may have been unfortunate in the weather when he went there, or perhaps he just shared the attitude common enough in the mid-nineteenth century that wild nature is a terrifying spectacle. Iona has become a place of pilgrimage in its own right. So far is it from being desolate and gloomy that it became the favourite theme with the group of painters known as the Scottish Colourists, and among these S. J. Peploe especially grew obsessed by the brilliant play of light on the dark rocks jutting from bays of silver sand and illumining the greens and purples of the water. By Hebridean standards it is not a spectacular island. Yet if any visitor find it disappointing he must be unfortunate indeed. The glories of Tara may have departed, but the glories of Iona are reconstituted with every dawn and sunset, and with every changing minute of the day. But of course it is no accident that the holy places of Celtic Christianity tend to be like no others in Christendom. The Celtic church grew among people who were not builders, who were not tempted to follow a tradition of containing their gods in temples but felt closer to them where they could feel the wind buffeting their faces, and see the flash of white wings against the sky, and smell the tangle or the sun-warmed bark of trees. This is no modern romantic fancy. That Irish monasticism saw value in such things is manifest in early records, recognising that tumbling waves and soaring clouds stimulate communion with God, and the simple pleasure taken by scribes in the play of dappled sunlight on their doorsteps is spontaneously recorded for all time in marginal notes in the gospels which they penned. Iona provided the perfect setting for their worship.

In trying to establish what sixth-century Iona was like I think the first thing we have to do is to re-orientate our thoughts. Today, we "escape" to the Hebrides. They are desirable because they are remote from the centres from which this country is ruled. Columba and his monks would have been astonished at and depressed by the state of Scotland's western seaboard now. I remember how the late Dr Arthur Geddes used to talk of the need for an atlas showing the familiar map of Britain upside down, London and Stornoway changing places. As things are those beautiful islands are treated with a mixture of neglect, cynicism and condescension, fostering a new clearance situation in which islands are traded between absentee landlords, while a thinning and ageing population is forgetting the basic skills, and imports its bread from Glasgow and sometimes even its fish from Aberdeen.

If we go back fourteen centuries, we find a very different state of affairs. These islands were not at the distant edge of a world but at the centre of one. This does not mean they were thickly populated; it certainly does not mean they had riches or power. What it means is that they were able to support balanced com-munities, growing crops, plying trade, fighting fiercely for their interests, being fought for as the Picts and Dalriadans fought for them. They were in fact not the fringe of anything, but a significant part of that potent Celtic world symbolised by the exquisite mantle spread before the eyes of Columba's mother in her dream, and Iona was as well-placed to command that world as, say, Augustine's Thanet would be for a modern Columba attempting to dominate the United Kingdom.

It is perhaps a little hard for anyone visiting the Hebrides now to believe they were ever viable as the homeland of a vigorous, forward-looking people, a people worth the strenuous effort to bring them within the Christian fold. A casual glance suggests that what our urban civilisation looks on as the amenities of life in the Hebrides can be found only in towns like Stornoway, still a port of call for little ships from far-off places such as Spain, and that the rest is heath and bog and lochan. A knowledgeable eye can detect that at one time things were different. The green richness of the *machair*, coastal stretches of grazing and cultivable land, is not difficult to recognise, but in many spots higher ground may be seen to show areas, often roughly rectangular, which look less black and sour than the rest of the brown, heathy hillsides, and those indicate where crofts once built up sweeter soil, crofts long abandoned, victims of the clearances or simply of the growth of a money-based economy. Such cultivated areas could have been much more extensive at one time. The two essentials for productive soil were always present: vast quantities of shell-sand on the beaches to lime the fields, and an endless supply of wrack and other seaweeds to feed them. True, areas of deep soil are limited, and rock protrudes all over the place. Also there is much rain, more especially in the landward, mountainous areas, and even more discouraging is the strength of the winds which blast in from the Atlantic heavy with scorching salt. Cultivation is a relentless task.

We know almost nothing about the agriculture of the sixth century. We do know a great deal about medieval farming, however, and about the marvellous achievement of the monastic communities then, and we know that large areas which were unproductive in the seventeenth and eighteenth centuries had provided rich harvests when they were worked by the monks or under their direction. Irish monastic communities may not have been as accomplished as the Cistercians of Melrose in the twelfth century or the Benedictines of Arbroath; but there are things in the pages of Adomnán which do hint at the standard of farming, and we do know that when Dalriada was founded in Alba the Scots incomers brought their farming methods with them, including grain-crops, by contrast with the pastoral Britons and Picts.

Iona itself offered many advantages. It is not large, about three miles north to south by half that distance at its widest, a matter of 3,000 acres in all. There are many rocky projections, but also some good cultivable areas and *machair* land, and of course the white coral sand of the beaches is blown across the island by the winter gales to scatter calcium carbonate like a benison on the pastures. Anyone going north from Clachanach, through little fields with fat, white sheep to the *machair* land behind the White Strand, may take in at a glance the richness of those pastures sweetened by the shell-sand drifting from the dunes. Arable for the growing of corn amounted to as much as 500 acres. There was a granary and a mill, the wheel of which was turned by an overflow from Lochan Mòr, the former mill-pond at the base of Dun I. It was what is known as a vertical water-mill, so efficient a type that the ninth-century Viking raiders, as T. Bedford Franklin, the authority on monastic farming, has explained, imitated it all over their dominions, even in Norway. The community practised mixed farming: corn, cattle and sheep were the basis of their agriculture. There are small hills enough to give protection from the westerly winds. Sheep were grazed on a small island to the south, and as time went on there would be contributory farms on other islands, certainly on Tiree, "the land of corn", where a daughter monastery was established. Cultivation of the land, indeed, is one of the features of Adomnán's *Life* which gives it a strong element of credibility to balance the unreality. In Book II, chapter xliv, for example, he relates how, in a time of drought during his own abbacy of Iona, to bring rain some elders walked round a new-sown field carrying the white tunic of Columba and then read from his books on the Hill of the Angels, now Sithean Mòr, the "great fairies' hill" on the *machair*. Rain then fell day and night, and the corn grew. There are other "wonders" which reveal that one of the crops was barley, and that the saint refused to bless a butcher's knife because

.the cattle were meant to be used for ploughing, not for meat. Franklin, with his expert eye, finds enough evidence to hazard a guess that the plough used was the ard or scratch-plough which, drawn by two oxen, only scratched its furrow in the earth without turning it over.

Iona is a latinised name. Reeves proved it a corruption of Ioua. The old Gaelic names for the island are Hii, Ia or simply I, the last still in use, and often it came to be called Icolmkill, the isle of Colum of the Church, because of Columba's association with it. Other features of the island too have naturally come to be associated with him, such as the bay known as Port-na-Churaich. The hill behind this bay, Carn-Cul-ri-Eirinn, literally "cairn of the back turned to Ireland", occurs in a remarkable poem included in an Irish manuscript in the Burgundian Library in Brussels. It is titled "Columcille fecit". Although there is nothing to confirm the saint's authorship of any of the early poems attributed to him, this one at least was written by someone who knew those islands . . .

> "That I might hear the thunder of the crowding waves
>   Upon the rocks;
> That I might hear the roar by the side of the church
>   Of the surrounding sea;
> That I might see its noble flocks
>   Over the watery ocean;
> That I might see the sea-monsters,
>   The greatest of all wonders;
> That I might see its ebb and flood
>   In their career;
> That my mystical name might be, I say,
>   *Cul ri Erin* . . ."

Skene quotes the poem in full. It is of course a hymn of praise to God, but it is also a song of thanksgiving for happy hours spent watching the glint of sun on the Atlantic swell, listening to the cries of gulls and sandpipers, even in fishing and "at times plucking *duilisc* from the rocks". The poet has, almost idly,

strung his memories of summer days together like beads on a
rosary, to be told and re-told in gratitude.

Nothing recognisable as part of the earliest settlement on Iona
survives, above ground at least. Reeves believed the oldest signs
of building are the foundations of a few stone huts above Port
Lavaichean, the Bay of Ruins, at the south end of the island.
Adomnán states that the early dwellings were of the usual wood-
and-wattle construction and that the church was of oak, as
Columba's own cell seems to have been. Reeves located the
monastery on the gentle, sloping ground north of the present
abbey; but Professor Charles Thomas, in his Hunter Marshall
lecture in Glasgow in 1968, put forward other views firmly
based on field-work. He chose to excavate a site just south of the
abbey, and was able to locate some of the monastic buildings.
O. G. S. Crawford had already mapped the *vallum*, the boundary
bank and ditch which surrounded the settlement, enclosing a site
of about eleven acres. To the west, this *vallum* is a fairly roughly-
executed fortification, but where sectioned to the south-west of
the abbey it seemed there had been a facing of large stones,
although subsequently these have been tumbled into the ditch.
The whole thing is only about five feet high from the bottom of
the ditch, so it was not a very formidable obstacle. Some features
may be located from references in Adomnán, though these are
tantalising in their brevity. For example, he tells us that where
Ernaan the priest died a cross was put up, before the door of the
kiln, and that another was raised where Columba stood, 24 paces
distant. From this Skene deduced the kiln lay between Columba's
cell and the landing-place. The site of the kiln helps to determine
the landing-place itself since the little creek called Port na muintir,
corresponding to a similar landing-place across the strait in Mull,
appears to be it. The settlement must have been similar to the
Irish settlements such as Clonmacnoise or Glendalough.

Thomas points out that the concept of such enclosures is alien
to western Britain at this period, and he suggests it may derive—
like the eremitical movement itself—from the East, comparing
it with monasteries in Egypt and the Levant. He makes the interesting comment that since the *vallum* has little defensive capacity,

the enclosure may rather have been for the enforcement of monastic rules, such as leaving without permission from a superior, for which a penance could be imposed. It might also mark the area of land gifted by the chief of a tribe, although in the case of Iona surely this was the whole island. But there is no object on the island which provides a firm visual link with Columba himself, unless it be the vestiges of a cell on Tor Abb. Professor Thomas writes to me that "it conforms to the loose description in Adomnán's *Life* of the saint's day-time cell in which he wrote", and adds that the existence of a cross-base may indicate that in earlier times it was believed this had a holy association. We must content ourselves with the thought that the boulders and other natural features on which our eyes rest were also familiar to the saint. Possibly the nearest we come to a link is the small slab with a rather elegantly-inscribed *Chi-Rho* cross, having two words incised on its upper edge which Professor Kenneth Jackson interprets as *Lapis Echodi*, the stone of Ecodius. It must have marked a grave, but is probably early seventh rather than late sixth century. Dr Henry thinks crosses of this kind may have been copied from initials in gospel- and service-books.

Skene has described in some detail the nature of the monastic *familia* on Iona. There were three classes. The seniors, older men on whom the abbot knew he could rely, carried out the services of the church and also devoted themselves to reading and transcribing the Scriptures. The working brothers laboured in the fields and attended to the cattle as well as preparing the food, and they also served in the workshops. The third class were the *alumni*, or pupils. All wore a white under-garment, and over it a surcoat and hood of the natural wool. Even on the sheltered side of the island it must have been a spartan existence when winter gales blew in from the west, but, reading between the lines of Adomnán as well as in the early verses, one gets the feeling the monks were fully appreciative of those idyllic summer days which turn many visitors today into addicts. Also, although their diet was simple it was plentiful, and could be supplemented when visitors arrived. The Duke of Argyll, as landlord, reviews at length the island's resources in his own time, now over a century ago, and compared with the picture today what he says is rather surprising. Although I remember sharing a ferry-boat with a load of cattle-beasts, there is no doubt tourism has replaced farming as the staple industry; and in Columba's day the produce probably exceeded the produce in the duke's time, for there were 150 monks to feed and open-door hospitality. The duke is quick to point out too the abundance of large flounders on the green, sandy bottom of the sound, and the brethren ate the flesh of the seals which abound on the skerries, seals which also supplied oil for the lamps of the community.

With the coming of Columba Iona became the mother-church not only of Alban Dalriada, but of Dalriada in Ireland, and Columba had become the recognised religious leader of his people. Something should be said about the form of worship practised. In general principles it is the form observed by the monastic order throughout Ireland, but it could be modified in detail by the abbot. Skene is careful to point out that the doctrine was the doctrine common to the Western church up to the fifth century, and that divergence in Britain and Ireland occurred only with the fall of the Empire. After the fifth century the Irish church held rigidly to practice laid down by the second general council of 381. The preaching of Columba was simply the Word of God as taught by the evangelists and apostles, which has persuaded many to see in it an affinity with Protestantism. Ritual evidently was not elaborate, and churches were small. Much time was devoted to recitation of the psalter. Celebration of the Eucharist took place during the fixed festivals, or when appointed by the abbot. The priest at the altar consecrated the elements, or he might invite a brother-presbyter to break bread with him as a token of equality. If a bishop were present he broke bread alone, and Adomnán records how on one occasion Columba gently reproached a visiting bishop for not identifying himself. The penitential discipline which marked the monastic movement has a special place. Ascetics who immersed themselves in water have been mentioned in an earlier chapter, and the practice of reciting the psalter with the body so immersed may have some reference to John the Baptist, or again to pagan preoccupation with springs and streams in Celtic countries, as elsewhere. Usually such penances were undergone under the direction or advice of a chosen "soul-friend", or *Ammchara*. Whether this is the equivalent of a confessor, or something more like a *guru*, is obscure.

It will be remembered that in Ireland monastic communities were usually associated with lay communities, tribal communities, with mutual obligations; and in the *Rule of Saint Columba* the first requirement is "to be alone in a separate place near a chief city, if thy conscience is not prepared to be in common with the crowd". The situation on Iona scarcely fits in with this. Nevertheless the monastery there must have been closely linked with the mainland, and it was the ecclesiastical "capital" of Dalriada, complementing Dunadd, the seat of secular rule. Dunadd, like Iona, is well-placed strategically. There is easy access by sea to the homeland, Ireland, by way of reasonably sheltered sea lanes, and to the Inner Hebrides, while there are good land communications with central Scotland by the low ground leading to Loch Fyne or along the shores of Loch Awe to Dalmally and Breadalbane.

In its way, the country around Dunadd is as interesting as Iona. It abounds with monuments significant of its past, although like those of Iona they date from long after Columba's time. The carved stones in the village of Kilmartin are medieval, but still reflect the Scotic invasion from Ireland; the same is true of the isolated monuments which occur near that beautiful road which strikes south from the Crinan Canal and divides around Loch Sween. Dunadd is a rocky hill a mile north of Kilmichael-Glassary, a village associated with the twelfth-century bronze bell-shrine, a late relic of the Celtic church, now in the National Museum of Antiquities in Edinburgh. A farm-track leads to the foot of the hill. A few minutes of scrambling brings one to the summit of what obviously has been a stronghold from very early times, what Mr R. B. K. Stevenson terms a "nuclear" fort because of its concentric rings of defence. This crag commands not only what used to be the Bog of Crinan, now reclaimed, but also a very wide stretch of country on which an invading army could be seen for two or three miles in any direction. On a summer evening, the Paps of Jura and other island outliers of Dalriada float between sea and sky like the mythical marine monsters which fascinated Columba and his contemporaries.

Bell-shrine of Kilmichael-Glassary. 12th cent.
National Museum of Antiquities of Scotland

But if we turn to look at the rock under our feet, we see one or two surprising things. One is a fine relief of a boar, wisely preserved under glass by the Department of the Environment. The boar was of course a cult animal of high importance, as mentioned earlier, and this looks to be Pictish, of perhaps the seventh century, a perplexing feature in the heart of a Scotic fortress. Or could it have been carved there in the eighth century, when the Pictish king, Angus MacFergus, stormed Dunadd? The other feature of much interest is the "print" of a foot hollowed from the rock. It is isolated, quite small, much worn, which is hardly surprising as thousands of visitors must have tried to fit a shoe into it. It is widely believed that to do this was one of the coronation rites of kings of Dalriada. Footprints have been looked on as a vehicle of sympathetic magic in many parts of the world, involving the transfer or investiture of power, and in ancient Denmark treaties were concluded by the parties sprinkling one another's footprints with blood. Close to this footprint is an ogham inscription. It has not yet been deciphered, but possibly some day it may throw light on the meaning of the print.

The commanding situation of Dunadd is almost the only pointer to its past importance. Excavation has yielded little evidence of the character of this Scotic stronghold. There must have been a township surrounding the hill, as the citadel is estimated to have contained 700 people at most. Finds on the site include a variety of agricultural implements as well as tools for such trades as bronze-casting. There is little by which to assess the cultural level of the place, but one piece of slate carries a working-drawing for a penannular brooch of quite sophisticated design. One odd find which could be linked to the boar carving is a carved stone ball of a type associated with the Picts, but this does not necessarily mean a Pictish presence. The only pointers to Christianity are a cross incised on one of a group of about 50 querns discovered, and a disc inscribed *in nomine* in Irish minuscules, but this is much later in date than Columba's time. For the rest, there were fragments of jet, a good comb, two ornamental bronze pins, some glass beads and a number of iron implements. Weapons found were surprisingly few: only a number of spearheads. Altogether, this amounts to few signs of a prosperous community or of a strong garrison, but then Celtic communities tend to leave few relics behind by comparison with other ancient peoples. Not even the royal sites of Ireland have yielded much; yet for the pagan period at least the quality of the finds is sometimes so high that one must accept that the people who made and used them were both technically advanced and culturally sophisticated.

It may be Dunadd's importance to Dalriada has nothing to do with the size of the township, for neither Tara nor Eamhain

VII

The Mission to the Picts

The mission to the Picts has usually been regarded as the climax to Columba's career, and the main reason for his coming to Alba. Most historians have accepted the complete success of this mission as a fact without seriously weighing the evidence. Thus Hume Brown: "This conversion of the Picts may fairly be regarded as the governing fact of Scottish history." Yet if we look carefully at all available evidence the outcome of the mission is far from clear.

Whether we accept Columba's main motive for going among the Picts as religious zeal—the traditional belief—or as determination to revive and expand the strength of Dalriada, or as a mixture of the two, we must assume he consulted with Conaill, the king, if only to get a picture of the situation and an estimate of the prospects. The saint was up against a problem far different from those which had faced him in Ireland. Certainly the Picts were in part at least Celts, but Columba had no family bonds to make things easier for him. In some degree tribal customs and patterns must have differed from those in Ireland. Above all he could not speak the Pictish tongue and would have to rely on interpreters, a considerable handicap for a man whose commanding voice and eloquence were among his most persuasive assets. And then again, who precisely were the Picts, where were they, and were they one nation or merely loose confederations? Was the key to his purpose one ruler, whose will all would obey, or did he have to devote years to converting tribe after tribe? To us, it is still a little obscure, but the King of Dalriada would be fairly well informed about his enemy.

In the first place, we can probably accept the division into southern and northern Picts. The barrier dividing them physically from 400 AD was The Mounth. We saw in Chapter II there were probably missions to those in the south, though not all agree about this or about the depth of penetration. The southern "nation"—if it was a separate nation—had its homeland roughly in the valley of the Tay and in Strathmore, the northern was concentrated around Inverness and eastwards through Morayshire and beyond. The so-called dorsal ridge separating south from north may have led to some difference in identity, although one must ask oneself whether a people who had menaced the Romans so effectively would really be divided by mountain passes which, in summer at least, were not very formidable barriers even allowing for forests and bogs which have since disappeared. King Brude or Bridei (the less-commonly used Pictish form of the name), whom Columba knew he had to reckon with, is described by Bede as *rex potentissimus*. This may be nothing more than a figure of speech, a chronicler's vague description; but whether it is because Brude had proved the threat to Dalriada or because he was thought to command all the Picts, Columba seems to have singled him out for his attentions.

It is at this point we should begin looking for some material evidence against which to check what we read in Adomnán and Bede. The Picts themselves left no written records of what happened, but they did leave those extraordinary works of art, the symbol-stones. Obviously, everything depends on dating. The date generally ascribed now to the earliest of them is the seventh century, although Dr Henderson quotes a possible range of 500–700, while Mrs Fowler pushes the date of the silver plaques with symbols found at Norrie's Law back into the sixth century, although not all agree with this. Yet if we put a seventh-century attribution on the stones, the symbols they bear, or some of them, are so perfectly and elegantly designed that they cannot possibly have been new inventions. They must have been evolving over a span of several generations, perhaps longer. They could well have been in existence in some form in Columba's time.

Leaving aside their significance for the moment, what concerns us first is the interesting theory of the "declining symbol", noticed by Mr R. B. K. Stevenson and discussed by Dr Henderson, which can be explained briefly by saying the correctly formed symbol declines in time to a less-correct form and finally to something virtually meaningless. It is found that correct symbols tend to appear on stones in the far north, as for example on the Golspie slab now at Dunrobin Castle, and that the decline can be seen as we go south. The argument from this is that the seat of power lay in the north, but also that there was a certain political unity throughout the Pictish region. Dr Henderson suggests a powerful ruler as the influence behind all this, but prefers Brude MacBili, successor to the Brude MacMaelcon of Columba's day, as the originator of the stones. However, it supports the theory that the main centre of power lay in the north in the sixth century, and that Columba believed that by going to Brude's court at Inverness he might convert the whole of Pictavia at a stroke.

Nothing in the old chroniclers is more baffling than the casual way in which Columba's mission is described. Bede merely says he "converted that nation to the faith of Christ by his preaching and example". Adomnán is not much more explicit, although he devotes more space to incidents during the mission, as Cuimine does also. The "Old Irish Life" gives only a few lines to the mission. What we can deduce with certainty, however, is that here we have a further pointer to Columba's steely determination and courage. For a few clerics to set out from Iona for the Great Glen of Alba and the Pictish stronghold at the other end of it is akin to a party of clergy going from Peshawar to Kabul by way of the Khyber in the days when the mullahs were preaching a holy war. Most of the journey may have been made by water, first turning east into the Sound of Lorne, then up Loch Linnhe. Even this early part of the route could have been dangerous, with lurking places for enemies in the sea lochs on either flank, but at the head of Loch Linnhe the saint and his party would have to disembark to follow the River Lochy into the mouth of the Great Glen itself. The rest of the way, for the most part, was probably done by boat, first through Loch Lochy, then Loch Oich, and finally Loch Ness, but all the way tribesmen could have fallen upon them out of the forests on the steep hillsides—on either flank stretched a hostile wilderness. The only precaution

Columba seems to have taken was to include in his party St Comgall, founder of Bangor, and St Canice, both Irish Picts from what is now Co. Down and South Antrim, men who must have had some knowledge of the Pictish speech of Alba.

The journey would have been suicidal if made without some prior agreement with the Pictish king. Moreover, I find it impossible to believe that Brude simply acceded to a request to receive a Christian mission. Columba's mission must have had an overt element of political purpose, made known to Brude in advance, and the king apparently saw an advantage in the meeting. Columba's reputation had gone before him, enhanced by his royal blood, and Brude may have looked upon him as a figure like one of those great statesmen-clerics of later times who were ambassadors of their country. Brude could also have been curious about him as a miracle-worker, a magician, and about the opportunity of confronting him with his druids. He was certainly not a complete stranger to Christian beliefs, and perhaps he wanted a first-hand exposition of them. However, I cannot accept Simpson's contention that the Picts were not pagan when Columba went among them. His claim that St Moluag founded churches at Rosemarkie, Mortlach and Clova implies that he forestalled Columba, and his claims for St Donnan and St Finbar of Moville are equally unproved. There may have been some pockets of Christians in the furthest parts of Pictavia, that is in the south and south-west and on some of the islands open to direct influence from Ireland; but the material evidence to be examined presently indicates the Pictish people were not Christian, and Adomnán's account of Columba's reception at Inverness, while largely symbolic and not factual, does nothing to suggest otherwise.

This colourful event is famous. Arrived at Inverness, Columba and his people join in vespers, *vespertinales laudes*, before Brude's palace. The druids try to prevent their singing, but Columba chants the 46th Psalm in a thunderous voice which terrifies the Picts. Columba then finds Brude's fortress barred against him. The king, we are told, was "elated with pride of royalty". Columba's next step is to go up to the gates and mark them with the sign of the cross, when he knocks and lays his hand upon them, and they fly open, "the bolts having been violently driven back". The saint and his party pass through. Thereupon the king and his "Senate" are much alarmed and go out of the palace "to meet the blessed man with reverence and address him with the most respectful and conciliatory words; and from that day ever afterwards that same ruler as long as he lived, honoured the holy and venerable man with the greatest honour, as was meet".

This is the incident which, naturally enough, has caught the imagination of later ages. William Hole's well-known mural in the National Portrait Gallery in Edinburgh depicts a Brude cowed by the stern glance of Columba with an upraised crucifix. What is always forgotten is that Cuimine, like Adomnán, who repeats him almost word for word, is writing in terms of symbolic imagery, and their aim is not to record facts but to establish the spiritual supremacy of their saint. Accuracy of detail mattered no more than it did in a devotional painting or a stained-glass window in a medieval church. What those hagiographers are really saying is that Columba's journey to Inverness met with success, and was to be hailed as epoch-making, and there is no reason to doubt the truth of this if we look at the long-term results. What sort of success it met with is another question. It is hard to credit that Brude was truly cowed, or even discomfited. Superstitious he would be, but he was a realist and a tough one, and had his own reasons for letting Columba come to his court. The success of the meeting cannot have been one-way. If anyone were discomfited it would be his druidical counsellors, who must have been suspicious of any rival influence.

What do Cuimine and Adomnán say about the druids? The pagan priesthood is concentrated in the person of one man, Broichan, the "Magus", who had been tutor to the king. Confrontations between Columba and Broichan are not debates on a theological or philosophical level. They are more like magical contests, as Moses competed with the high-priest at the court of Pharaoh, or for that matter as St Patrick did against the druid before King Laogaire at Tara. Some writers maintain the druidism of Pictland was more a kind of shamanism than the sophisticated cult practised in Gaul. If so, Adomnán implies Columba brought himself down to the druids' level; but in fairness to Columba we must judge the tales of magical "successes" as we do so much else in the hagiologies, as contrivances to symbolise the power of the saint.

Those magical confrontations are not many, but they are described in considerable detail. Some may have a basis of truth. First—and this, unlike some other incidents, seems to begin at least in the king's presence—there is the request by Columba that Broichan set free an Irish handmaid, which the druid refused to do "with hard and doltish obstinacy". Columba then said: "Know, Broichan, if thou refuse to deliver to me this captive stranger before I return from this province, thou wilt surely die." Columba and his followers go down to the River Ness, and Columba selects a white pebble, saying God will effect many cures among the heathen by its means, and he goes on to say that an angel has smitten Broichan, shattered a drinking-glass in his hand and reduced him to a state near death. He adds that Broichan is now ready to set free the maid. Two horsemen arrive from the king, confirming Columba's words and bearing a message from the king begging the saint to save Broichan from death. Columba at once sends two of his companions to Brude with the white stone, directing that if Broichan agrees to free the girl he is to dip the stone in water and drink it. The messengers return to Brude. Broichan yields the girl and the stone is placed in water, where it floats "contrary to its nature", and when the druid drinks he is cured. The king retains the stone and achieves many cures by its aid; but it is added that if the sick person should be near death the stone would not be found, and tradition has it this happened at the death of Brude himself.

In a second confrontation Broichan essayed a challenge. It seems the saint was about to make a voyage on Loch Ness, perhaps returning to Iona, when Broichan threatened to make a tempest that would stop him. The saint came down to the shore of the loch accompanied by a great crowd, and there was rejoicing among the druids when the sky darkened and a great wind began to blow up the loch from the south. Adomnán here makes the interesting comment that it is quite within the powers of demons to arouse such tempests, if God were willing; and he cites the precedent of St Germanus, against whose voyage to Britain legions of devils stirred up a storm that was quelled by the prayers of the saint. Columba called upon Christ and went aboard, ordering the sail to be raised in spite of the contrary hurricane. Speedily the boat sailed into the wind, which then veered and blew from the opposite direction, carrying Columba and his party safely to their destination. This of course could have a basis in a good knowledge of seamanship, which Columba probably possessed.

And there is another example of a confrontation in which superior knowledge could have played a part. The son of a peasant whom Columba had baptised fell dangerously ill, and the druids bitterly reviled the parents because they had turned away from the old faith which could have cured the boy. He died, but Columba brought him back to life and confounded the druids. There was, too, the "fountain" sacred to the pagan gods, to drink from which brought leprosy or other ill, but when Columba blessed the water he and his disciples drank from it and washed in it, without harm. From that day the demons departed from the fountain, which became a healing spring.

It is not difficult to find rational explanations for some at least of the miracles recorded of far-off times, but neither is it particularly rewarding. I have stressed the context of wonder in which men like Adomnán wrote. But it is also right to be cautious about incredulity. We live in an age of doubt when even the churches look with a critical eye on miracles. Yet I have been told that when modern missionaries left some gospel-books behind in Ethiopia and returned many years later they found not only a flourishing church, but a community of believers among whom miracles like those mentioned in the New Testament happened every day—because there had been no missionaries to teach that such things were not to be taken literally. Materialism can shrivel certain faculties just as surely as it can destroy morality, health and simple happiness. We may yet have to weigh very carefully

the doubts of the doubters. We have already learned that primitive societies are not so primitive as had been thought, that the
practices of so-called witch-doctors are not to be dismissed out
of hand as hocus-pocus, nor as necessarily evil or anti-social. And
when we examine, or try to examine Pictish society in relation
to the Columban mission, not only do we have to avoid
polarising the situation into a confrontation between evil and
good, as no serious student today would do, but we have to
keep reminding ourselves that Columba was no modern missionary. He believed in the Pictish deities, and he believed in their
powers. They were as real to him as his own God. The atmosphere
of wonder and miracle was not imposed upon him by the
hagiologists: he lived in it, all the while pursuing the interests
of his people. I say it is not rewarding to try to rationalise the
miracles credited to him because I am sure he himself had no
doubt about miracles and may well have achieved things which
we should call miraculous, even if so many of the examples
cited by Adomnán appear to be naïve. While, therefore,
Adomnán's miracles are to be taken as symbolic, there may be
a profound truth behind them, the astonishing accomplishments
of a dominating personality.

Naturally we can only speculate about Columba's beliefs.
What looms up for us through the dark glass of Adomnán is,
in the main, a conventional figure of a saint. But, as we have
already seen, there are chinks in the darkness. Sometimes
Adomnán is disconcerted into a half-admission, as in the evasive
references to the synod of Teilte, and occasionally he betrays
knowledge that the saint could be tortured by a struggle within
himself. Demons were as real to him as angels. Skene draws
attention to this, and cites in particular an event located by
Adomnán as happening on Iona, when Columba went to seek a
place remote from men in which to pray. Afterwards the saint
told a few of his brethren he had seen "a very black host of
demons fighting against him with iron darts". The Holy Spirit,
he said, revealed to him the demons were about to attack the
monastery and slay the brethren, but he was clad in the armour
of the Apostle Paul and fought with the utmost bravery for most

of the day but was only able to conquer when a few angels of God came to his aid and drove off the demons in terror. The cloud of demons departed for Tiree, where they would attack the community of brethren and cause many to die. Skene attributes this to a dark thundercloud which Columba peopled with demons, a cloud which passed on towards Tiree; but if there is anything in the tale at all I think there must be more to it than a passing cloud—a conflict within him, surely, responding to a mood of nature. It is probably Adomnán's way of saying, symbolically, that Columba had his deep doubts and fears.

Even in Adomnán's pages, then, reading between the lines, there is enough to dispel the sentimental, rather Pre-Raphaelite image. The man who emerges is far more credible in the sixth-century context, and if one agrees with this the open-and-shut case for the conversion of the Picts as usually presented is no longer acceptable and demands much more investigation. Seen in this way Columba could not dismiss the beliefs of the Picts summarily in his own mind as Livingstone was able to dismiss the superstitions of his Africans. We are left wondering about the very nature of the Christianity which he carried to the Picts. Many times he had copied the gospel-books, which were the basis of his belief, the same gospels familiar to us all in the Authorised Version, but we have to divest them of a centuries' old build-up of imagery to arrive at Columba's attitude. Like the Africans of modern times, he had no heritage of Byzantine icons and medieval frescoes and Renaissance paintings to pre-determine his visions, no great weight of dogma to restrict his thinking. For want of those things, was his Christ a less or a more real shield to him when he went among a pagan people? An image will emerge in the great gospel-books of the eighth century, and that will be strange enough, as we shall see in due course, but all Columba had to rally his spirit was the symbol of a cross, probably rudely-scratched at that. Through his pagan heritage he could think of Deity only in terms of symbols. Did he see Christ truly as the Son of Man, with all that implies, or as a kind of Cuchulainn figure striding fantastically down the corridors of Celtic mythology, maybe as shape-changing as the hero himself, but commanding a legion of angels who could be called down to defeat the demons who lurked in the mountain-springs or peopled the thunderclouds? All we can be sure of is that Columba's concept of Christ would be of a being stranger and more inscrutable than any mosaic image in Ravenna.

Adomnán describes several encounters between Columba and monsters while he was among the Picts. One occurred on the Isle of Skye. The saint had left his companions to go into a wood to pray when he met a boar of huge size running from the hounds. He stood still and watched the animal, then raised his hand and commanded it to come no further, but to die where it was. As soon as the command rang through the wood the boar fell dead. The boar was a cult animal among the Celts, and as I commented in the first chapter this incident seems to have a symbolic significance.

The monster story which is best known, for obvious reasons, is the fabled meeting between the saint and the creature which emerged from Loch Ness. He had crossed the River Ness when he found a party burying the body of a man who had been attacked by a monster when swimming. The saint commanded one of his companions to swim across the river to fetch back a coble beached on the opposite bank. The man, Lugne Mocumin, stripped to his tunic and dived in; but the monster lay in wait on the river bed and rose to the attack, rushing up with a great roar, mouth agape. All who were there, the brethren as well as pagans, were filled with terror. Columba made the sign of the cross in the air and invoked the name of God, ordering the monster to keep off and go away. Although no more than the length of a punt-pole separated the animal from its prey it fled in fear. Even the "barbarous heathens" there present marvelled and "magnified the God of the Christians". The aquatic monster story is inevitable in any collection of Celtic legends, because most streams and lakes were credited with denizens of this sort.

Other saints elsewhere did what Columba did at Loch Ness, and legends of such monsters are not only widespread but long-lived. Reeves instances in his own time the fearful Bran, the "direful wurrum" of a lake in Co. Kerry, which could be heard

The Monymusk Reliquary

Gartan, Co Donegal: Birthplace of Columba

Battlefield of Cul Dreimne, Co Sligo

Derry

Iona: St Columba's Bay

Iona: St Martin's Cross

The *Cathach* of Columba

Iona: The Abbey Church

Book of Kells: Incarnation
Initial Page

Ahenny, Co Tipperaray: The North Cross

Monastic settlement of Skellig Michael, Co Kerry

Monasterboice, Co Louth: Cross of Muiredach

Birsay, Orkney: Three Pictish Warriors

The Guthrie Bell-shrine

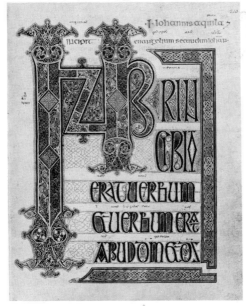

Lindisfarne Gospels: first page of St John

Lindisfarne

on stormy nights bellowing like a young bull. Today in the West Highlands there are many who would not scoff at the thought of the dreaded water-horse, and belief in the monster of Loch Ness is by no means limited to transatlantic scientific expeditions. In short, monsters were an everyday challenge to the powers of any Christian holy man, whose ability to deal with them had to be placed firmly on record.

It is a pity we know so little about that *rex potentissimus*, Brude MacMaelcon. Even his stronghold or "palace" cannot be identified with any certainy. Reeves thought it must have been the vitrified fort of Craig Phadrig, two miles west of where the Ness enters the sea. Skene, understandably, rejected this because the fort stands nearly 500 feet above sea-level. He prefers the gravelly ridge of Torvean, a mile south-west of the town of Inverness, and now dominating the golf-course. There are ditches and ramparts indicating an old hill-fort encircling part of the ridge. Here, where the Caledonian Canal is cut, workmen in 1808 found an object now in the National Museum of Antiquities of Scotland: a heavy silver chain. It comprises 33 double links, each carefully channelled. Its length is 18 inches, its weight 92 ounces. Skene mentions the chain in a footnote but, perhaps prudently, draws no conclusions from it. I shall be a trifle more indiscreet.

Several such chains have been found in Scotland, some with terminal rings bearing Pictish symbols. They are massive assemblages of the precious metal, ingeniously contrived, and they seem to indicate a wearer of special importance. It is known that in ancient Wales kings wore not crowns but ceremonial chains of gold, and it is tempting to believe the Pictish chains were royal insignia of this kind. Now Brude's father, Maelcon, may have been Maelgwn, King of North Wales, for among the Picts the queen might choose the father of her children in this way. Clearly it would be foolish to put much weight on the chain as a pointer to the site of Brude's stronghold—chains of this kind have been found in areas as far apart as Lanarkshire and Aberdeenshire—but it would be equally foolish to reject it as an indication of the presence of a Pictish royal personage in the vicinity. True, the chain is usually dated to the seventh century, and Brude died

in 583; but 583 is not so far out, and in any case none would be
so bold as to claim this as Brude's own chain of office. It could
have been made in the Welsh tradition by his successor and still
link the area with Brude's seat.

That Inverness was the capital of the northern Picts is in itself
an assumption, based on the probable location of Brude's stronghold. There is no archaeological evidence of an important
settlement here. There are some vitrified forts in the area, proving
only there were settlers there long before the Picts. There are
also some symbol-stones (Class I), but only a few. On the other
hand, if the seat of the king was here it is hardly likely to have
been an isolated fort, and it is the natural point of focus of the
territories controlled by the king, with good communications in
all directions. If one stands on the Great North Road, the A9,
just where it begins the long descent from Drummossie Muir to
the town, the picture becomes clear. The broad waters of the
Moray Firth funnel in to the mouth of the Ness, and for a sea-
going people like the Picts this is of high importance. The low
lands of Moray and Nairn are fertile and easy to cultivate, and
that they sustained communities from early times is plain from
the surviving remains, ranging from the Clava Stones down by
the Nairn to the site at Burghead where the bull-sculptures were
found. Beyond the firth are the equally-fertile lands of the Black
Isle and the sheltered waters of the Cromarty and Dornoch
firths; then turning westward past Ben Wyvis are the long routes
to Skye and the islands by way of Strathbran and the Dirrie
Mor. South-west is Glen Albyn. Inverness is at the hub.

However, the issue is the degree of success achieved by Columba
among the Picts. He led at least two further missions after the
first. Adomnán gives us little hard information. We are told this
or that happened "beyond the dorsal ridge of Britain", or when
the saint was "sojourning in the province of the Picts", but the
good abbot mentions only haphazard incidents. So we read of the
healing of Fintan, son of Aedh, and learn that the youth later
founded a monastery at Kailli-an-Inde, an unidentified place
which has been located, on no good grounds, in Perthshire. Or
again, there is the boy raised from the dead whose parents were

abused by the druids for letting him fall into the hands of the Christians, until Columba confounded them with a miracle, the most significant thing we learn being that the saint was still using an interpreter. Geographical pointers are more interesting. There is more than one reference to Columba in Skye, among them the baptism of the aged chief of what is called the "Geona cohort", followed immediately by the death and burial of the old man. There is also a prophecy relating to the voyage of Cormac, when Columba spoke to Brude with the Under-King of the Orkneys present, commending this "soldier of Christ" to the under-king's protection. Nowhere do we read of those gifts of land or the founding of churches and settlements which formed the pattern of conversion in Ireland. Skene takes from this last tale a sign of the saint's authority at the Pictish court, and he assumes that Brude, won over to the Christian faith, must have been facilitating the spread of the new religion. Bede is no more helpful than Adomnán. He accepts without question that the Picts had followed their king and become Christian to a man. But all we are justified in concluding is that the king, for his own good reasons, did not order Columba out of his kingdom, or persecute him.

If Columba's dealings with Brude were substantially political, of course, the king might consider it was in his own interests to tolerate his teaching. Is it possible, too, that his teaching was less radical, less uncompromising than we have supposed? The Saints of Ireland won success not so much by preaching as by example. Columba comes through to us as literally a *miles Christi*. He could treat his adversaries like the great boar in Skye. His time among the Picts is marked much more by magical duels with his arch-enemies, the druids, than by examples of Christian compassion. In his *History of the Church of Scotland to the Reformation* Dr Duke puts his finger on this when he says: "Columba does not seem to have employed the most approved means of commending, in the face of such superstition, the Christian Faith: to endeavour to out-match the druids at their own profession, and to meet magic with what seemed to be merely a more successful kind of magic, was a poor substitute for the proclamation of the simple Christian message." His methods were far different from those of Paul among the Galatians—who also, be it remembered, were Celts. But Dr Duke goes further. "The truth of the matter seems to have been that St Columba himself had not advanced very far out of the darkness which surrounded him; and that his own mind was shadowed by many of the superstitions of his age." This may seem heresy, impiety even, to those who cling to the traditional picture of the saint but, as Dr Duke claims, it is a judgment based on Adomnán. Yet I think Dr Duke is as guilty as the traditionalists of examining Columba out of context. We are merely back with what I keep on stressing: the ever-presence of the pagan heritage. And, *pace* Dr Simpson, the Picts had not had the equivalent of a St Patrick, so that to think of their nation as true converts to Christianity in the accepted sense after a few years of missionary work is surely unrealistic. Impressed many may have been by Columba's dominating personality and superior magic, but how many had abandoned their ancient beliefs?

There are two ways of trying to get a little nearer to the truth. The first has been discussed over a century and more, and consists in tracing through place-names possible sites of churches founded by Columba or his immediate followers. In Chapter II this method was applied to the missions of Ninian, and showed how careful one must be to check that dedications were not made merely as tributes to a saint at a later time. The cult of Columba was more widespread than Ninian's. Dr Henderson reviews this practice briefly but effectively. It was usual in the Celtic church to name a church after its founder, but churches built later yet within the *familia* of the saint were also named after him, bestowing much honour and power on them. There may or may not have been a personal connection with the saint. In Wales there was a practice of "re-culting" of saints in the case of churches with traditional connections, which means that even if a dedication is known to be later it is not necessarily wrong or unfounded. The Pictish area has numerous sites named after Irish saints. They must represent missionary activity at one time or another, but Dr Henderson reasons that most of them simply reflect the swamping of Pictish national identity by the Dalriadic Scots after AD 850. Bede claims all the monasteries in Pictland were Columban. Iona, Dr Henderson suggests, "may have kept a fairly firm hold on the Columban church in Pictland, particularly after the defection of Northumbria". In fact, none of the foundations in Pictland can be substantiated in any way, and the absence of any evident Pictish saints among them is very strange if Columba indeed converted the entire people. On the other hand, it can hardly be doubted that over the years there was much Columban influence on the fringes of Pictland at least, especially among the western isles.

The second and surely more rewarding way of testing claims for conversion of the Picts is by examining the sculptured stones. Early in this chapter the symbol-stones were referred to as pointers to where the main power in Pictland lay. Now we have to speculate on the message of the symbols. Dating is vital, and it need hardly be said that any new discovery forcing us to change the dating could make nonsense of theories about the message. Likewise, any well-substantiated new evidence affecting the origin of the symbol-stones—and by this I mean notably the non-animal symbols—could drastically alter the issue. I have already suggested the symbols had been evolving for a considerable time before sculptors began to carve them on the stones, so it is probably reasonable to suppose the symbol-language in some form was in use in Brude's reign and, likely as not, much earlier. The signs could have been inscribed on perishable materials such as wood or bone, tattooed on the skin, or even scratched in the dust as aboriginals in Australia scratch their symbol-patterns. The meaning of the symbols remains a matter for speculation, and perhaps will always be so. What matters now is that if the theory of a longish evolutionary period is accepted, then the symbols can have no Christian significance, although it would be difficult to avoid that conclusion anyway. This view, of course, contradicts the opinion of that almost legendary figure in Scottish archaeology, Dr Joseph Anderson, which Simpson regards as "unassailable", but then I find Anderson's theory curious, if not bizarre. He argues that since the symbols occur on later stones together with the cross they must therefore be Christian, and that where the symbols stand alone "there is no suggestion of paganism connected with them". What suggestion of paganism does he look for?—He says that "only two stones bearing symbols have been found in direct association with pagan burials". He devotes the entire fourth Rhind lecture of 1880 to asserting that all the symbols must be Christian, and that they are "disguised and degraded" variants of "the higher art of the primitive Church" elsewhere. But in fact the symbols are unique to the Picts, and so far from being degraded variants of church art, some of them—the animal symbols—were actually copied, and relatively clumsily, by scribes illuminating the gospel-books of a later time, so that Anderson's conclusion is untenable. It is likely the symbols had a magical purpose, perhaps totemistic, or denoted some personal or tribal distinction, or both. If the purpose were magical, they were pagan and the concern of the druids. The argument for their being of secular significance is strengthened by the fact that symbols and crosses appear together on later slabs, implying there was no conflict, but I am not convinced by this—we have only to look again at the reliquaries with their pagan symbolism to see why. Secular or religious in significance, those symbols are very difficult to reconcile with a wholesale conversion of the Picts to Christianity in the sixth century. It is difficult to believe the appearance of so many obviously important monuments happened except under royal approval, and if the king had become Christian would such a momentous event not have been reflected in such a nation-wide manifestation as those stones?

"The message of the symbolism," writes Dr Henderson, "was the prime motive for the erection of these monuments, and not the message of the Christian Church." What was this important message? Those Class I symbol-stones are scattered all over the north-east of Scotland, the greatest concentration in the territory of the northern Picts. Professor Charles Thomas, who subscribes to the tattoo theory mentioned earlier, suggests that a ruling caste in Pictish society began, perhaps in the late fifth century, to erect monuments to the dead analogous to the ogham-inscribed stones of Ireland, using pictorial symbols derived from Iron Age art; and he points to the Moray Firth area as the place of origination, an area "not converted to Christianity until the late seventh or eighth centuries". Since the Moray Firth area is the heartland of the northern Picts, this is virtually to say the rulers of the Picts were pagans until long after Columba's day.

The animal symbols, while not in themselves necessarily evidence of surviving paganism, do hint at something of the sort. If they are tribal totems, as Lethbridge suggested, they might just possibly have existed in Christian communities but if they are "objects of power", as C. A. Gordon thought, bestowing magical power over cattle or objects of the chase, they point to the survival of ancient superstitions. And because they are not rudely scratched but exquisitely done by artists of outstanding ability they must, I think, have had the approval of those in authority. Whatever their meaning, they surely derive from prehistoric cults, and one is tempted to believe those cults were still very much alive. Look, for example, at the boar on a stone at Knocknagael, not far from Inverness, and compare him with the animal sculptured in relief on the little boar-god figure from

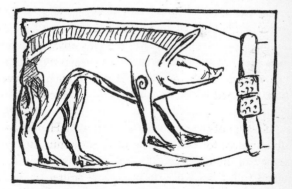

Relief on boar-god from Euffigneix. 1st cent. Musée des Antiquités Nationales, St Germain-en-Laye

Euffigneix in the Musée des Antiquités Nationales at St Germain-en-Laye. The resemblance is startling. What is more, although the Knocknagael stone is badly weathered the boar on it has been as beautifully executed as the little French boar, and one cannot but suspect the boar-god cult inspired it. There is some kind of link here with Adomnán's tale of Columba's encounter with the great boar on Skye. Then look carefully at those magnificent bulls from Burghead, mighty in their maleness, the best in the

Boar on stone at Knocknagael, nr. Inverness.
Poss. 7th cent.

British Museum although fortunately the small museum in Elgin possesses an example. They are such assured and potent images that there must have been bull sacrifices where and when they were carved, in the seventh century. It is only fair to say that what appears to be an actual bull sacrifice is depicted on a stone with Christian attributes in the St Vigeans museum; but the execution is weak compared with any of the Burghead bulls, and Dr Henderson has commented on the habit of later sculptors who filled in empty spaces with random motifs which have no significance. There is no conviction, no "witness", to borrow a Christian term, in the St Vigeans stone.

Dr Henderson has kindly drawn my attention to the grave-markers, stones marked with incised crosses, which she worked on for some years and discussed in the second of her Rhind Lectures in 1977. She points out those markers might be associated with the Columban missions' introduction of Christian burial. Professor Thomas published a map of the distribution of markers

(*Early Christian Archaeology of North Britain*, p. 124), although I understand many other sites could be added. Such markers are nearly impossible to date, but may yet yield evidence of penetration of the Columban church. There is a marker-cross at the seventh-century burial on Eilean-na-Naoimh, in the Garvellochs which traditionally was the grave of Columba's mother, Eithne.

The Class II stones, on the other hand, the cross-slabs, assert boldly the faith of those who set them up. The cross dominates. Indeed it determines the shape of the monument. The symbol-stones were usually rough monoliths, like the roadside stone at Aberlemno or the Dunnichen stone, but the new type had to be shaped to frame the cross, and the surface suitably dressed. There are other new features. The shallow incised lines of the symbol are deepened so they almost produce relief sculpture; and complicated interlace work is introduced, perfectly and surely executed, with no transitional, tentative stage which can be discerned. The Picts were certainly consummate sculptors long before this, but we are given the impression they are now suddenly working under a new edict. I say suddenly because there are no signs of hesitation or experiment, and it is too much to believe such trial pieces were all lost or destroyed. Clearly something momentous has happened. Apart from the appearance of the cross itself, there are several clues. One is the interlace which is in the Hiberno-Saxon style. Another is the distribution, which is denser in the south. The cross itself is evidently borrowed from representations in the gospel-books. Everything, in fact, points to Northumbrian influence.

In terms of chronology I am anticipating, as the Class II stones date from a century and more after Columba's death, and it seems probable the event which brought them about is the Pictish king Nechton's invitation of 710 to Ceolfrith of Jarrow to send instruction in the Roman practices and architects to build churches. In Bede's very full description of the event there is not a single mention of the Columban church in Pictland, but the existence of a church there is certainly implied, and Bede declares that as a result of Ceolfrith's letter "all the ministers of the altar and monks had the crown shorn" in accordance with

Roman practice. We are faced, then, with a dilemma. The early chroniclers would have it the Picts were Christian, that under Nechton their church was "reformed". Yet the first Christian monuments appear only about the time of this reformation. Does the combination of symbols and cross on the "transitional", and therefore earliest cross-slabs throw any light on the problem? The official HMSO guidebook, *The Early Christian and Pictish Monuments of Scotland*, cites Pope Gregory's letter recommending the reconciliation of pagan and Christian practices by sanctifying the pagan element. It proceeds cautiously to suggest "the symbols might be pagan when occurring without the Cross, converted pagan when with it, and eventually to be dropped from the artist's repertory altogether." It then draws attention to two monuments, the Glamis stone and Meigle No. 5, both apparently symbol-stones to which a cross has been added. I find this a persuasive argument, but if it is right it does mean there was no general conversion of the Picts until, probably, the reign of Nechton. Dr Henderson writes to me she believes the Picts were "thoroughly Christian" by this time. It seems to me to be a question, an apparently insoluble question, of degree. Bede's insistence that Nechton and Ceolfrith brought about the reformation of an existing church can be explained if we allow there had been a considerable penetration by Columban monks during the saint's lifetime and the century which followed; but if Iona had had the authority in Pictland which it possessed in other Celtic lands it is difficult to believe the Northumbrian mission would have prevailed so easily.

I believe the real success of Columba's missions to the Picts is to be measured in political terms. Adomnán was concerned with his spiritual fame alone, and if Columba had discussions with Brude about the relations between Dalriadans and Picts, as is probable, the abbot would not record them. Conversion of pagans to his faith must always have occupied Columba's thoughts, but he was a prince-abbot fiercely loyal to his people, and in his mind politics and religion were probably inseparable. He knew that to further the cause of his people, and to realise his ambition to carry his faith deeper into Britain, the bridgehead in Dalriada must be held. He knew the greatest threat to it was Brude and his Picts. He knew that to convert the Picts could well solve his problem, but he was a realist and must have been well aware such a conversion would take many years. Meanwhile, he had to stop Brude from treating Conaill, King of Dalriada, as he had treated his predecessor. Another invasion could drive the Scots into the sea. So he went north to Brude not only as Abbot of Iona but as a prince of the Uí Néill. Status, lineage were of supreme importance among the Celtic peoples, and even if Brude never accepted Christian baptism he would receive with honour one who had a place in the line of succession to the throne of Tara of the Kings. The abbot-prince had a commanding presence. He had to obtain the respect of Brude, and did so. The next two and a half centuries show he had laid the foundations of victory for his people.

VIII

Columba the King-Maker

Columba is said to have laboured nine years among the Picts. This does not mean he did nothing else during those nine years. Probably it does not even mean Pictish missions were his main preoccupation. He does seem to have paid several visits in person, but much of the missionary work must have been entrusted to his followers, men such as Cormac, whose dangers and difficulties Adomnán describes so vividly in chapter xlii of Book I—Cormac, "who now, by voyaging too far, has ventured beyond the bounds of human discovery, and now suffers horrible alarms from monsters never before seen and almost indescribable". It will be asked why Brude tolerated such evangelism in his territories if he was not himself a convert, but I have indicated the king may have had political reasons for coming to an understanding with Columba. To be more explicit, he could have seen advantages in treating with the Scots of Dalriada because he had become uneasy about the strength of the Angles in Northumbria, to whom his southern lands across The Mounth were exposed. It is difficult to accept Simpson's view that the saint did not enjoy Brude's support if we allow he had any access at all to the Pictish tribes; but Simpson is right, I think, in believing his activities were chiefly among tribes immediately to the north of Dalriada and in Strathtay, and his emphasis on the apparent absence of any church or monastic foundation in Brude's capital is surely significant. Incidents in Pictland take up a relatively small part of Adomnán's *Life*, compared with those happening on Iona, and we must conclude that Iona was not only the centre but the main ground of the saint's activities.

But the familiar picture of Columba on Iona, devoting his life to prayer in his cell, varied by writing his books, welcoming strangers and watching the birds, has an air of unreality if we keep in mind all that has been told about him. Quite apart from any conclusions we may reach that he was proud and ambitious, politician and statesman as well as cleric, we find his piety and devotion were often forgotten in surges of impatience or anger, or on impulses generated by his enormous energy. Iona was his base, but it is too small an island to contain such a man. Iona became his spiritual stronghold. He could dream there, and plan, and build up his strength of purpose, and as we shall see later in the chapter he seems to have regarded it as the religious capital of the Scotic people and to have had far-seeing ideas about the part it would play in the future. There is, of course, no hard evidence on which to anchor those speculations. Unlike Whithorn, Iona has no stones of the time into which we can read meanings. Can we therefore read anything about the influence of Iona from the distribution of Pictish monuments? The symbol-stones are scattered over a wide arc, almost as far from Iona and Dalriada as they could be. There are none on the nearer sections of the main routes into Pictland: the Great Glen, Glen Spean, the route through Glencoe and over the Moor of Rannoch to Tayside. If the symbol-stones are evidence of paganism surviving into the sixth and seventh centuries, then why are they absent or nearly so from Knoydart and Lochaber, Badenoch and Breadalbane? There are a few in the Hebrides, such as the rather crude one known as *Clach Ard* at Skeabost in Skye, a part of the island which Columba is supposed to have evangelised. Did the Christian influence emanating from Iona inhibit pagan symbols in those areas, or is it just a question of distance from the heartland, which stretched from the shores of the Moray Firth and Easter Ross to Donside and Deeside? Then if we look at the distribution of the cross-slabs we find the strongest concentration in Tayside and Strathmore. Perhaps Columban missions had weakened the grip of paganism among the southern Picts, at the end of the main west–east penetration route. The *Amhra Choluimchille* has it that Columba himself got this far and had "shut the mouths of the fierce ones who dwelt with Tay's High King". Northumbrian influence in the eighth century would do the rest. So that even if the northern Picts were unconverted until Nechton's reign, as I have suggested, the Pictish threat to Dalriada in the sixth century had been rolled back by the end of the seventh and the Dalriad Scots were no longer at bay with their backs to the sea. Columba did not live to see it, but he had turned the tide and his people had regained the initiative. And although I cannot agree with Skene about the the conversion of Brude, he does say that at the end of the nine years Columba also appears to have "attained the political object of his mission".

Columba had to look in another direction: towards the Britons of Strathclyde. The problem here did not perhaps hold the same urgency, but good relations with the Britons were essential. Here St Kentigern had been at work, like St Ninian before him. Kentigern had been exiled to Wales by the kin of the pagan King of Cumbria after working in the area where Glasgow now is—as St Mungo he is the patron saint of that city— but when the pagan cause was defeated at the battle of Arthuret, north of Carlisle, Kentigern was able to return. Rydderch Hael had been made King of Cumbria, and he is said to have gone out to welcome Kentigern and his monks at Hoddam. There is not even dedicatory evidence of Kentigern in south-west Scotland, but nevertheless he may have returned to the Glasgow area and made it his base. An account of his life was not written until some centuries after his death, so that records of him are very much hearsay, but the belief that he went on missions to "Albania" might just be borne out by some of the dedications in upper Deeside. If so, this further indicates a Christian wedge being driven between the northern Picts and the pagan Angles of Northumbria, driven by pressures both from Iona and Strathclyde.

There is a tradition that Kentigern and Columba met in Tayside about the year 584. Jocelyn's life of Kentigern is probably largely invention, but it contains a detailed description of the meeting. Columba, says Jocelyn, had a great desire to see Kentigern, "to approach him, to visit him, to behold him, to come into his close intimacy, and to consult the sanctuary of his holy breath regarding the things which lay near his own heart".

The place of meeting is given as Mellindonor. Each saint brought
up the rear of a solemn procession, the two processions advancing
with singing, and Kentigern and Columba embraced and kissed,
then "after a spiritual banquet of divine words" they refreshed
themselves with "bodily food". The two exchanged pastoral
staves. Columba's staff was preserved afterwards, so Jocelyn
relates, in the church of St Wilfrid at Ripon. Adomnán makes
no mention of Kentigern but, as Skene comments, he does say
there was intercourse between Columba and the King of Strathclyde, Rydderch, Kentigern's patron, and that clerics came from
Iona to Rydderch's capital at Dumbarton, so that a meeting with
Kentigern would at least seem likely. Jocelyn ends his account of
the meeting "then saying farewell, with mutual love, they
returned to their homes, never to meet again".

Within ten years of his coming from Ireland Columba had
transformed the situation which he found when he first arrived.
We hear of no fighting-men brought over to reinforce Dalriada,
yet the *milites Christi* and the saint's own prestige between them
had restored the country's status. Even if the Picts were not
converted, one senses they were no longer an immediate menace,
because what in modern terms would be called a dialogue had
been established between Columba and Brude. The saint had
become a presence in the "waist" of Alba, and had an understanding with the King of Strathclyde. Moreover, such repute
had he built up in the church in Ireland that not only did Iona
form the religious centre of the two Dalriadas, Irish and Alban,
but it may have become already the premier establishment of
Irish Christianity.

Perhaps the only weakness in the standing of Dalriada was its
king, for Conaill, son of Comgall, was not another Brude nor
yet a Rydderch, but more on the level of a *toiseach*, a tribal chief.
Columba must have been well aware of this weakness and of the
fact that he, not the king, had become the central figure. In 574,
eleven years after his coming, the death of Conaill in Kintyre
brought a crisis and at the same time presented an opportunity.
In Ireland, the law of tanistry determined the succession. The
tanist, the heir-apparent, usually was the king's son or a near

relative and succeeded the king; but there was no question of primogeniture, of automatic succession, since Celtic tribes laid much store on their ruler being the worthiest man of the blood. Conaill's heir was Eogan, his cousin, a man said to have been much beloved by Columba, who for purely personal reasons would have liked to see him on the throne. Columba the statesman had other ideas. Perhaps Eogan was not a man of forceful character. He was the son of Gabrain, Conaill's predecessor, the king who had been defeated by Brude in 557, and Columba may have sensed Eogan had not the qualities of mind and character needed to raise the kingship and the kingdom above the level to which they had fallen. Apparently he had no such doubts about Eogan's brother, Aidan. He had fought for the Britons for some time, and may have shown more military capacity than had his father, Gabrain. How Columba went about ensuring Aidan's succession is perhaps best told in the words of Cuimine:

At another time the holy man, while staying in the island of Hynba [Eilean-na-Naoimh], one night, when in an ecstasy of mind, saw an angel of the Lord sent unto him, who held in his hand the glass book of the ordination of kings. This book he received from the hand of the angel, and began to read. Refusing to ordain Aidan as he was directed (for he loved his brother more), the angel suddenly stretched forth his hand and smote the saint with a whip, the mark of the bruise whereof remained on his side all the days of his life. He also addressed to him this word: "Know for certain that I am sent by God, in order that thou mayest ordain Aidan king, which if thou wilt not do I will smite thee again." The angel of the Lord giving him the same things in charge concerning the ordination of Aidan on three consecutive nights, the saint sailed over to the island of Iona, and Aidan coming thither, he ordained him king.

Adomnán repeats the story in words which are nearly identical. Many will say that if there is any ground of truth in this tale it reveals Columba as an unscrupulous manipulator of the credulous, making an unpopular decision and blaming it on divine intervention. However, there are several good reasons for being cautious. The most obvious is that the story may have been concocted to justify Columba's setting aside of Eogan in the interest of the kingdom, an interference with the succession which must have shocked many at the time. We must never forget Cuimine and Adomnán were not historians, and that they would not hesitate to protect the memory of their saint by introducing fables to add to his sanctity. But then again the story may not be a hagiographer's invention. It is not impossible that Columba himself let it be known that something of this kind occurred, and that he actually believed it had occurred. We have been subjected to logic and commonsense for so many centuries, and so much to the dictatorship of scientific truths over the past hundred years, that anyone justifying an action by saying an angel told him to do it would be regarded either as a humbug or as a candidate for the psychiatrist's couch. We do not have to suggest the angel really came to Columba and scourged him to exonerate the saint from blame. All we have to do is to project ourselves back into the sixth century, a prerequisite for the study of Columba which I have recommended before. The situation was a critical and probably dangerous one for the saint, who must undoubtedly have believed his work had the blessing of God, and such were the pressures upon him that I, for one, am not prepared to doubt he could have had a vision of this kind, which he would certainly have attributed to the guidance of God. The story does nothing to reduce his stature either as cleric or as leader of his people.

Before saying something about the consecration ceremony, it is only right to insert here another version of the relations between Columba and Aidan, a version which claims open hostility between the two. Dr Bannerman points out that the commentary to the Bodleian *Amhra Choluimchille* shows Aidan as "determined to prove Colum Cille a liar and a fool", although Columba is his *ammchara* or spiritual director, and elsewhere it is said Aidan summoned 47 druids to curse the saint. Columba naturally has the best of the dispute. There may well be something behind this, some difference of opinion between hot-blooded Celts. Aidan may even have resented Columba's authority in the matter of his own elevation to the kingship. But the weight of evidence seems to support the probability of a close tie between the two, at least after Aidan became king.

The most interesting aspect of the enthronement of Aidan, of course, is the implication of this authority wielded by Columba. I have stressed the influence he had built up in his first ten years in Alba, but it still does seem remarkable that the Abbot of Iona should have been able to select the new King of Dalriada. There is no information that he was invited to choose. One gathers that he intervened himself, proffering his triple dream as the excuse. That his vision took place on Hynba, one of the Garvelloch islands and much closer to Dunadd, the Dalriadic capital, than Iona itself, is seen by Simpson as indicating a *coup d'état* by Columba; but this is surely a rather extravagant attempt to invest the saint with an atmosphere of cloak-and-dagger intrigue. His power, after all, was not exerted through physical force but through spiritual sanctions. His decision, however, does seem to have resulted in trouble, perhaps bloodshed. Alexander Scott in *The Pictish Nation*, basing his view on a reference to great slaughter of "the allies of the sons of Gabhran" in the *Annals of Tigernach*, says the election of Aidan brought civil war to Dalriada, cul- minating in a fierce battle somewhere in Kintyre in which the late king's son, Duncan MacConaill, was killed and Aidan secured victory. Here again the facts are obscure. More recent writers have said the battle may have been with Picts, or even the Irish. Yet a controversial decision such as Columba's is bound to provoke violence among men whose hands were never far from their sword-hilts, and the embers of the battle of Cul Dreimne seem to glow again. It is hard not to wonder whether, in a crisis involving a political decision, the prince did not take precedence over the prelate, the warrior over the saint.

Columba certainly used the occasion to seal the power and prestige of his abbacy by bringing the new king, Aidan, to Iona for his consecration. This seems to be the first consecration of any king in the history of Britain, and as matters have turned

out the blood of Columba's nominee still runs in the British
monarchy, so that the dreams of this remarkable man have surely
been fulfilled. Columba seems to have left Aidan in no doubt
of his, Columba's, function as a king-maker. If we accept
Adomnán's account, based on Cuimine's, the words he used
were:

> Believe me unhesitatingly, O Aidan, none of thy enemies shall
> be able to resist thee, unless thou first act unjustly towards
> me and my successors. Wherefore direct thou thy children
> to commend to their children, their grandchildren, and their
> posterity, not to let the sceptre pass out of their hands through
> evil counsels. For at whatever time they turn against me or
> my relatives that are in Ireland, the scourge which I suffered
> on thy account from the Angel shall bring great disgrace upon
> them by the hand of God, and the hearts of men shall be turned
> away from them, and their foes shall be greatly strengthened
> against them.

Only after this adjuration did the saint lay his hand on the king's
head and bless him. Columba emerges as a grand Old Testament
theocrat. There under the Atlantic skies he reconstitutes Judah,
dons the mantle of Jehoiada the Priest . . . "He commanded them,
saying, This is the thing that ye shall do . . . And he brought forth
the king's son, and put the crown upon him, and gave him the
testimony; and they made him king and anointed him; and they
clapped their hands and said, God save the King." The mystical
description of the ordination of Aidan is a calculated borrowing
of Biblical precedent to confirm the new king's rights, the *liber
vitreus* from Revelation, the act of ordination from Samuel. From
that day the ruler of Dalriada ceased to be a mere *toiseach*, but
the power behind the throne was the man who consecrated him.

There is a significant note in the very first sentence of Columba's
address to Aidan. Who were the enemies who would be unable
to resist the king?—Not, at that time at any rate, the Britons of
Strathclyde. Not the Angles. Those enemies could only be the
Picts. Aidan had become an independent king, in status the equal

of Brude, and, as Skene remarks, the ceremony of Iona was calculated to "induce" Brude to recognise this. No monarch of those days or any other time could fail to interpret such a gesture as a challenge, and as hostile. If further proof were needed that Columba had not converted the Pictish king and nation to his own faith, this seems to point to it. The "Apostle of the Picts" was not likely to throw such a gauntlet in the teeth of the Pictish king if he had achieved what he wanted to achieve. We know Columba to have been an impatient man, but there is an element of exasperation in his words. Either his hopes for converting the Picts were not being fulfilled swiftly enough to satisfy him, or he knew or suspected Brude would never tolerate his plans for the expansion of Dalriada. The Iona consecration amounted to a declaration of intent, a policy statement, and war was the burden of the message. As always, we must qualify this by saying Columba may never have uttered such words, and that the description of the consecration may be just another myth, but the consecration was an event of supreme importance and must have been described to Cuimine by men who were present at it.

The new King of Dalriada was strong, and also ambitious. Aidan did not at once grasp the sword. Many preparations had to be made. He had to consolidate his position, and Dalriada could not be made into a power overnight, for the country's military strength had shrunk and it had been on the retreat for too long. Preparations may have been spread over several years, for there is no record of any action against the Picts until 580, six years after Aidan's succession. In that year, we are told in the *Annals of Tigernach*, he sent or led a fleet to the Orkneys. It has been suggested Aidan's fleet may have operated in alliance with the Picts, or on behalf of the Picts; but such an alliance sounds a little strange, following shortly after Columba's consecration address, and the expedition suggests rather an attempt to harass Brude from the north, perhaps to divert his strength from the south, where he was faced with difficulties. Here we have to anticipate events in order to round off an account of the progress of Aidan's plans. Two years after the Orkney incident he is recorded as winning a victory at a place called Manu, which

H. M. Chadwick identifies with what is now Slamannan, south of the Forth. This is a long way from Dalriada, and unless he had exposed his lines of communication on his Pictish flank to a dangerous extent it would seem he had conquered a large part of Breadalbane and left garrisons from Lorne to the Flanders Moss. But Chadwick's identification of Manu with Slamannan is not altogether convincing. An alternative is the Isle of Man, and this appears to me preferable, as will be seen in the next chapter in dealing with the naval aspect of Aidan's expansion. In 584 Brude's death took place. He seems to have been killed in battle at Circinn on Tayside, a battle with Picts on both sides, which may mean an attempt by the northern Picts to suppress dis-affection among the southern Picts of Fortrenn and Strathmore, and while this may have been a purely internal affair it is possible it had something to do with pressure exerted by Aidan.

For lack of reliable evidence, the problem of Aidan's campaigns against the Picts remains in dispute. Adomnán has him victorious over the Miathi, which Simpson claims to be a tribe of southern Picts occupying Clackmannanshire, a tribe whose main fortress he places on Dumyat, one of the summits in the Ochil hills. The Miathi have also been identified with a British tribe near the Roman Wall, but this seems unlikely, because Adomnán represents Columba as having the bell rung on Iona to call the brethren to pray for victory, and when he announces success it is over "the barbarians". It was dearly won, for Aidan lost many men, including two of his sons, Arthur and Echoid Find, so there have been doubts as to whether it brought him much advantage. Chadwick, however, asserts he conquered "a con-siderable part of the kingdom of the Picts", by which presumably is meant the southern Picts. He quotes a prophecy in the *Tripartite Life of St Patrick* that Fergus' descendants would reign over Fortrenn for ever, a prophecy fulfilled by Aidan. Chadwick estimates he must have overrun the whole length of Fortrenn. Fortrenn or Fortriu is the old province of the Verturiones, whose tribal capital was at Dundurn, a frowning outlier of the hills near St Fillans, from which they defied the Romans in the fort at Dalginross. Following the River Earn eastwards there is much flat, cultivable land, so Fortrenn must always have been a coveted prize.

Chadwick claims Aidan also possessed Menteith, because in the *Life of St Berach* he is named as presenting the saint with his fort at Aberfoyle: another fertile area, although it hardly seems possible the Dalriadans could ever have possessed places like Fortrenn or the lands bordering southern Pictland in the sense of being able to settle or profit by them, for they were much too far from their western bases. The upper Forth area is perhaps where he concentrated his attention, for several reasons. The flat, alluvial straths stretch far to the west, to Aberfoyle and by way of the Teith to the Pass of Leny, within a couple of days of forced march from the borders of Dalriada. Aidan's southern flank here met Strathclyde. His relations with this Christian kingdom were presumably good, since Kentigern and Columba had been friendly. There is even a possibility Aidan had some hereditary claim to this district through his mother, although this is not clear. If he were able to establish himself here and keep open his communications through Glen Ogle and Glen Dochart, he might have been strong enough to push expeditions eastwards, towards Fife and Lothian and the southern Picts. Chadwick considers he was successful in this. He bases this on a reference to his son, Eochaid Buide, in the *Annals of Ulster*, where he is described as "King of the Picts", interpreting this as meaning he had usurped the kingship in such Pictish territory as he had annexed.

Whatever the results of Aidan's campaigns against the Picts—and Dr Henderson has doubts about their success, as there is no sure evidence in the records that he ever had a victory over them—his expansion eastwards brought him into confrontation with a dangerous new enemy, Aethelfrith, King of Northumbria. The outcome is described in one short chapter of Bede, the last in Book I. Bede exalts Aethelfrith, which is curious, because Aethelfrith of course was a pagan. He calls him "a most worthy king, and ambitious of glory", who was ravaging the Britons. He compares him with King Saul, except for the one short-coming—"that he was ignorant of the true religion". This pious monk of Jarrow appears to have had a kind of admiration for the pagan English, among whose "great men" he gives pride of place to Aethelfrith. Aidan, he says, "King of the Scots that inhabit Britain, being concerned at his success, came against him with an immense and mighty army". And Bede goes on to say Aidan was beaten by an inferior force and put to flight. One might almost say that this earnest and likeable scholar who never left his monastery is the initiator of an Anglo-Scottish rivalry which has continued ever since, for he ends the chapter with the near-gleeful comment that "from that time no King of the Scots durst come into Britain to make war on the English to this day". According to him, nearly all Aidan's army was slain, and the battle was fought at a "famous" place called Degsastan, or Degsa-stone, in 603. It is possible Aidan's army was indeed large, swelled perhaps by a contingent of the Britons of Strathclyde, who were certainly threatened by the pagan English at that time, and it is said even Irish princes fell in the fight. Aethelfrith evidently had to pay a price for his victory, for Bede records that his brother Theodbald was killed with most of his army.

The battle of Degsastan did not take place until some years after Columba's death, but it is a convenient point at which to assess the short-term outcome of the saint's policies for Dalriada. In the long view, this defeat counted as no more than an incident. The very fact that Aidan had the resources to lead a big army so far out of Dalriada in itself reflects a transformed situation. He had restored the status and initiative of what seems to have been a moribund colony of Scots in Argyllshire. He had made it respected by its neighbours to north and south. He may well have secured an alliance with the Britons of Strathclyde. More important than any of those things, the spiritual capital of Dalriada had grown into the religious centre of the Celtic world, the fame of which in both piety and learning had earned the respect and admiration of Christendom.

IX

The Convention of Drum Ceatt

The growing importance and the new status of Aidan's kingdom of Dalriada is confirmed by the event known as the Convention of Drum Ceatt, which took place in 575.

Drum Ceatt is, or was, on the River Roe, close to Limavady in Co. Londonderry. It is known now as The Mullagh, or Daisy Hill. The convention has been built up by historians as a highly significant happening, and legends have grown around it. Dr Bannerman has tried to strip it of the legendary material and cut it down to size, but for most of us it has been like one of those inadequately posted roundabouts which leave us uncertain about which way to go. Adomnán refers to it as a *condictus regum*, a conference of kings, which Bannerman equates with the later *rígdál*, from which is to be inferred that it was not unique, summoned specially perhaps at the prompting of Columba himself, which the myth and legend surrounding it seem to imply. Whatever we make of the convention, it does throw some light on what was happening, and however baffled we may be about the part taken by Columba we are left with the feeling that at least it went the way he would have wanted it to go. There are those who think he had little more than a watching brief; but if it is conceded he attended the convention—and this does not really seem to be in doubt—I find it hard to credit that a man of his dominant character would fail to have his way in the discussions.

The agenda for the convention is recorded in the preface to the *Amhra Choluimchille* as coming under three heads. First is the freeing of Scandlán Mór, son of Cenn-fáelad, King of Ossory, a hostage in the hands of Aedh, King of the Irish Dalriada. Second is the plea for the poets of Ireland, under threat of banishment because they were burdensome. Third is the relationship between the Irish and Alban kingdoms of Dalriada, probably strained since Aidan's power had grown. Dr Bannerman makes a strong case for the third being the only real purpose of the convention. Nevertheless the traditional agenda in full should be dealt with, *pace* the myths and the miracles, even if only because the first two items are firmly entwined with the story of Columba.

Adomnán says little about the Scandlán affair. We have to turn to the *Amhra* for a full account, and the *Amhra* being what it is we cannot accept any part of the story as factual, or that the case of Scandlán was raised at all. However, Adomnán does relate that Columba had been concerned about Scandlán, and the continuing close relations between Columba and his home-land after years of "exile" are emphasised, so an account of what may have happened is useful. Evidently Scandlán's father gave him as hostage to Aedh, with Columba standing surety for his release within a year, but Aedh would not release him or accept an alternative hostage. Instead, a hut of wicker was built round him, and they loaded him with nine chains. There were 50 sentinels, and they gave him only salt food and a small quantity of ale, so that when anyone passed he used to plead for drink, which caused him to be known as Scandlán the Thirsty. All this had been reported to Columba on Iona, and the *Amhra* tells that he wept and set out for Ireland with a black cloth over his eyes, his collar and hood further preventing him from seeing Ireland, so that his prophecy be fulfilled and his "grey eye" not fall on the men and women of Ireland again—a somewhat awkward attempt by the author of the eulogy to evade a climb-down over the prophecy. When King Aedh was told Columba had arrived for the convention he is said to have been so disturbed that he threatened revenge—in one version, death—upon any member of the assembly who showed the saint respect. Aedh's son, Conaill, went so far as to rouse some of those attending against Columba, and Columba cursed him "until thrice nine bells were rung against him", then declared him disqualified from succeeding his father. This is a remarkably bold gesture on the part of a cleric whom the king had declared unwelcome; but if there is any truth in it at all it indicates his towering status. We are also told Columba came in company with King Aidan of Alban Dalriada, and according to the poet Dallan Forgaill he had with him a great company:

> Forty priests was their number,
> Twenty bishops, noble, worthy,
> For singing psalms, a practice without blame,
> Fifty deacons, thirty students.

As Skene notes, Drum Ceatt is near the monastery of Derry, Columba's own foundation, so that he could well have recruited a massive delegation if he wanted to, and even if the poet has exercised licence there is something convincing about such a show of strength. The convention was the locus of a critical confrontation with the king. As a Celtic prince, he would be aware that a meek appearance would count for nothing and that he must present himself with a semblance of the trappings of regality.

After cursing Conaill, Columba turned to another son of Aedh, Domhnall. Domhnall welcomed him and kissed his cheek, giving him his own seat. Columba blessed Domhnall and prophesied he would be 50 years a king, and that he would be "battle-victorious". Here the story flies off into fantasy. We are told that when they informed the queen of the cursing of her son and of the promises to Domhnall, who was her stepson, she flew into a rage and instructed her handmaid to tell her husband that if he tolerated "that crane-cleric" she would make trouble; which drove Columba to change the queen and her maid into, not cranes, but herons, which haunted a nearby stretch of the River Roe ever after. In his enthusiasm, the poet helped himself liberally to the vast store of pagan Celtic lore on the subject of cranes and herons and the metamorphosis of women into such birds. But to pursue the story, Columba and Domhnall went to see King Aedh, and the saint demanded the release of Scandlán. Aedh refused, saying the prisoner would die in his hut. Columba retorted that in whatever place he found himself that night, it would be Scandlán who would take off his shoes for him. Columba went to the Black Abbey church at Derry; and after he left the convention a thunderbolt fell and all those present "turned their faces to the ground". At the same moment a bright cloud appeared above Scandlán's prison, and an angel freed the prisoner from his chains and conducted him to Derry. As Columba passed through the chancel screen of his church, Scandlán helped to remove his shoes. Then followed a curious dialogue, in which Scandlán persisted in his demand for a drink until the saint impatiently told him his successors would be cursed by "delay in answering"; but Scandlán promised Columba he should have their rents, tributes and customs, and Columba in return promised him his race would be of bishops and kings for ever. He thereupon gave Scandlán a vast drink of ale, which the other consumed at once, following it with seven joints of old bacon and ten wheaten cakes, after which he slept, not surprisingly, for three days and nights. In due course he succeeded his father as King of Ossory. It will be noted that the whole tenor of the tale, down to the Gargantuan appetite for bacon, follows an ancient traditional pattern. The narrator barely troubles to find even an insubstantial peg to hang it on.

Adomnán says nothing of such happenings. He refers to Domhnall as a mere boy at the time, and as for Scandlán, he records only that Columba gave him comfort and promised he would outlive King Aedh, with no hint the saint was able to do anything for him. As to Columba's reception at the convention, Dr Bannerman is of the view there has been confusion with another conference, that at Teilte described in Chapter V, when Brendan of Birr alone among the clerics rose to greet Columba. There seems to be a strong probability that Scandlán was not on the agenda at Drum Ceatt, and that any steps which Columba may or may not have taken on this issue had nothing to do with the convention.

The second supposed item on the agenda has a very odd sound in our ears: the "staying" of the poets or bards. To make sense of it one must look at the history of a very ancient institution among the Celtic peoples, highly developed both in Wales and Ireland.

The poets in Ireland formed a section of the *aes dána*, the second of three social classes, the others being warrior-aristocracy and the serfs. In the first chapter the druids were mentioned as belonging also to this class, a professional class. Not birth but skill and wisdom were the qualifications for belonging to it, and it conferred extraordinary privileges. The bard's high status can be traced back to classical times, to writers such as Caesar, Strabo and Diodorus Siculus. In its general features Celtic society changed little. The main task of the bard was to extol his patron, to recite his genealogy when necessary. He composed complicated eulogies, which he sang or intoned to the assembled company at feasts, and those colourful and wildly boastful praise-sessions were as much a part of a warrior-chieftain's panoply and pomp as his rich weapons and jewellery and his horses and chariots. Unreal though they might be, the eulogies seem to have followed a stylised pattern readily comparable with the deeply-meaningful patterns wrought by the artist-craftsmen; and while the superficial beauty of both is apparent to everyone, the significance was hid from all but other Celts. Diodorus and others refer to the bards' baffling speech—they speak, he says, in riddles. There is no doubt that an ability to devise and sing those paeans, those epics, was highly prized by their patrons, the kings and chieftains. And there was another side to the bards' function, because they could turn from praise to contumely. They were masters of satire, which seems to have been feared as much as—and perhaps more than—the keenest weapon. A bard could rip to shreds the honour of a prince, and in a society so hag-ridden by customs and taboos a satirist protected by his status found himself in a powerful position. It can be understood readily, then, what pressures bards could exert on their patrons, pressures probably amounting at times to a sort of blackmail.

Bards may have acquired even greater powers through certain developments in Christian Ireland. It has been suggested earlier that druidism was not driven out by Christianity as swiftly as tradition implies, as for example among the Picts; but there is no doubt that in Ireland itself by Columba's time it was on the retreat, and it seems possible the bards acquired some of the functions of the druids. The poet, the *fili*, as Dillon and Chadwick remark, inherited some of the druidical prestige, in particular a reputation for exercising the priestly powers of divination and magic. This must have lent his rhetoric or satire a new dimension, even though the *fili* did not overtly claim to possess such powers, and it can be imagined how his emotional and impressionable audiences were swayed by awe, fear or delight as his eloquence and his imagery enslaved them. They gave him credit for an ability to harm people physically by his words, even to kill. And the system was on a highly professional basis, involving years of training in the schools, where the instruction was entirely by word of mouth, so that not just anyone could assert he was a poet. The trained *fili* must have been a quite remarkable man. Not only did he possess a formidable store of knowledge, but he had to attain a very high standard indeed in composition expressed in metres as strictly regulated as, we must suppose, was the visual symbolism practised by craftsmen. But rewards were high. In the eye of the law, if he achieved the status of *ollamh* he could travel beyond the territory of his *tuath* and sell his services to chiefs other than his own, claiming hospitality not only for himself but also for as many as 24 retainers, his rights in the matter being fully protected. This freedom to roam the whole country and invite himself to strange courts, saying what he chose to say and influencing his listeners wherever he went like a kind of perambulating oracle in some respects made him more favoured than a king. The situation invited abuse. It is small wonder, therefore, if King Aedh decided things had got out of hand. It appears that not only had the numbers of the poets grown to excess, but that they were getting together and making progresses with unlimited retinues, and probably they were using their status and guaranteed safety to make trouble wherever they went.

Dr Bannerman believes the poets were not on the agenda at Drum Ceatt. He points out that the preface to the *Amhra* provides the only evidence that the problem was discussed there, and says a decision to banish the poets of all Ireland is something not to be taken seriously, the reason being that Aedh of course had not got jurisdiction over the whole country. Is it possible Aedh was demanding only the expulsion of the poets from his own kingdom of Dalriada? This would have been a perfectly proper matter for discussion at his *condictum regum*, and one in which Columba would certainly have interested himself since he had decided to come to the assembly anyway. If tradition means anything, he himself indulged constantly in verse composition, although there is no reason to think he may have been identified with the poets as a body. Aedh is said to have insisted on the banishment, and Columba to have retorted on behalf of the poets "the praises they will sing for him are enduring for Cormac, grandson of Conn. And the treasures that are given for them were transitory, while the praises live after them." In short, the poets were cheap at the price. Aedh then relented.

The sequel is supposed to have been the *Amhra Choluimchille* itself. Dallan Forgaill, the chief *ollamh*, composed it, a eulogy of the saint in gratitude for his intercession on the poets' behalf. In return Columba is said to have "promised to Dallan the gifts and produce of the earth for this praising; and he took not them, but heaven, for himself and for every one who would recite it each day and would understand it between sense and sound." This curious record brings us back to fantasy, yet it does emphasise the extraordinary value placed on eulogies by the recipients.

The one subject under discussion at the convention corroborated by sources other than the *Amhra* is Dalriada, the mother-kingdom in Ireland and the new kingdom in Alba. The two rulers involved in this "conference of kings", according to Adomnán, were Aedh, son of Ainmire, and Aidan, son of Gabrain, who attended with Columba. Dr Bannerman believes Columba was there in a secondary capacity, as adviser to Aidan, and that the prominence given to Columba and indeed to the assembly itself is due to the process of magnification of the saint which went on through the centuries following his death. I would not presume to contest this. Technically of course he could not be more than an adviser; but he had only recently completed successfully the elevation to the kingship of the man he had come to advise, so it is not unreasonable to suppose his presence may have been influential in the deliberations, in whatever capacity he attended.

The point at issue was the status of Aidan's new kingdom of Dalriada in Alba. Until the coming of Columba it had been, as we have seen, little more than a province of the Irish Dalriada, and a shrinking province at that under threat from the Picts. But the Irish kingdom itself seems to have been in a rather precarious position. Although its ruling dynasty claimed to be "of the seed of Conaine Mór", a pre-Goidelic, prehistoric king, the Dalriads had been pushed by the eastward expansion of the Uí Néill right to the Antrim coast, where they had their backs to the sea. They were pressed also by the Dal Fiatach to their south. Their crossing to Alba, then, was due not so much to any ferment and boiling-over of their vigour and capacities, such as compelled the Elizabethans to expand, as to the need for an escape route, for a refuge: perhaps not the best auspices for a new settlement. Columba's positive thinking had transformed the situation. By securing the throne for an able and determined man like Aidan, he had made the province a more effective force than the kingdom from which it sprang. A colony, as Skene emphasised, was liable for a long list of tributes, rents known as *cain* and *cobach*, and there were military obligations to the superior king, who could command the colony's support for any adventure he chose to indulge in.

The *Amhra* records Columba's behaviour in this matter in its usual baffling way, introducing a story about how Columba appointed Colman, son of Comgellan, to decide between the claims of Erin and the men of Alba; but what apparently is meant is that Columba appointed Colman to deliver a judgment which may well have been of his own devising. The judgment he gave was: "Their *fecht* and their *sloged* with the men of Erin always; their *cain* and their *cobach* with the men of Alban, but all beyond that with the men of Erin." This somewhat Delphic utterance is interpreted by Skene as meaning that "Dalriada in Scotland was to be freed from all tribute to the supreme king of Ireland, but that they were to join in expeditions and hostings when called upon, with the exception of the sea-gathering or

maritime expedition". That is, Aidan became virtually independent of Ireland. Bannerman confidently states that Aidan
was also considered king of the Irish kingdom.

There are times when Columba's actions, or their outcome,
makes him look more hawk than dove, and even if he were
merely at Aidan's elbow at the convention, Drum Ceatt is one
of them. Aidan quite plainly regarded the judgment delivered
there as licence not only to consolidate but to expand his power.
At this point it can be said with assurance that his military ability
together with Columba's political sagacity laid a foundation on
which ultimately the kingdom of Scotland was built. Aidan's
landward wars were briefly described in the last chapter, anticipating the result of the convention, but his maritime enterprises
complete the picture of the new situation. Dalriada straddled the
sea, and so Aidan seems to have made a big naval effort. Most
accounts of the early history of Dalriada are tantalisingly vague
about what this amounted to and content themselves with
references to a battle or two in sources such as the *Irish Annals*,
but there is a good deal of information in the *Senchus Fer nAlban*,
the *History of the Men of Scotland*, a seventh-century document
which Dr Bannerman has re-examined in some detail. A glance
at the map shows how essential control of the sea would be even
for the internal control of Alban Dalriada, especially as overland
routes were complicated by mountains, forests and morasses. The
fortress of Dunadd is well positioned to control the seaways.
Although not itself on the sea, three sea lochs reach in towards it:
lochs Gilp, Sween and Crinan. All have snug anchorages for
shallow-draft vessels. There is direct access to Ireland down the
Sound of Jura, with the Pictish borderland by way of the Firth
of Lorne and Loch Linnhe, with Ardnamurchan and the Hebrides
through the sheltered channel of the Sound of Mull. Control of
Cowal, Bute and the Kilbrannan Sound would demand a fleet
stationed at Lochgilphead, but the land-link here is only a few
miles, the route now taken by the Crinan Canal. Most of the
larger land areas of the region—Mull, for example, or Lorne—are
so pierced by sea lochs that men and supplies could be ferried
into the heart of them with ease. Those people were in and out

of boats all the time. Adomnán constantly refers to sea trips, naming destinations. Bannerman enumerates 55 of them.

It is generally accepted that Columba was familiar with boats and navigation, as Adomnán seems to have been. In view of the importance of sea power to the Dalriadans, it may be useful to say a little more about the ships available. *Navis* is Adomnán's usual word for a ship, although sometimes he uses *navicula*, *navis longa*, or occasionally *curucus*, a *curach*, this last plainly the equivalent of a rowing-boat. But he also has references to features of ships which imply craft of some size. He mentions sails, prows and stems, yards and rigging, and tells of Columba and his sailors trying to bail out the *sentina* or bailing-well, while the *Senchus* uses the term "seven-benchers" which, allowing two oarsmen to a bench, indicates fourteen oarsmen. Bannerman shows this is small compared with a Norse boat of perhaps as early as the fourth century, excavated at Nydam, so the Dalriadans might have had ships as large as or larger than this. As well as oarsmen there had to be sailors to work the sails and man the helm, and to those must be added a complement of fighting-men. That such vessels were numerous enough to constitute war-fleets is clear from the *Senchus*, which refers to a recruiting system requiring every twenty houses to provide two seven-benchers, which is to say 28 oarsmen. Some of the expeditions which may have involved such types of ship are listed by Tigernach, and in the *Annals of Ulster*. They include, against the year 582, the *Bellum Manonn*, in which Aidan was the victor.

This probably refers to the Isle of Man. There is a record that the king of the Dal Fiatach of Ulster (Co. Down), Báetan mac Cairill, expelled the "foreigners" from Man and affirmed his rule over the island; also that Aidan made submission to him in Co. Antrim. Now there is also a record that the Dal Fiatach left Man in the second year after Báetan's death (581). The "foreigners" were presumably Britons from North Wales. It seems likely that Aidan took over the island in 582, bringing it under Dalriada for a time, maybe after a defeat of the Dal Fiatach rulers in view of the *Annals* entry quoted at the end of the last paragraph. It is tantalising that we do not know what happened after, or how long Man remained in the hands of the Dalriads. It would be interesting to know if Columba became involved in this episode. He must have discussed it with Aidan, but there is nothing to indicate he ever set foot on Man, nor do any of its churches seem to have been dedicated to him. Traditionally it is the name of St Patrick which is associated with the island's conversion, commemorated in, for example, St Patrick's Chair at Kirk Marowan. The carved monuments indicate nothing. Some of the simple, linear engraved crosses probably date from the sixth century, or even earlier, but stylistically they suggest links neither with Ireland nor Scotland, and the effective impact of those countries upon Man, in visual terms, comes at a much later time.

Not in itself a decisive event, the Convention of Drum Ceatt nevertheless set the seal on the emergence of Dalriada as an independent, viable Scottish kingdom, with its destiny in Britain. Its religious and cultural bonds with Ireland were to remain close for centuries, and were a major factor in determining the ultimate character of Scotland. Ambition grew with independence. The tribal wars and jealousies rife in an Ireland isolated and cut off by the sea from the Roman world were replaced by a more serious kind of challenge, by bigger dangers but also by bigger opportunities. For all his military abilities, it is too much to see in Aidan the man who really wrote this new chapter in history. One may say, of course, there was nothing remarkable about what happened in the sixth century, and that the future course of events is something else; but it is not easy to dismiss the feeling that the grey eminence on Iona looms large in all the critical happenings leading to Dalriada's recovery: the battle of Cul Dreimne, the staying of Pictish threats, the choosing of Aidan, and Drum Ceatt. Columba became a legend for more than his saintliness. Even if we allow generously for exaggeration in the encomiums and eulogies which grew around his name, he gleams through the fog of myth as one of those personalities who emerge from time to time to dominate an epoch. Can it be doubted he found tribal Ireland too confined to hold him? Or that he was driven by the consuming sense of power in himself to find opposition worthy of his mettle? Britain was dark and menacing, a salient of the pagan world thrusting forward towards his own, a pagan world which had rolled back the legions and with them the frontiers of Christendom. Long before Gregory the Great, Columba may well have dreamed of restoring the situation; but whether he did or no he had ensured that the rivalry of Roman and Celtic churches for possession of Britain must come about.

Never during Columba's lifetime, however, did Dalriada cease to be embroiled in the affairs of Ireland. By the terms of the convention, Aidan had been committed to the "hostings" or military expeditions of his Irish counterpart. It is not very clear what this meant. There was continual strife in Ireland, but whether Aidan had to divert a large proportion of his fighting-men from his maritime adventures is not known. But we do know of two battles in which he may have been concerned. More important, Columba was concerned in them.

First is the battle of Coleraine, fought about 579. It seems a dispute arose between Columba and Comgall about the church at Ross-Torathair, near Coleraine. At times tempers appear to have been as short between the early saints as between the warriors, and this persisted for several centuries if we are to believe writers such as Giraldus Cambrensis in his *Topography of Ireland*. The Ross-Torathair dispute was at once taken up by the Uí Néill on behalf of Columba, and by the Dal-Araidhe for Comgall. The nature of the trouble is not clear, but Reeves remarks that Comgall's abbey-church of Camus was close to Coleraine, and that territory hereabout was debatable ground in any case between the rival tribes. The result of the battle is not recorded, but the pattern of the affair resembles the lead-up to the battle of Cul Dreimne—basically tribal ambitions, and the tribal loyalties of the abbots.

The second battle took place in 587, near Clonard. The combatants were the northern and southern branches of the Uí Néill. The respective leaders were Aedh and Colman MacDiarmada, and the cause of the battle was a violation of Columba's sanctuary at Leim-an-eich by Cuimin, Colman's son, who slew Baodan, son of Finneadh. Colman is said to have been killed together with 5,000 of his men, so the fight must have been on the scale of Cul

Dreimne. It is interesting that Aedh should have been willing to fight on Columba's account, unless the obligation as regards "hostings" was binding on both Dalriadas, or unless Aedh had his own reasons for making war on Colman.

Some writers have grouped all three battles together, Cul Dreimne and the two later ones, as contributing to the "guilt" for which Columba had to suffer, or chose to suffer, "exile". If the dates given are in any way reliable, only the battle of Cul Dreimne can have been involved in the departure from Ireland, in which case we have to conclude that despite the blame Cul Dreimne brought upon him Columba twice again sought to involve his people, the Uí Néill, in bloody fighting on his behalf. The sources of information are, of course, confused and often much later than the time of Adomnán, so that we can look for no accuracy in the accounts, yet although later ages had deep reverence for the saint's memory this does not stop the chroniclers from hinting at Columba's part in turbulent incidents. We look in vain for some historical guidance, for some evidence from an utterance of the man himself. The nearest thing to it is the *Altus Prosator*, which has survived in the *Leabhar Breac*, the Speckled Book. Unlike most of the poems attributed to the saint, this hymn could be from his pen. It is written in Latin rhymed couplets, but the preface contains some comment on how it came to be composed, and one version has it that Columba was "beseeching forgiveness for the battle of Cul Dreimne which he had gained over Diarmaid son of Cerbail, *and the other battles that were gained on his account*". The italics are mine. This clearly states that in later life Columba was still concerned about his responsibility for Cul Dreimne, and that he had added to it.

When could he have written the hymn? The preface says that for seven years he "searched it out" in the Dubh regles, his own church in Derry. This cannot be before his "exile", as only two years elapsed between Cul Dreimne and his going. Did he spend seven years at Derry later? We know he was in Ireland about 585, visiting his monastery at Durrow and St Ciaran's foundation at Clonmacnoise, but a long period at Derry surely can be ruled out, so the preface to the *Altus* is dubious evidence except, maybe, as an indication of a belief that Columba did feel himself guilty of certain battles—in short, a persistent tradition of such guilt. My own feeling is that far too much has been made of this guilt, and of the need for expiation, and that it has been contributed mainly by the chroniclers of later times, who found the records embarrassing to their sense of propriety as to how a saint should behave.

The ancient priesthood—as Reeves emphasises—had no aversion to taking part in war, and seemed to be able to reconcile Christian beliefs with a more primitive morality. Giraldus, as Huyshe reminds us, as late as the twelfth century found Irish churches had to be fortified against marauding bands and that clerics must be prepared to punish evil-doers in the only way they understood. If the hints of Columba's irascibility are accepted, it is hardly surprising if sometimes he tried to settle his quarrels with the sword, or with the swords of others. Nevertheless it is perfectly consistent with the Celtic temperament if times of anger and vengefulness alternated with times of profound regret for what he had done expressed in penitential austerities or humble bathing of his disciples' feet. I think he could be both New Testament saint and Old Testament prophet. There is, I am sure, something of him in the *Altus* itself. Quite different from the familiar sentimental verses associated with him, it is deeply impressive and moving, and some stanzas have a menacing grandeur which, like the books of Job or Isaiah, makes us suddenly aware we are in the presence of greatness. Whether Columba is or is not the author, we are given a glimpse into the mind of a remarkable being.

The political aspect of Columba's work constantly obtrudes itself, but there is no reason to think him in any sense a precursor of statesmen-ecclesiastics like Wolsey or Richelieu. Wolsey was a secular prince obsessed with the vanity of power, not a servant of his church; Richelieu secured his cardinal's hat by subjugating his king. But Columba, surely by any reading of the legend that surrounds him, sincerely served both his faith and his people. He had immense pride, pride which could bring trouble down on his head, but it was not the kind of pride which expresses itself in palaces and sycophantic followings and high offices of state. To the end of his days he remained a simple monk and presbyter. He possessed bounding ambition, but devoted it to furthering the interest of church and tribe, and it remained incompletely fulfilled until after his death. Ironically, since he was a cleric, his tribal loyalty in the long run brought his greatest achievement; but his spiritual zeal created in a remote island the metropolitan centre of the Celtic church, famed throughout Europe as a bulwark of the Christian faith and as a fount of learning and scholarship.

X

An Atmosphere of Miracle

A great deal may be gleaned from Adomnán about the life of the community on Iona, but we have to try to assess the nature of the emerging Celtic church which has left so few remains on the island to guide us. Was it part of the main stream of the Roman faith, differing only in minor details due to remoteness? As Thomas puts it, "The result of peripheral survival, not the outcome of separatist heresy." Or was it, as some have insisted, a wholly different church, in some ways anticipating the Reformers?

Leaving aside documentary evidence, one has only to look at the rich store of material remains of the early church in Italy, from *cella* to *schola* and *basilica*, to realise how little solid basis there is for speculation about the practices of the early Celtic church. The very fact that a Roman saw every achievement in terms of a stone monument, whereas a Celt barely understood the idea of a monument at all, in itself ensured a totally different attitude to worship. The Roman bent nature to his purposes, the Celt adapted himself to nature. Therefore, although there is nothing on Iona to help us visualise the worship there, it should be remembered the island in itself is significant: the characteristic site of Irish monastic tradition. Many of those sites have a haunting quality, comparable to temple or cathedral. Glendalough has it, even Lindisfarne from far off; and as for Iona, the impression it made upon Dr Johnson has been shared by thousands—on the right day its pearly, ethereal light, once experienced, is unforgettable. The early Christians of Rome came together instinctively in congregations to follow certain recognised rituals; but the Celtic faith, as we have seen, grew out of a longing for a life of contemplation, when the individual could try to seek out for himself the essence of Christian belief. It is not to be supposed the ordinary worshipper, or even the ordinary priest in a Celtic community was questioning accepted doctrine; but just as a religion is shaped by being contained in certain buildings, so it must be influenced by the choice of sites associated with the rejection of conformity.

In its beginnings, the eremitical movement was reformist. Obviously this does not mean Columba was some kind of reformer, anticipating John Knox by a thousand years. The spiritual environment of the sixth century, still coloured by the pagan world, was utterly different from the environment of the sixteenth. Where there is a parallel between Knox and Columba is in the fact that for both the truth lay firmly in the scriptures: *Verbum Dei*, the Word of God. So instead of searching for the foundations of ancient churches we turn to that fateful book the *Cathach*, and the other gospel-books which Columba and his companions transcribed so diligently. The dominant picture of the early church which materialises is of hundreds of dedicated men, without worldly possessions or trappings or dignities, unceasingly copying the Word of God in humble cells in lonely places. Throughout his life, Columba became deeply embroiled in the affairs of the world about him, often preoccupied with secular causes, as we know, but almost at the beginning of his life and again at the very end he is seen copying the Word, symbol and vehicle of his belief. Bede says of the Columban monks "they only practised such works of piety and chastity as they could learn from the prophetical, evangelical and apostolic writings", the reason "their being so far away from the rest of the world". He implies they had a limited understanding, had not the benefit of the wisdom of orthodox ways, but at least he underlines what their faith is founded upon.

Contemplation occupied much of the time of the monks, and it was private. The little oratories scattered around the coasts of Ireland and the Hebrides, and the reliquaries modelled upon them, emphasise the privacy. In those tiny cells the monks fought their personal fights with the devils who attacked them, and with those temptations with which Flaubert so graphically surrounds St Anthony. As Professor Thomas says, the materialist world of today might call them escapists or drop-outs, but in their own time they were in the front line of battle, *milites Christi*. I have already remarked that the pagan motifs on the reliquaries suggest the old beliefs were not necessarily looked on as hostile to the new faith, that a strange dualism could have existed for a time, but agonies of indecision must often have driven those solitary contemplatives to seek their huts and, in the dark, pray for their souls, while the sounds of wind and wave, of every bird-cry in the world outside, subtly threatened them or coaxed them with siren voices, for in the ancient teaching all those things had meaning. The confined space within an oratory may have been as much as a monk felt his prayers could fill with the Holy Spirit to protect him.

At first those cells seem to have been the only churches. They were expanded in size, but in early times accommodation was usually increased by building a group of little churches instead of one larger one, as if privacy were a necessary feature of worship. However small, they ranked as churches and were given the Gaelic term *teampull*. Teampull Beannachadh on the Flannen Isles, Teampull Sula Sgeir and the far-flung Teampull Rona: they crop up in deserted places all over the Celtic west.

It should be remembered, however, that not all those deserted places were as deserted in the sixth century as they are today. M'Laughlan contrasts the Roman practice of seeking out populous centres, "covetous of place and power", such as Canterbury and York, with the Celtic emphasis on contemplation in lonely, difficult places, "exalting Christ, and crucifying self", as he puts it. This is only part-true. It ignores the fact that in the Empire there was a pattern of administrative centres, towns and cities linked by roads, whereas in Ireland and northern Britain there were probably no towns, far less cities. It also ignores the close link between the Irish monasteries and the tribal communities they served, and from which they had their land. In short the Roman church merely fell heir to the existing system of civil and military administration, as the church in Ireland did to the system of Irish tribalism. But on the other hand it did mean the Roman church was held together by a hierarchy of power on the imperial

pattern, totally foreign to Celtic ways. The church in Ireland
had no Primus. It had not the equivalent of the assembly in
Protestant churches. The abbot of a monastery had supreme
power over his community and did not have to refer back to
anyone. The Bishop of Rome does not come into the reckoning
at all. There were bishops in authority in Ireland at least until

the seventh or eighth centuries, but
on Iona their standing was peculiar
and rather puzzling. They were
owed a certain deference, and
Columba would invite a visiting
bishop to preside over the Mass
instead of doing so himself. As
mentioned earlier, he actually
chided one such visitor for not
disclosing he was a bishop; yet
bishops do not seem to have exercised any particular authority or
function except to confer Holy
Orders, and then agreement of the
abbot first had to be signified.
Bishops, however, could also be
abbots, although on Iona the abbot
was invariably a presbyter.

The liturgy seems to have been
Gallican rather than Roman. The
Gallican liturgy had its origins in
the East, but Dr Duke warns against

Stone figure of bishop, 9th cent.   reading too much significance into
White Island, Co. Fermanagh   this. The name of St Martin of
                                     Tours apparently was normally
commemorated in the Eucharist, for Adomnán relates how
Columba on one occasion substituted the name of St Columban
the bishop, who had died; and St Martin of course is a link with
the eremitical movement in southern France. Easter was the
principal festival. Adomnán is quite specific in describing details
of worship, for example in observance of the Eucharist. He gives

no information about music, but he does mention choristers and that prayers were sung, but it is thought the music was the old Gallican Chant, not the Gregorian, as Bede states (IV. xviii) that only in 680 did John, the singer of the Apostolic See, bring to Britain the method of singing "as it was practised at St Peter's at Rome".

The sign of the cross—*Signum Salutare*, the "sign of deliverance, or healing"—was made on occasions both notable and everyday. We are told Columba made it before Brude's palace, also preparatory to the use of tools or milking-pails. The most extraordinary instance of its casual use is the saint's absent-minded blessing of a dirk without raising his eyes from a book he was writing, so that afterwards he had to ask why he had done it. The Duke of Argyll notes the absence of the "cultus" of the Virgin. This is not significant, as it did not become a part of orthodox practice in the Roman church until after the Council of Ephesus in 431. But comparisons between the two churches are not particularly profitable, because in the sixth century the practices of neither were clearly defined. The pope had not then the dominating position which he was to attain. It would never have occurred to Columba to consult him before any of his great undertakings, and a century later Adomnán mentions the pope not once; but then a continental cleric of the time would have been unlikely to consult him either.

Of very great interest, I think, is what the Duke of Argyll a century ago called "the atmosphere of miracle", an atmosphere in which all accounts of life on Iona in Columba's time are set. The duke's assessment cannot be bettered. The exasperating first impression is dispelled on closer study. There is, as he says, "real mystery" here: a problem, that is, of disentangling what could be true from what is manifestly false, and further, of trying to reconstitute a credible picture not only of the happenings on Iona but of the attitudes of those who lived there. There is a good deal of miracle-material which can be dismissed at once as childish. An obvious example is the chapter "Concerning the Expulsion of a Demon that lurked in a Milk-Pail"; another is the case of a staff left behind on the island by a departing visitor

miraculously transported to the visitor's destination in Ireland by
the prayers of Columba. The duke's comments on this category
are scathing, and he is equally scathing about the acceptance of
such tales of the saint on the ground of their being "picturesque".
Nor does he have much patience with the theory that "the belief
of the times is part of the record of the times". Here he is wrong.

What must be avoided is the impression so easily produced
by the more childish miracles that Adomnán was a credulous,
foolish and thoroughly unreliable writer who recorded every
bit of hearsay without question. We have to remember two
things. First, it was customary among the Celts to commemorate
great men by extolling their deeds extravagantly and without
too much regard for facts, just as when in later times the *orain
mhora*, the "great songs", were written in praise of highland
chiefs. Secondly, in the sixth century the "atmosphere of miracle"
did exist and rational explanations of happenings that seemed a
little untoward were less common than attributing them to
supernatural intervention. And of course no Celt could pass on
a story without adding to it, for he delighted in supplying the
"corroborative detail to an otherwise unconvincing narrative",
if Gilbert may be quoted in this context without seeming
flippancy.

It is interesting to compare the gospel miracles with those in
Adomnán. In the gospels miracles are part and parcel of a coherent
whole, elements in an argument leading up to a climax. As
Hoskyns and Davey put it in *The Riddle of the New Testament*,
Matthew and Luke modified Mark "for the sake of clarifying
and emphasising the significance which they found attached by
him to miracles", and they even tend to edit or omit stories
which they think "unedifying or capable of misunderstanding".
They instance the omission of the healing of a deaf stammerer
and the restoration of sight to a blind man because those miracles
are "recorded in such a manner as to present Jesus as a superstitious wonder-worker". Those apostolic editors were deeply
anxious that Jesus be not shown as any ordinary purveyor of
marvels such as the rabbis denounced. Miracles, in short, had to
add up to proof that the ancient messianic prophecies had been

fulfilled. Some of the miracles and wonders in Adomnán are as casual and inconsequent as thistledown blowing on the wind. They add up to little except the light they shed on the people who recount or listen to such tales.

Columba's healing power comes into a different class. Some stories appear to have their origins in the gospels. The raising of a Pictish boy from the dead is one of them, and indeed Adomnán concludes the tale by saying: "Let our Columba, then, share this miracle of might in common with Elias and Eliseus, the prophets, and have equal honour with the apostles Peter and Paul and John in the raising up of the dead." Other healing miracles, again, involve the exercise of simple common sense, such as when Columba stopped Lugne Mocumin's nose bleeding by pinching his nostrils between his fingers. This time the very childishness of the story seems to imply its truth. But we should be foolish to dismiss as mere eulogy Columba's saintly powers of healing the genuinely sick, as for example Diarmaid, his attendant, or Fintan, son of Aedh, or the woman in childbirth. There is abundant evidence today of spiritual healing. Columba must have been a man endowed with immense authority and personal magnetism, and I would certainly accept he had the ability to heal by faith and prayer, the more so since he was among men and women who would never doubt his power. Failures are not of course recorded by the hagiographers, which lends, if I may so put it, a false air of unreality to what they wrote, persuading the doubters to doubt everything.

Both Adomnán and the "Old Irish Life" present a picture of Columba himself very much at odds with the one which has developed up to this point. Predominantly he has been shown as the astute politician or statesman, champion of the Uí Néill, the churchman imperious and intolerant of desecration of the right of sanctuary and willing to invoke the test of battle, the stentorian-voiced challenger of the druids. But in the old descriptions of life on Iona the holy abbot appears a meek figure. The "Old Irish Life" dwells at length on his humility. He is said to have taken off the shoes of his monks and washed their feet, as Christ did for his disciples. He carried his share of corn to the mill, ground it, and brought home the flour. He would not wear linen or wool next his skin, would sleep on the bare ground with a stone for his pillow, and then only if his friend Diarmaid recited three chapters of the Beati. When he woke he would get up and recite the psalms. During the day he went about his offices and attended the sick. His eating habits were sparing: he ate no meat, drank no ale, and refused any food prepared with dripping or seasoning. In every way he made do with little. This is not necessarily typical of the whole community, for the monks seem to have eaten well and there are hints of the equivalent of the fatted calf being killed for visitors. However, a certain austerity was the rule in Irish monastic settlements and this is underlined by the known simplicity of dwelling-huts and oratories. As we have seen, it is this very simplicity, and the fact that monks were seen to be living in accordance with the gospels, which brought early success to the Christian missions in Ireland. We have to be watchful, however, of gaining from the hagiographers an exaggerated impression of pietism. Life on Iona may have been rather less austere than appears at first sight. The "Columcille fecit" poem mentioned in Chapter VI is a helpful corrective. It possesses a happy spontaneity which reaches out across the centuries to convey glimpses of contentment, of pleasure in the roar of those blue-and-silver seas and the white glow of sun on sand, in scraping dulse from the rocks, in the sound of seabirds, and glimpses too of constant delight in the reading and writing of books. There is nostalgia, but no sentimentality or affectation: nothing to anticipate Fiona Macleod or the Celtic Twilight. And there are simple, human incidents in the pages of Adomnán, incidents such as the book falling into the water-jar, the upsetting of the ink-horn. They reflect a sort of family atmosphere. There is even a hint of a sense of humour. But there is really no inconsistency between the simple-living abbot with his everyday pleasures and the fiery, resolute champion of Dalriada. Like so many great men, he was a complex character. In Bede (Book III, chapter iv) there is a curious reference to him: "Whatsoever he was himself, this we know for certain, that he left successors renowned for their continency, their love of God, and observance of monastic rules." It may mean no more than that Bede knew little about Columba; but it is just possible there is more to it, that the monk of Wearmouth and Jarrow had heard tales of the Abbot of Iona which disturbed him in the seclusion of his narrow cell.

At this point it should be remembered that monasticism had sprung up elsewhere than in Ireland. The fundamental aims of the movement, the seeking of purification and atonement through a life of self-denial, occur in all religions. Extreme asceticism is typical of the Eastern attitude, and here is where the more rigorous ascetics of Irish monasticism, those for example who stood for hours in cold water, seem to have had their roots. In the West as a whole, strict discipline was preferred to rigorous self-denial which, in cases like St Anthony or St Simeon Stylites, could reach a point where it was repugnant to human feelings; and discipline was the practice of, for example, the Benedictines, who conformed to a firm rule and at the same time faithfully served the lay community, not only through their religious services but also, if less importantly, in the example they set by bringing the land under cultivation with much skill. As on Iona or in Ireland, the Benedictine abbot presided over his "family", but his relationship with the monks was carefully regulated and he was enjoined to consult them before decisions were taken. The Columban abbot was free to make his own decisions. On the other hand his family does not seem to have been bound to remain with him, and Adomnán provides many instances of brethren appearing or disappearing, usually coming from or going to Ireland. The free flow of missionaries presumably would have been impossible under Benedictine rule, and the seemingly haphazard movements of Irish monks would have been unthinkable. Unfortunately no reliable guide has survived to such regulations as existed for the Irish communities, although I understand the early Irish canons do stress the need for permission before journeys are undertaken.

The document known as the "Rule of St Columba", another of the Irish possessions of the Burgundian Library in Brussels, is doubtfully authentic in being what the title claims, although it is likely enough that the requirements listed in it do reflect the practice on Iona. Most of the rules are connected with prayer, vigils, abstinence from indulgence and the like, and are on predictable lines; but there are also counsels of another sort which bring us closer to the brethren themselves. An example is the warning against gossip:

A person who would talk with thee in idle words, or of the world; or who murmurs at what he cannot remedy or prevent, but who would distress thee more should he be a tattler between friends and foes, thou shalt not admit him to thee, but at once give him thy benediction should he deserve it.

And then again: "Let thy servant be a discreet, religious, not tale-telling man, who is to attend continually on thee, with moderate labour of course, but always ready." And the shrewd final direction:

The measure of prayers shall be until thy tears come; or thy measure of work of labour until thy tears come; or thy measure of thy work of labour, or of thy genuflections, until thy perspiration often comes, if thy tears are not free.

As mentioned earlier, Adomnán throws no light on what kind of music the monks used, but he does refer to a book of hymns for the week, written by the hand of St Columba, a book which survived long immersion in a river although the satchel containing it had rotted. No such book has survived the centuries. Early hymnals do exist, the *Antiphonary of Bangor*, the *Liber Hymnorum* at Trinity College, Dublin, but nothing attributable to Columba; yet there is good reason to believe the saint must have been deeply interested in this aspect of worship, since he was himself a poet and possessed a remarkable singing voice:

> The sound of his voice, Columcille's,
> Great its sweetness above every company.

So Dallan Forgaill claims in the *Amhra*. Forgaill mentions the clarity of his voice at 1,500 paces, and for his capability of producing thunderous tones there is the story of his approach to Brude's palace. It is reasonable to accept the tradition that he had a remarkable voice. What is a little difficult to comprehend is how the choral element in the services can have been developed in a place which had no sizeable church. I referred to the use of Gallican Chant, but this would be effective only in the right setting. Oratories even as large as the one at Kells would scarcely be adequate. Worship in the open air took place, notably at points marked by a stone or a cross, but this must have set considerable limitations in a region notoriously exposed to gales and heavy rainfall, and formal ritual of any sort, far less singing, would be nearly impossible for half the year. Here and there one finds natural amphitheatres—services are still held occasionally in summer in one such in Torridon, Wester Ross—but there does not seem to be anything of the kind on Iona, nor is it mentioned by Adomnán. It is baffling, but I think it must be assumed that in the absence of churches worship in all its aspects must have been informal by comparison with Roman practices. On the other hand, the bards appear to have solved the problem of effective chanting of their epics and praises, so it is difficult to believe the monks did not attempt to produce an equivalent, or that the celebration of the Eucharist as described by Adomnán depended on the vagaries of the weather.

But the question posed at the beginning of this chapter, the question whether the Columban church is a "separatist heresy" or a "peripheral survival" is not fundamentally a question to be answered by comparing rituals or organisation but by examining loyalties. One may over-emphasise papal authority in the earlier days of the Roman church, but Rome had been the centre of the Empire. Enough has been said about the relationship between the Irish monastic community and the *tuath*, the tribe, to make plain that the bond between church and tribe was a close one. The Brehon Laws refer to "the Church of the Tribe of the Saint", and lay down that while there is a member of the tribe of the saint fit to be an abbot it is he must succeed to the vacant office of abbot—"even if there be but a psalm-singer it is he will obtain the abbacy". What is really meant here by "tribe" is kindred, not the *tuath*. In practice, kindred of the founder might or might not retain an interest, and a monastery could become independent of any ties or jurisdiction from without. Not that inherited monastic office was peculiar to Ireland. But what we can say, I think, is that the roots which the Christian faith put down in Irish soil produced a church whose allegiance was primarily to the Irish people, who in turn gave it their allegiance. There is no "heresy" here, nor is it "peripheral survival". This is a limb of the Christian tree, but with a banyan-like independent existence. It is true enough that the churches of the continent in this era were under no particular direction from Rome, and were in a sense independent; but the attitudes of continental and Celtic clerics were surely deeply different.

Whereas Rome, with its imperial heritage, embodied its faith in an art and an architecture born of the humanist tradition, Iona's equivalent is sky and sea and that "atmosphere of miracle" which contrives to linger there. This is not a romantic solecism. The pages of Adomnán show that Columba and his brethren reckoned the elements of the world about them were the fabric of their house of God, as much so as the mosaic-lined walls of any Roman basilica. If to understand the spirit of the early Christians one must walk in the catacombs, to understand the Columban spirit one must know the Hebrides. Only by scrambling to the top of Carn-cul-ri-Eirinn and looking down on those seas where the "marvellous monster" threatened Cormac's voyage, is it possible fully to realise the profundity of difference between a faith which grew on the Atlantic seaboard and a faith nurtured in the rich gloom of San Vitale and the marble splendours o St Peter's.

XI

The Last Days of Columba

The "atmosphere of miracle" which enfolds the whole of Adomnán's account of the saint continues to the end, but in Book II, chapter xxiii, the last chapter, there is a marked change in treatment. It is a long chapter, with an unusual content of sustained narrative. Much of it is written in the present tense, giving it a feeling of intimacy, and the result is passages of beauty, which often are also moving. There are signs and wonders, as there are at the time of the saint's birth, but they are simpler and more credible, here and there with incidents suggesting the writer's thoughts had strayed to the garden of Gethsemane.

The prelude to the end comes in the penultimate chapter. We are told the face of the saint suddenly became filled with joy, with delight and rejoicing, which in a moment turned to sadness. Lugne Mocumin saw this and so did Pilu, a "Saxon", and they were deeply troubled. Columba at first told them to go, and not be troubled about his gladness and sorrow, but they wept and beseeched him to say something. So he replied "Because I love you and I am loath you should be sad"; and, making them promise to say nothing to anyone, he told them he had been 30 years in Alba, and had begged God to take him. He had had a vision of angels, sent to lead his soul from the flesh, and they were standing on a rock beyond the narrow Sound between Iona and Mull, yet they were unable to approach because, in answer to many prayers from churches, God had granted him another four years of life, years which he did not want; but at the end of those years he would be taken, suddenly and without sickness. It is among the more convincing of his prophetic utterances, and one senses that all at once he has become an old man, tired of the stress, perhaps drained of the ambition, the more worldly ambition certainly, which seems to have supplied much of his driving force. To translate his feelings into visions was a simple process, and inevitable. For him, or for Adomnán after him, to look across that Sound, with its green waters and silver surf swirling around the pink and purple rocks, a longing eye may well have filled the eastern sky with beckoning angels, white clouds tipped with haloes by the rising sun.

The four years of deferment ended in the early summer of the year 597, when Columba had come close to the age of 76. Weary, and in the knowledge he was about to die, he had his brethren take him in a cart to visit others who were at work on the far side of the island, facing the western sea. It was a day in May, when the unearthly colours of the place are sharpened by showers from the trailing edges of the cloud-banks beginning their climb over the mountains of Mull. He told his people that during the Paschal services in the previous month "with desire he desired" to depart to Christ, but that he had delayed his going rather than turn a festival of joy into sorrow. Even to the very quoted words, there is an air of the feast of the passover in Adomnán's description of the incident. He tried to comfort his disconsolate monks; then, seated in the cart, he turned his face to the east and blessed the island and those who lived on it. He went on to the prophecy which Adomnán records in full in Book III, chapter xxviii: "My children, I know that from this day you will never again be able to see my face anywhere in this field. From this moment the poisons of all reptiles shall in no wise be able to hurt either man or beast in this island so long as the inhabitants continue to observe the commandments of Christ." He is believed to have spoken from one of the "fairy hills" overlooking the *machair*, after which he was carried back to the monastery. It is a curious passage, this, for it seems to link up with the tradition that St Patrick banished snakes from Ireland, an odd tradition since, as far as Iona is concerned, the only poisonous snake in Dalriada is the common adder, which cannot have been held in great dread.

A few days later, on Sunday, 2 June, the saint celebrated Mass in his chapel as usual. Suddenly he raised his eyes to heaven, and his face was seen to be filled with a "ruddy glow" and with rapture, for he had a vision of an angel of the Lord within the walls of his oratory. This he told the company himself. "For behold," he said, "an angel of the Lord was sent to demand a certain deposit, dear to God, and after looking down upon us and blessing us he went back through the roof of the church and left no trace of his going." None of the company could understand what had been meant by a deposit, but Adomnán explains the term referred to the soul of the saint, entrusted to him by God.

On the following Saturday Columba called his servant Diarmaid and walked to the barn nearby. He entered and blessed it, then blessed two heaps of winnowed corn that lay there, saying, "Greatly do I congratulate the monks of my household that this year also, if I should perchance have to leave you, you will have bread sufficient for the year." Diarmaid, cast down, remarked that his abbot frequently referred to his passing "at this time of the year". Columba replied he "had a little secret message to give him if Diarmaid would promise not to disclose it to anyone before his death". Diarmaid promised on his knees. His master then said:

"In the Holy Scriptures this day is called the Sabbath, which is to be interpreted as the day of rest. A true Sabbath is it for me, for it is the last day of my present laborious life, and upon it I rest from my labours; and this night, at midnight, when begins the solemn day of the Lord, according to the Scriptures, I shall go the way of my fathers. For already my Lord Jesus Christ deigns to invite me, to Whom, I say, in the middle of the night, He Himself inviting me, I shall depart. For so it has been revealed to me by the Lord Himself."

The saint left the barn to return to the monastery. He sat down by the wayside to rest at a point where afterwards a cross was erected, fixed into a millstone. Here occurred the incident of the white horse, the horse which had been used to carry milk-pails from the byre to the monastery. It came up to Columba and pressed its muzzle into his bosom, "inspired by God, as every animal is endowed with the knowledge of things according to the will of the Creator". As it thrust its head against the saint it whinnied plaintively and shed tears, its mouth foaming. Diarmaid tried to drive it away, but Columba forbade him, saying:

"Let it alone, let our friend alone, let him pour out his bitter grief into my bosom. Behold thou, as thou art a man and hast a rational soul, canst know nothing of my departure beyond what I myself have just told thee; but to this brute beast, devoid of reason, the Creator Himself has in some way manifestly made it known that its master is about to leave it."

And he blessed the horse, which turned away mournfully. Skene, while he notes that Adomnán has inserted the incident of the horse into Cuimine's narrative, makes no comment on it.

After resting for a while, Columba got up and climbed a little hill overlooking the monastery. Skene identifies it with the rocky knoll behind Clachanach known as Cnoc an bristeclach, but he locates it from the supposed position of the saint's cell, and more recent work on the site perhaps throws doubt on this. There are many rocky knolls in this part of the island. He stood for a time on the summit, probably scanning the familiar scene for the last time, maybe looking down on the spot from which he had seen the vision of angels four years earlier. Then, raising both arms above him as in a benediction, he blessed his monastery and prophesied, saying: "On this place, small and mean though it be, shall not only the kings of the Scots and their people, but also the rulers of foreign and barbarous nations and their subjects confer great and unusual honour; the saints also of other churches even shall regard it with no common reverence." The final part of the utterance is especially interesting, though too much may be read into it. Did Cuimine and Adomnán, and of course Columba himself if the words attributed to him are truly what he said, not hereby make it clear that by "other churches" they meant Rome?

When he came down from the hill to the monastery, he went to his cell to continue his daily task of transcribing the psalter. It was the thirty-third psalm he was working at (in the modern version, the thirty-fourth). Coming to the verse where it is written, "They that seek the Lord shall not want any good thing," he completed the page and put down his pen. "Here," he said, "I think I can write no more, but let Baithen write what follows." It is an appropriate verse to end on, as the old chroniclers comment, and the verse which comes after is equally apt for his successor: "Come, ye children, hearken unto me; I will teach you the fear of the Lord." This successor, Baithen, a cousin and close friend of Columba, was at the time superior of the daughter monastery of Maigh Lunga on Tiree, and was of course of the clan, the Cinel Conaill Gulban. He may have been designated by Columba previously. Whether the instruction for him to continue with the writing of the psalter was the saint's way of making his wish known to his people is not clear, but it certainly confirmed Baithen's rôle as writer and as teacher. An allusive direction of this kind is precisely the sort of oblique speech which a Celt would choose for an important utterance. It helps just a little to build up the feeling of authenticity which invests the description of those last days.

His pen laid down, the saint crossed to the church for the vesper Mass of the vigil of the Lord's Day. This completed he returned to his cell and lay down on his bed, a bare flagstone, for his pillow another stone which, say Cuimine and Adomnán, is "to this day" his gravestone. Nothing is more likely than that his pillow-stone should have been set up to mark his grave; but there is no evidence that the stone shown as his pillow in the abbey building is the actual stone, and the wheel-cross carved on it is certainly much later than his time. Lying there on his comfortless couch, he took leave of the brethren.

"These, my last words, I commend to you," [he said] "O my sons, that ye have mutual and unfeigned charity among yourselves, with peace; and if, according to the holy Fathers, ye shall observe this God, the comforter of the good, will help you; and not only will the necessaries of the present life be sufficiently supplied by Him, but the rewards of the good things of Eternity, prepared for those who keep His Divine commandments, shall also be bestowed."

Columba then fell silent. When presently the bell began to toll for midnight, there came that strange, indeed eerie last scene recounted by the chroniclers. The saint is described as rising from his bed in haste, and as "running faster than the others" to be the first in the church. He fell on his knees before the altar and Diarmaid, following, saw the interior filled with an angelic light, the source of which was around the kneeling man. Others also saw this. Suddenly the brilliant light was gone. Diarmaid, blinded by the contrasting darkness, cried out "Father, where art thou?" Other monks ran in with lights, and Diarmaid found Columba lying before the altar. He raised him a little in his arms and supported his head on his breast, while the monks around wept. Columba's eyes were open, his face filled with joy at the sight of angels coming to meet him. Diarmaid took his right hand to raise it in blessing. The saint could not speak, but was able to make a movement of the hand in token of blessing, and then he breathed forth his spirit. It was remarked that he seemed to be asleep, not dead, for his face remained "ruddy and lit up in a wonderful way by the angelic vision". But his joy found no reflection in the brethren, who filled the church with their lamentations.

The chroniclers describe how the passing of Columba was announced to the world by many wonders, visions and revelations. One of the most elaborate tales was told by a *miles Christi* called Ernene, latinised as Ferreolus, when a very old man, to the young Adomnán in Donegal. He stated that on the night when Columba passed away he and others were fishing in the River Finn when the entire eastern sky became bright, and it seemed as though an immense pillar of fire rose up at midnight "to lighten the whole world as does the summer and meridian sun". Others fishing the pools of the river, as they said afterwards, had been terror-struck by the sight. In Ireland too, Lugud son of Tailchan had a vision which he related to one Fergno in the morning.

"In the middle of the past night," [he told him] "the holy Columba, pillar of many churches, passed away to the Lord;

and in the hour of his blessed departure I saw in spirit the island of Iona, to which I have never been in the body, all resplendent with the brightness of angels, and the whole space of the sky, up to the heaven of heavens, illumined by the splendour of the same. Angels were sent from heaven, and came down in troops to bear upward his holy soul. High-sounding hymns also, and exceeding sweet canticles of the Angelic Hosts, did I hear in the same moment that his holy soul departed amidst the angelic choirs as they soared on high."

This tale Adomnán says he not only heard from "several well-informed aged men" to whom Fergno had spoken, but also from records in books.

The obsequies were simple. When the morning hymns were sung chanting brethren bore Columba's body back from the church to his cell, and for three days and three nights it lay there. It seems one of the monks had said to Columba that on his death the people would flock in multitudes from Mull and elsewhere in Dalriada in order to do him reverence. He may have had in mind the practical problems of coping with such numbers, thinking their coming might endanger the resources of the community; but Columba had replied it would not be so, that no multitudes would come, and that his beloved monks alone would perform the rites and grace the last offices. He did not explain why they should fail to come but his prophecy, says Adomnán, came true. A rainless tempest raged for three days and nights, so that no one could row across the Sound. Such a succession of miraculous events is today perhaps difficult to credit, but it is far from impossible that there may be some substance in them. Did an electric storm burst over the narrow sea between Alba and Ireland on that night, filling the little church with lurid lights and terrifying shadows, and amazing the fishermen over in Donegal? It was a season of the year when such things happen. As for the rainless tempest, Skene, who has a way of looking at natural phenomena for explanations, as in the case of the cloud of demons, remarks in a footnote that such things happen when the wind blows strongly out of the south-west. It drives the sea through the channel between Mull and Iona so that a powerful motor-boat has difficulty in making the crossing. But to return to Columba's obsequies, these being completed the body was wrapped in fine linen and committed to the ground. The word used by Adomnán for the place of burial is an obscure one, *ratabusta*, unknown to Latin scholars, and has been translated variously as sepulchre or coffin; but Reeves prefers coffin, and it is probable this was placed in a simple grave in the precincts of the monastery. Adomnán assures us that as soon as the interment had taken place "the tempest fell, the wind ceased, and the whole ocean became calm". The day was Sunday, 9 June.

The one thing we know for certain about Columba is that he was a supremely remarkable man, a man so remarkable that no one for centuries could speak or write of him in any but extravagant terms. A careful assessment of him therefore depends a great deal on interpretation of his known achievements. The hagiographers virtually rejected all the tales or records which did not contribute to the image of a man of high virtue and spirituality. That they built this image on a basis of reality is not in doubt, but if much of it is truth it is not the whole truth. The volume of praise and wonder crowded all else out and, as I have suggested earlier, there are also hints of deliberate suppression. The claim that "he was vindictive, passionate, bold, a man of strife, born a soldier rather than a monk, and known, praised and blamed as a soldier" is explicit only in much later writers such as O'Donnell, and the tradition—it has been called the "popular tradition", although certainly not the popular notion of him now—that he was both saint and soldier was formulated by Montalembert, whose words I have quoted. Skene, to me incomprehensibly, comes down totally on the side of Adomnán and the hagiographers. Montalembert's view is based, he says, on "questionable statements", as in O'Donnell's biography, and this of course is true. Adomnán's expression *insulanus miles*, he claims, has been misunderstood by the Frenchman. But essential as the writings of Adomnán and his fellows obviously are to our knowledge of Columba, it is quite evident they were not telling the whole story: it was not their purpose to do anything other than to confirm and maintain the repute of Columba as a great saint. What is more, they were justified. They were not writing for readers of another millenium. The very existence of their church depended on such extravagant eulogies. The fabric of their faith was a precarious screen between them and the pagan world, and any rent in it could be disastrous for the society which pious men like Adomnán were striving to hold together. Skene's rejection of the idea of a militant saint for a wholly angelic one seems to me possible only by taking him out of his sixth-century environment. The hagiographers are not meant to be taken literally: no one knew this better than Skene. Why then does he sweep aside Montalembert uncompromisingly and accept Adomnán and even Dallan Forgaill? It is fashionable today to weigh our saints and heroes in the balance. Perhaps Adomnán was wiser. But in exalting the saint he left out some of the heroic qualities of a man who must have been both saint and hero to his own people, his own tribe.

There is nothing inconsistent in believing Columba was both a truly great Christian evangelist and teacher and also an ambitious and resolute statesman. Nor is there any reason why he should not have been tender, devoted, angelic, and yet passionate, irascible and, on occasion, even ruthless in achieving his ends. The Celtic temperament runs to extremes. If we take into consideration the Iron Age state from which he and his people had barely emerged—indeed had not emerged, as I have argued—it would be astonishing if Columba had shed the characteristics of his race. Add to temperament pride in his royal blood and loyalty to his clan and he would have had to be meek indeed to have suppressed his traditions and his instincts in a time of crisis for his people. It has been made clear that in Ireland the church was the church of the tribe. It had a duty to promote the interests of the tribe. Many a saint was of international repute, but saints were not internationalists in the modern sense of the term, and there would be no difficulty in justifying siding with their own people against another in battle. This is why I would put Columba in the category of Moses or Joshua rather than a New Testament evangelist. There is every reason to believe he preached Christian virtues; but he was a true Celt, brimming over with the qualities, good and sometimes not so good, which are looked for in a Celt, not least of them mercurial inconsistencies to be found even in the pages of those who eulogised him.

It is hard to pin down the Celtic temperament, but those who have tried to do so often might have found examples in the life of Columba. Of sensibility Matthew Arnold says he should not wish the Celt had less of it, but that he had been more master of it: Columba's swift, delicate response to the needs of others, even his white horse, is matched by his hair-trigger reaction to wrong done him or his friends, which could have lethal results. There is quickness of perception: the saint could "read" a stranger at a glance, and also signs and portents of the weather, as we are told in the *Amhra*. There is the gift of rhetoric, and of the felicitous phrase: all agree it was one of Columba's greatest assets. There is the practical idealism which, Dr Sophie Bryant claims, makes the Celt a man of action: the multiplicity of his monasteries and other enterprises is proof of this quality in Columba. There is the hot temper and the joy in fighting: these cannot be denied in Columba unless one reads his chroniclers with blinkers on, and by this I do not mean misinterpreting *insulanus miles* as a fighting-man. And some would say that like so many of his race, his fighting was for lost causes. As Ossian sang: "They went forth to the war, but they always fell." In his lifetime Columba had success in plenty, but it might be held that the cause of the church he founded in the long run was lost, and that the doom of it lurked in the heart of his success—did not Augustine land in England in the very year of Columba's death? He was yet another hero marching in the shadowy procession towards the Blessed Isles, a procession of dim ghosts that included Boudicca and Vercingetorix and chiefs and princes of the chariot-tombs of the Rhineland and Gaul, and warriors from those humbler graves in the valley high above the lake of Hallstatt.

There is no way of discovering what the saint really looked like. There is no way of building up a convincing picture of him from what has been written in books. He lived too early for anyone who knew him to have attempted to draw or paint or sculpt a likeness of him. The earliest representation of him, so far as I am aware, is in a ninth-century copy of Adomnán's *Vita Sancti Columbae* now in the Stiftsbibliothek at St Gallen in Switzerland, but one can say no more than that it is a picture of a man in monkish habit. The only "facts" we have to go on are the "soft grey eye" referred to in the poem, much later in date than Columba, and the knowledge that like other Irish monks he was tonsured not on the crown of the head but from ear to ear, leaving the forepart of the head bare. The rest is conjecture. It may be taken that his face was weatherbeaten and his glance keen because, despite his labours as a scribe in his cell, he spent much of his time in the open and exposed in boats going from island to island, and the salt winds of the west soon produce a permanent tan. His character determines that his presence must have been commanding, his abstemiousness that he was lean-faced. One must also take into consideration, however, Skene's conclusion that to be the object of such love and devotion "softer and more amiable features" would be present, although I do not think it necessary to agree with Skene that they predominated. Bishop Reeves writes of his martial character, and in the times he lived through amiability would not have won him much success. If fire flashed in that grey eye it was the fire of anger, not of fanaticism, for there do not seem to have been any Savonarolas in the early Celtic church. I am sure too that the grey eye could twinkle with humour, because no Irish Celt could have found himself in some of the "miracle" situations recorded in the hagiologies without seeing the funny side of it, and the expression on Broichan's face when his opponent contrived to shame him by sailing into the wind must surely have earned a chuckle. Columba knew well enough that a laugh at a discomfited foe can be more profitable than a shout of triumph, especially in terms of converts. It is an error to think the great personages of history behaved as solemnly at all times as the chroniclers would lead us to believe.

The bones of the saint were still in their place of interment on the island in Adomnán's day, and remained there until the Vikings came. What happened to them then will be told in due

XII

Confrontation with Canterbury

"Let Baithen finish it." Whether or no this was Columba's only direction concerning his successor to the abbacy of Iona, there seems no doubt he wished his cousin to take over, or so his monks believed. Two of them arrived in Ireland and met there St Fintan and a cleric named Colum Crag, who asked them about their travels. They replied they had "rowed" across from Britain, and had just come "from the Oakwood of Calgach". Colum asked, "Is your holy father Columba well?" Only then—the casualness of Adomnán's tale is odd—did the two fall down and weep bitterly, telling of their abbot's death. Fintan asked about the succession and was told Baithen would be the man. Fintan thereupon sailed to Iona to see Baithen, saying, "If he will take me I will have him for Abbot." There he told Baithen Columba had prophesied that he, Baithen, would be Abbot of Iona.

Baithen's abbacy was brief. So was that of the man who followed him, Laisren, son of Feradach, another member of the Cinel Conaill Gulban. Most of the succeeding abbots are unfamiliar by name until Adomnán himself, who held the post from 679 until 704, a century after Columba; yet that century was a momentous one for the monastery of Iona, which held the primacy of a Celtic church whose influence spread deep into England. Whatever the situation may have been among the Picts, the main deployment of the "soldiers of Christ" now was towards south and east, towards the territories of the pagan Saxons. Rome looked on this as a direct challenge to its authority. The pope had sent Augustine to Britain in the year Columba died, and his remit and that of his eventual successor, Laurentius, was not merely to bring back into the fold the British church but specifically the Scots—which is to say the Irish—whose "independence" manifestly had caused disquiet in Rome. This disquiet must have been intensified by the success of the Irish missions to the continent. One of the most remarkable is that of Columbanus to Gaul before the end of the sixth century, pressed forward until he founded the great monastery of Bobbio in the Apennines, almost, one might say, on the doorstep of Rome. The immediate issue on which the main conflict raged around Columbanus seems to us a trivial one: the notorious issue of the date of Easter. It became central in the whole struggle between the churches. So it is worth defining.

On certain occasions—when the fourteenth day of the lunar month fell on a Sunday—the Celts held their Easter on the day the Jews held their Feast of the Passover, commemorating the destroying angel's exemption of Israelite houses from the slaying of the firstborn in Egypt. Rome calculated the day on a cycle which could determine it late in the month. How, demanded Columbanus, can we celebrate the triumph of Christ over death when the night is moonless, when the dark is supreme? The Easter of Rome was, in his words, "a dark Pasch". If we put ourselves in his place, in an era when symbolism was of supreme significance, Columbanus may be thought to have had a point. Rome saw symbolism in a quite different light. Poetic notions about moonlessness were less important than tokens of conformity. Pope Honorius wrote directly to the Celts on this point, reminding them they were few, and asking them if they thought they "in the utmost borders of the earth" were wiser than all the "ancient and modern churches of Christ".

It is perhaps a rational enough argument, but today we are again so sensitive to such issues that we can share the feelings of those on whose ears it fell thirteen centuries ago. Then, as now, there were conformers. Honorius' exhortation persuaded a section of the Celtic church. About 632 Abbot Cummian of Durrow wrote to the Abbot of Iona, Segine, to say the clergy of southern Ireland had accepted the Roman Easter. Durrow, though a Columban foundation, seems to have been cut off from the influence of Iona and come within the jurisdiction of the south. Cummian's letter, which still exists, explains how he became convinced that to conform was right. What could be deemed worse, he asks, than to say "Rome errs, Jerusalem errs, Alexandria errs, Antioch errs, the whole world errs; only the Scots and Britons know what is right". He is apologetic, and he might well be, since he is writing to a successor of Columba. He claims he resisted the Roman mode, but that for a year he examined the scriptures, historical documents and the alternative cycles, then consulted other clerics about the threatened excommunication by the Apostolic See, and finally delegates were sent to Rome "as children to their mother", where they remained for three years and returned convinced by all they heard and saw, including miraculous cures and exorcisms. We are apt to interpret such apologies as abject and contemptible, but this is to lose sight of the bewilderment which must genuinely have seized many of the Irish communities in view of the already legendary wisdom of a church which had inherited the status of the one-time Empire. If they had had a leader of Columba's confidence and pride and stature, it might have gone differently.

The northern Irish, which of course includes the Columban clerics, were more stubborn. In the year 640 they wrote the pope stating they could not follow their southern brethren. He had died, and the papal reply came from the Archpriest Hilarius to the leaders of the Celtic church, who included Segine of Iona, accusing them of trying to revive a new heresy out of an old one, "rejecting with a cloudy darkness our Easter, in which Christ was sacrificed, and striving to celebrate it on the fourteenth moon with the Jews". Whether by accident or design, Hilarius had not told the new pope that the Celtic Easter coincided with the Passover only when the fourteenth day fell on a Sunday. He may have implied a deliberate link with Jewish practice; but Bede, writing of Aidan, who adhered to the Celtic Easter, puts the record right in this respect.

Aidan's name marks the period of greatest expansion in the Columban church, the abbot of the time being Segine. Some years earlier the sons of Aethelfrith, King of Bernicia, had fled north when their father was slain, and they remained in banishment among the Picts and Scots. They had been pagans, but they were baptised, and Oswald in particular, the second son, seems to have spent a number of years on Iona. In time he succeeded to the throne of Bernicia, defeating the pagans under Cadwalla at the battle of the Heavenly Field, near Hexham, so called because Oswald erected a cross before the battle and prayed for victory beside it. At once the victor sent to Iona for someone to preach the Christian faith to his people. He asked for a bishop. The monk Aidan was consecrated, "a man of singular meekness, piety and moderation", and he proceeded to Northumbria. There, predictably, he chose for the seat of his episcopate a long, rocky island not unlike Iona in situation, Lindisfarne, an island less remote from the mainland than its Dalriadan counterpart since it is linked to the shore of the mainland at low tide by a causeway, yet possessing an atmosphere of otherworldliness reminiscent of the western isles and, like them, a haunt of seals and sea-birds. The landward area and the Fenham Flats, on the other hand, close to where the Great North Road now runs, might have been a rather dreary sight to Celtic eyes, and more acceptable to Jute or Angle or any of those other incoming strangers from the low lands of Denmark or the estuary of the Elbe, especially when the *haar* or sea-mist drifts in; but the rocks of what was to be the Holy Isle float on the mist like an Atlantic skerry.

Bishop though he had been created, Aidan inaugurated an abbacy precisely on the lines of Iona. He remained a monk, surrounded by his community of brethren: a bishop only in the curious, unhierarchical Celtic sense. He had had a predecessor in Northumbria, Paulinus, sent there by Augustine of Canterbury and with a seat at York, but he had been driven out by the pagans. Oswald may have envisaged Aidan replacing Paulinus at York, but he certainly did not oppose the choice of Lindisfarne and, after his years on Iona, must have understood and been sympathetic to it. He accepted also the Celtic Easter. This, says Bede, "was patiently tolerated by all men" because of Aidan's piety and the love in which he was held. Saxon though he is, Bede has nothing but the warmest tributes for the establishment on Lindisfarne. It is the simplicity and discipline of Aidan and his people which Bede singles out for special praise, contrasting these with the "slothfulness" of the times.

The relationship between Aidan and King Oswald was remarkable. The kings of those days were still warrior leaders and their greatness was measured by their conquests, but Oswald under the influence of his spiritual adviser was a new kind of ruler. He himself interpreted the words of Aidan and his missionaries to his people. His piety is illustrated by the well-known tale of how, when he feasted with his thegns and his bishop, he was told of a multitude patiently fasting outside his gates, and gave orders that the food before him should be taken out to his people. The great silver vessel in which it was carried they broke up and gave to the poor. Aidan is said to have grasped his hand and blessed it, praying that it never grow old. The tale is important because it underlines the simple virtues of the Columban faith.

But here in Northumbria the church of Columba had carried the cross to the very borders of embattled pagandom. Penda of Mercia stood at bay, hemmed in by Christian kingdoms but a formidable fighter. He knew well that the dominant figure among his enemies was Oswald of Northumbria, whose dominions stretched from the Firth of Forth to the heart of what was to become England. Oswald led an army to overthrow Penda and wrest control of East Anglia from him, but at the battle of the Maserfield the pagans were victorious and Oswald was slain. They displayed his severed head and arms on lofty poles driven deep into the ground, which were not taken down until his brother and successor a year later rescued them and placed the head in the monastery of Lindisfarne. This defeat threatened the entire Christian cause. The King of Wessex abandoned the faith. Penda and his Mercians drove north against Northumbria until they came to Bamborough, the royal stronghold. This fortress, built on a rocky headland protected on three sides by the sea, seemed impregnable. Legend has it that Aidan and his monks on Lindisfarne, across the sea and Fenham Flats, watched the siege anxiously. Penda's army demolished the houses of Bamborough and its neighbouring villages and piled the timber and thatch high against the fortress walls and set the material on fire. The west wind drove the flames against the walls and must have burned or choked the defenders; but it is said that Aidan in his

agony cried out: "Lord—see what ill Penda is doing!" Thereafter
the wind changed into the east and drove the flames back on
the besieging pagans. Baffled, Penda retreated south. The tide
had turned. Oswald's brother, Oswiu, built up his strength,
reconquered neighbouring Deira, encouraged his old allies of
Wessex; and the indefatigable missionaries of Lindisfarne went
out again and ultimately converted Penda's own son, the governor
of East Anglia. Penda himself did not oppose the missionaries,
even in Mercia—Bede, in fact, says the pagan king kept his hatred
and scorn for converts who had not the courage of their con-
victions—but the growing strength of Oswiu forced him to
attack Northumbria again. In 655, at Winwaedfield near Leeds,
this savage old warrior in his 80th year led a great army against
Oswiu, was defeated, and himself fell to his pursuers when being
carried wounded from the field. As Freeman put it, the strife
between the creeds of Christ and Woden had been finally decided.

But if Oswiu was a Christian champion, he was no champion
of the Columban church.

Under Columba, church and state virtually had been one, if not
in every sphere of interest. The family of Iona and the kingdom of
Dalriada were two sides of the same coin, or better, two edges of
the Scotic blade driven into Alba; but Northumbria was a
different matter, for the invitation to Iona to send a mission there
brought no advantage to the Dalriads. Certainly the spiritual
dominion of Iona now extended over realms it had never penetrated before. Not only did Lindisfarne become a second Iona,
sending its missions deep into England, but the fields of Lothian
and the rich rolling valleys of what is now the Borders came under
the influence of Columban establishments, chief among them the
monastery of Melrose. This lay on a characteristic site, a little
promontory in the Tweed nearly surrounded by the river and
protected by natural features. Its first abbot was Eata, one of
twelve Saxon boys who had been instructed by Aidan himself.
Not far off was the nunnery of Coldingham, near St Abbs Head,
named after the founder-abbess, Aebha, half-sister of Oswald and
Oswiu of Northumbria, although, since Aebha had received the
veil from a Saxon bishop, her establishment cannot perhaps be

called a Columban one. But those mission-stations, widely separated, were in any case precarious strongholds of the faith in a wilderness only nominally Christian, many of its inhabitants in reality Anglian pagans at heart, accepting the cross only because their thegns commanded it. Green relates how a mishap to some logs drifted down the Tyne for the building of a monastery drove the peasants to complain of the loss of their old religion and to cry out upon the monks. But if her church was the church of Northumbria, politically Dalriada had no influence there. Rather the reverse is the case. Northumbria had grown to be the strongest power south of the Forth. Under Oswiu she thrust vigorously in all directions and even seems to have dominated the Britons of Strathclyde. Dalriada was remote, between the salients of Strathclyde and the southern Picts, but the *Irish Annals* tell of a victory by Oswiu's nephew Talorcan over the Dalriads. It seems the Northumbrians also occupied some parts of the land of the Picts, probably Fife, although Dr Henderson states they may have penetrated as far as The Mounth. It is a curious situation, in that the secular power in this vast territory from Forth to Humber was Anglian, while the spiritual influence was Celtic, but it is also an impossible situation, with a predictable outcome.

At this point it is necessary to look far to the south. It has been mentioned that Augustine had landed in England in the year Columba died, sent by Pope Gregory as his emissary to convert the Saxons of England to the faith. The successors to the Roman legions established themselves at Canterbury, and from here their influence spread rapidly. The King of Kent's queen was a Frankish princess, and soon the men of Kent were at least paying lip-service to the religion which had existed in their country under the Empire. Beyond the bounds of Kent Christian progress had been slow. Paulinus, as we saw, had to retreat from Northumbria, and his place had been filled by the Columbans. In the west, Augustine had another big rebuff. His claim to be head of all British Christians since he had been commissioned by the pontiff was angrily rejected by the clergy and monks of Wales at a conference on the Severn. Even London remained stubbornly pagan and unfriendly, although in those times this held less importance. However, in the long term the See of Canterbury occupied a strong strategic position. Where the Columban monasteries of the north were oases in a religious desert of moors and hills and bogs of Lothian and Northumbria, Augustine's Canterbury lay in country rich in potential which the industrious Saxons were gradually bringing into production, and south of it the routes lay open to the Christian Franks and Rome itself. Moreover, the Saxon pagans seem to have exchanged the worship of Woden for Christianity openly at their kings' command, whatever their private superstitions and reservations. Soon enough Augustine recognised that the real barrier to his spreading influence was not the pantheon of Valhalla but those cheerful and courageous Celtic missionaries who, without worldly possessions or any place of worship more impressive than a hut, trudged vast distances to carry the message of the gospels. When even a great man of Augustine's own persuasion admired them, what was to be done about them?

King Oswiu of Northumbria, baptised in the Columban church, might have been its main pillar in the north but for his queen, Eanfled. She was a Kentish princess, and of the Roman persuasion. Her priestly adviser actually was called Romanus. To say this produced some awkward situations at court is an understatement. The king and his consort observed Easter at different times. As Bede has it, when the king ended his fast and "was keeping the Lord's Feast, the queen and her friends were still fasting and celebrating the Day of Palms". It is not hard to imagine the resulting atmosphere or the pressures exerted by the queen on her husband, as Margaret was to do with Malcolm, King of the Scots, on much the same issue centuries later. The result is perhaps predictable, especially as the queen had the support of her son Alchfrid, instructed in the Roman mode by Wilfrid of Ripon; but Oswiu resolved to decide the issue once and for all, and in 664 he called a synod in the monastery of Streaneshalch—"the Bay of the Lighthouse"—a synod to become famous in British history under the place's Danish name of Whitby.

By this time the Abbot and Bishop of Lindisfarne was Colman, and it fell to him to lead the Columban delegation at this fateful conference. Colman had the support of Scotic clerics and of the Abbess Hilda, head of the double monastery for priests and nuns in which the synod was held, and with them came Bishop Cedd of Essex, ordained by the Columbans, to act as interpreter between Celts and Saxons. One gets the feeling Colman was not a masterful figure. He seems to have been a man of simple faith such as the Celtic church bred in plenty, without the guile or skill needed to sway debate, and it is tempting to speculate how the issue might have gone if someone of Columba's calibre had been chief protagonist on the Celtic side. Columba himself must have foreseen the eventual confrontation. His eastward urge made it inevitable if the faith was not to go under to the pagans. His learning and eloquence would have been hard to match in such a contest and if they had not prevailed his proud temper would have yielded no more ground than the Welsh clerics did to Augustine. The Roman delegation comprised Alchfrid, Oswiu's son, the Frankish Bishop of the West Saxons, Agilbert by name, a priest called Agatho, Romanus, the queen's Kentish chaplain, a deacon who had been with Paulinus, James, and leading them the Abbot of Ripon, Wilfrid, who, although trained on Lindisfarne, had travelled to Rome and been converted to its practices. He and Benedict Biscop, since their return from Rome, never ceased to arraign the Columban church as schismatic.

What happened at the synod is recorded in detail by Bede, and sometimes I wonder if historians who summarise its results briefly in passing ever go back to this source-book and attempt to reconstitute the temper of the proceedings from plentiful evidence provided. The king presided and made the introductory speech. His will on the issue is apparent from the first. Those who serve one God, he said, should observe the same rule of life, "as they all expected the same kingdom in heaven" and should not differ in celebration of the divine mysteries, but should determine which is the true tradition, then follow it one and all. As he did not expect Wilfrid to conform to the Columban ritual, but at most to tolerate it, this was tantamount to a directive to

Colman. He then commanded Colman to justify his "custom".
The issue turned entirely on the date of Easter. Colman replied:

> "The Easter which I keep I received from my elders, who sent
> me bishop hither; all our forefathers, men beloved of God, are
> known to have kept it in the same manner; and that the same
> may not seem to any contemptible or worthy to be rejected,
> it is the same which St John the Evangelist, the disciple
> beloved of our Lord, with all the churches over which he
> presided, is recorded to have observed."

Bede of course gives no description of the scene, or of the
chamber in which the synod took place, and the mood of the
speakers has to be read from their words, which is not difficult.
Plainly, Colman's back was to the wall, and he knew it. He was
a man being asked to justify something he had never seen reason
to question, and he had little to say, no real arguments to offer.
So the king turned to the Frankish bishop, Agilbert, to put the
case for the Roman Easter. Agilbert made the excuse that his
disciple Wilfrid was better versed in the English language than
he, and begged for him to speak for Rome.

Wilfrid was of different mettle from Colman. He was a skilled
and subtle debater, and aggressive with it to the point of being
contemptuous of his opponent, as will appear. Immediately he
makes Colman look like a provincial. "The Easter which we
observe, we saw celebrated by all at Rome, where the blessed
apostles, Peter and Paul, lived, taught, suffered and were buried."
So he begins. Then—and one can imagine the impatient gestures
of his arms—he proceeds to say how on his pilgrimages through
France and Italy he saw the same thing done; and that he found
the same practised in Greece, Africa, Egypt and Asia "and all the
world wherever the church of Christ is spread abroad". An
adversary more cunning than Colman might have probed and
dissected those sweeping claims—Wilfrid had never, so far as we
know, travelled further than Rome—and by doing it could have
jolted his confidence; but the bishop went on to throw scorn at
those "accomplices in obstinacy", the Picts and Britons, fools

who stood out against "the rest of the universe". At this point
Colman was stung into an expostulation. Was it so foolish to
follow the example of the Apostle John? But Wilfrid threw at
him a theological broadside, arguing that the early church still
laboured under judaistic practices for fear of offending the Jews.
Did not Paul circumcise Timothy? Did he not sacrifice in the
temple? Did he not shave his head with Aquila and Priscilla at
Corinth? So John began his Easter on the fourteenth day of the
first month, whether it happened on a Saturday or any other
day; but when Peter preached at Rome he regularised all that.
And what Peter laid down "all successors of St John in Asia,
since his death, all the church throughout the world, have since
followed". He had crushed Colman with a verbal almanac of
Easter which must have hit the weak Abbot of Lindisfarne like
a bulky volume thrown at his head. He told Colman he neither
followed John's example, as he imagined he did, nor yet Peter's,
whose traditions he "knowingly contradicted". And he went on
to demolish the Celtic practice with a mass of facts and figures
in a style which might have won him thunderous applause in a
union debate, ending, "You agree neither with John nor Peter,
nor with the law, nor the Gospel, in the celebration of the
greatest festival." It was a shattering performance and left the
Roman delegation in a commanding position.

Worse was to follow. The unhappy Abbot of Lindisfarne tried
to defend himself by quoting Anatolius of Laodicea, the third-
century controversialist, as an authority, then reverted to the
infallibility of the saints.

"Is it to be believed," [he pled] "that our most reverend Father
Columba and his successors, men beloved by God, who kept
Easter after the same manner, thought or acted contrary to
the divine writings? Whereas there were many among them
whose sanctity is testified by heavenly signs and the working
of miracles, whose life, customs and disciplines I never cease
to follow, not questioning their being saints in heaven."

An appeal to the authority of Columba was begging the question.

One can see the glint of triumph in the eye of the learned Abbot of Ripon. Obviously, Wilfrid admits, Anatolius was holy, learned and commendable—"but what is that to you, since you don't follow his decrees?" Again he confounds Colman with his facts and figures, showing that Anatolius' Easter was not in conflict with the Roman Easter. "Either you are ignorant of this," he proceeds, "or if you know it, though it is kept by the whole church of Christ yet you despise it!" And then he added what, to any monk of Iona, was the unforgivable thing:

"Concerning your Father Columba and his followers, whose sanctity you say you imitate, and whose rules and precepts you observe, which have been confirmed by signs from heaven, I may answer that when many, on the day of judgment, shall say to our Lord, 'That in his name they prophesied and cast out devils and wrought many wonders,' our Lord will reply 'That he never knew them'."

It was an insufferable retort for one man of God to make to another, a glimpse of pride and arrogance of spirit in total contrast to the traditional meek and humble attitude of Celtic monasticism. That sneer—if the words "whose sanctity you say you imitate" carry with them the curl of the lip which they seem to do—reflects a shameful contempt for the church which trained him. Then perhaps the faces of the pious Abbess Hilda and her companions, maybe a glance from the king himself, warned him he had gone too far, for he goes on:

"Far be it from me that I say so of your fathers, because it is much more just to believe what is good, than what is evil, of persons whom one does not know. Wherefore I do not deny those to have been God's servants, and beloved by Him, who with rustic simplicity, but pious intentions, have themselves loved Him."

And he proceeds to say he is sure that if any "catholic adviser" had come among them they would have conformed to his admonitions. It is a lame and clumsy apology, the arrogance scarcely veiled, and even at this late stage it could have brought his case to grief if his opponent had been capable of a ready thrust. Colman was past defending himself further and those with him seem to have been struck silent too. Wilfrid therefore swept into his final denunciation:

"As for you and your companions, you certainly sin if, having heard the decrees of the Apostolic See, and of the universal church, and that the same is confirmed by holy writ, you refuse to follow them . . . And if that Columba of yours (and, I may say, ours also, if he was Christ's servant) was a holy man and powerful in miracles, yet could he be preferred before the most blessed prince of the apostles, to whom our Lord said, 'Thou art Peter and upon this rock I will build my church, and the gates of hell shall not prevail against it, and to thee I will give the keys of the kingdom of heaven'?"

It is a resounding piece of rhetoric to complete his arguments. One may imagine the ensuing silence, the deep discomfiture of Colman. It was for the king to speak. He was at a loss for what to say, perhaps, since he must have been embarrassed by the plight of his bishop. "Is it true, Colman," he asked, "that these words were spoken to Peter by our Lord?" Colman replied: "It is true, O king." "Can you show any such power given to your Columba?" the king then demanded, and that "your Columba" must have wounded his bishop deeply. Colman admitted Columba had no such power entrusted to him. The king proceeded with a somewhat unconvincing attempt at judicial impartiality. "Do you," he asked, "both agree the words were principally directed to Peter, and that the keys of heaven were given to him by our Lord?" They assented. So the king concluded the matter by declaring his allegiance to Peter, somewhat naïvely adding "lest when I come to the gates of the kingdom of heaven, there should be none to open them, he being my adversary who is proved to have the keys".

It is difficult to read this 25th chapter of Book III of Bede's

History without a rising sense of indignation at the conduct of the synod. It has to be allowed to die down a little before one tries to weigh up the significance of the affair. The outcome is not merely the beginning of the end of the Columban church, protracted though that was: it is one of the more momentous happenings in the early history of this country. English historians have tended to set the seal of approval on the result, whether uncompromisingly as in Green's verdict that "England was saved by the victory of Rome", or more critically, as when Trevelyan concedes that victory "contained the seeds of all the trouble with Rome, down the ages to come", though it promoted "unity". Toynbee, on the other hand, sees the decision at Whitby as the first turn of a screw in a long history of coercion which persisted against the Celtic remnants in the Scottish Highlands and the bogs of Ireland, and fostered habits even carried across the Atlantic to be "practised at the expense of the North American Indians". If the last view looks a shade far-fetched, it has only to be remembered that had the monks with Cortez and Pizarro been Celtic the Indians of South America would have fared very differently than they did.

It should be possible to take a balanced view of the Synod of Whitby after thirteen centuries, but the truth is the issues are still alive, still emotive. Place, politics, prejudice: all those continue to colour our judgment. If one happens to be standing in St Thomas's Chapel in Canterbury Cathedral, contemplating that symbol of English expansionism, the tomb of Edward the Black Prince, a pageant of achievements unfolds that makes any verdict upon Whitby not in accord with Green's look a trifle eccentric. We remember how only four years after the synod Rome sent the Greek monk Theodore of Tarsus to be archbishop of this diocese, and how he organised the episcopate and built the foundations of what would become the church of England. What is a church which could only produce the Monymusk reliquary beside this in the eyes of the world? Had the church of Aidan won, says Green, the ecclesiastical history of England would have been like that of Ireland: tribal quarrels and controversies became confounded, and "the clergy, robbed of all really spiritual influence, contributed no element save that of disorder to the state". And the Victorian historian goes on to paint a picture of hundreds of wandering bishops, of piety divorced from morality, of domination by chieftains, and of "the absence of those larger and more humanizing influences which contact with a wider world alone can give". Oswiu, he concludes, had the instinct of a statesman when he set aside "the love and gratitude of his youth" to link England with Rome. Did Green ever really read with close attention that chapter in Bede? But he is a little odd in other ways. A largely Anglo-Saxon population is never likely to have developed along the lines of a purely Celtic one no matter what its ecclesiastical affiliations were, and it asserted its attitude anyway at the Reformation. Quite as odd is his estimate of the cultural isolation likely to have occurred under a Celtic church, but the brilliant cultural eclecticism of the Celt will be seen on nearly every page of the chapter which follows this so there is no need to expand upon it here. Yet Green and those historians who think like him do have a powerful case. Without the tectonic skills and the urge to organise and build which flowed into England through Canterbury, cathedrals like Canterbury might never have been erected, and certainly English history would have been far different, even if it is idle to speculate about the course it could have taken. The English genius made use of Rome until, in the sixteenth century, its interests were no longer served by Rome.

Whitby is almost as far from Iona as it is from Canterbury, but somehow it looms larger from that island. The modest cathedral of Iona is in a timeless setting and, seated with one's back to its ferny wall, the thin cries of gulls quivering in the void between here and the unchanging slopes of Ben More in Mull, it is not difficult to think about the synod as Colman must have done. Perhaps this should be qualified, because Colman seems to have been so gentle, so exemplary in his way of life as a follower of Christ, that it might not be easy for us to adopt his outlook. Empires, civil or ecclesiastical, were phenomena beyond his ken. It is tempting, in the soft, seductive Iona air, to fall under the Celtic spell and to see Colman's very simplicity and meekness as entirely virtuous and desirable and so to condemn out of hand the progress of more worldly churches over there on the mainland of Britain and beyond; but meekness can be weakness, and here I think we have to substitute for Colman the figure of Columba. Even Skene himself seems to resist acceptance of the realistic, ambitious, worldly aspect of Columba's personality, yet without those qualities Columba could never have set his church on the course which brought it into collision with Rome, and without an equivalent determination and energy and vision the Irish fathers could never have set up their foundations on the continent. It was not the church that failed at Whitby, but the man to whom it fell to speak for it. From the first he tried to defend, where Columba would have swung into attack. There was an immense strength in this church, the more since it sprang from the tribal roots which Green deplores. And if Columba, with his learning, his rhetoric and his commanding presence had been in the chamber at Whitby and prevailed there might have been a different England, and not necessarily a worse. One thing is virtually certain: there would have been a Britain long centuries before this in fact came about, and it might have been a Britain without an Irish problem, or Welsh or Scottish problems. The Celtic genius may be poorly gifted where a capacity to organise and build is concerned, but it is insatiably eclectic and able to transform the capacities of others. The Book of Kells is a symbol of it. The Synod of Whitby was about much more than the date of Easter.

Rejected, Colman gathered around him those of like mind who would accept neither the Roman Easter nor the Roman tonsure, and this sad company made its way across the Northumbrian moors and through the valleys beyond Cheviot on the long road back to Iona, and ultimately to Ireland. With Colman went the Scottish monks who were at Lindisfarne, and also about 30 Anglian monks. They carried with them some of the bones of Father Aidan, as sacred relics. Bede, whose respect for the integrity and virtues of the Columban church is constant, if he did not agree with its doctrines, supplies a brief but significant description of conditions on Lindisfarne at the time of the

Columbans' departure. Apart from the church there were few houses: dwellings only just sufficient to accommodate the little community. They had some cattle, but no money, for if anyone gave them money they passed it on at once to the poor. There was no provision for entertaining "the great men of the world", for such never came to the church but to pray and to hear the Word of God. Even the king came with only a few servants, and if he had need to eat he shared the simple food of the monks. Bede adds generous praise for the veneration and joy which these devout practices generated in the people, who flocked to hear the preaching when any priest came into a village.

Yet the retreat of Colman into the north-western fastnesses did not immediately bring about a retreat of his church. Nor did that church cease to be a threat to the domination of Canterbury in mainland Britain. It was incapable of militancy, except perhaps in the person of a man like Columba, but the influence of its teaching seems to have been profound, and so eagerly accepted over a large part of the country that it persisted in the face of all efforts to eradicate it. In Northumbria, York became the official ecclesiastical centre, its bishop a supporter of Roman usage; but there is no indication that Lindisfarne altered its ancient customs, despite a presumably new community, and there is small doubt that other monastic establishments in the north such as Melrose continued to observe the Columban rules. Even Whitby itself does not seem to have surrendered. It is not recorded that its devout abbess said anything during the deliberations, but she never ceased to oppose Wilfrid. Some years after the synod Wilfrid became Bishop of Northumbria, but he had no lasting triumph and in 677 was driven from his see by the enmity of the queen. And Northumbria, although at its most powerful under Ecgfrith, was not the whole of England. Irish monks continued to preach in the south and west for a century or more after Whitby, indeed until specifically forbidden to function in 810.

In Alba, not only did Iona continue to exercise the primacy as under Columba, but its missionary work expanded and its repute as a scholastic and cultural centre rapidly grew. In 679 Adomnán became the ninth abbot and continued the family tradition, for he too was of the lineage of Conaill Gulban. Circumstances combined to facilitate the enhanced prestige of the island establishment, now re-housed by Adomnán with the help of a supply of timber brought from oak forests in Lorne. Theodore at Canterbury divided the bishopric of Northumbria into three, and placed the northern part under Eata of Melrose, a man of Columban sympathies, and when King Ecgfrith led his army into Pictland and was utterly defeated at Dunnichen in 685 both Dalriada and Iona too were released from Anglian pressure. At this point Adomnán was persuaded by the Northumbrians to conform to Roman practices, but not all the monks of Iona or those of the many other establishments of the west would follow his example, and Columban ways continued. Adomnán became an absentee abbot. He returned to Iona in the year of his death, but the Columban foundation clung to their traditional mode even when, by the Synod of Tara in 692, the vast majority of the Scots of Ireland conformed to Rome.

Presumably the greater part of the north-western seaboard of Scotland had come under the Columban church. We know the man chiefly responsible for this is Maelrubha, a member of the northern Uí Néill, who made his centre at Aporcrosan (Applecross). It was then virtually an island site, for until the new road from Shieldaig was completed as recently as 1976 the only access to it lay by the difficult Bealach nam Bo or by boat, so that it served mainly the Hebrides and the isolated coasts of Wester Ross. Whether the main territories of the northern Picts also were widely evangelised from Iona and its satellite establishments is obscure, but we have to keep in mind Tigernach tells us that King Nechton expelled "the Family of Iona" from Pictland, as described in Chapter VII, and as I commented there, Iona does not seem to have had complete authority there, if we read the sculptured stones correctly.

Much of the strength of the Celtic church lay in its capacity to win adherents by example, an example based on a fairly literal interpretation of the gospels, in other words by the simple faith which Bede so much admired. Few societies find it possible even to attempt to follow such a faith. Piety, self-denial and earnest scholarship conducted in a mean hut are not everyone's ideal of the virtuous life. It is doubtful if a church professing such an ideal could ever have become the church of the Western world, of a society too deeply-committed to material power. But perhaps the seeds of ultimate failure lay deep in the Celts themselves. Ever since he looked down from his Alpine passes the Celt had nursed a mixture of envy and admiration for the achievements of that Mediterranean civilisation which he would help destroy; and now with one hand he was reaching out to save some of its heritage, its literary heritage. It is said that one of the aims of the pilgrim Aeneas Sylvius Piccolomini in coming to Scotland in 1435 was the hope of finding the lost books of Livy in the library on Iona. He got no further than the Lothians, where he caught a chill, on which afterwards he blamed his life-long rheumatism; but he was no foolish eccentric, and his hope may just have had some foundation. He was to become Pope Pius II.

XIII

Art and the Celtic Church

At this point I am going to propose an exercise which, in the eyes of some serious scholars, may seem childish and a waste of time. For those less familiar with the Celtic aspect of our cultural history, on the other hand, it might just spark off a flash of something like a revelation. It needs no special knowledge: mainly an elementary understanding of Latin. All else that is needed is a good reproduction of the front page of one of the gospel-books, let us say St John in the Book of Lindisfarne. Beside it place a Bible open at Chapter I of the same gospel. At first sight there is no connection between the two: the jewelled page from Lindisfarne seems nothing but a bewildering maze of decoration, a concourse of designs so intricate that it is impossible to disentangle them. The colours of the page are alluring, like a garden glimpsed through a gate; but it is a gate whose wrought traceries seem to bar entry to us and leave us baffled by the mystery beyond. We can recognise some of the characters of the Irish script which forms the framework of the design, but they seem nearly as baffling as the intricate detail. However, like all their Columban brethren, the monks of Lindisfarne wrote in Latin; so referring to the Bible the text should read: "In the beginning was the Word, and the Word was with God . . ." With this reminder, the fantastic column forming the left margin of the gospel-page gradually emerges as the capital letter "I". What had looked like an "Z" becomes an "N" on its side linked to a strange "P"; then all at once "RINCIPIO" takes shape, giving us *IN PRINCIPIO*. This is followed by *erat* and *verbum*, then comes a conjunctive link and *verbum* again, and again *erat*, and finally there is *apud* weirdly attached to the name of God. We have the first sentence.

Quaint though it may sound, even now I can recapture the

sense of wonder I felt when, after staring for the first time at the open page in the British Museum for minutes on end I realised I had received a recognisable communication from a man who wrote it down in a distant age. Of course one can get such communications from even earlier times simply by reading the very clear inscriptions on, for example, the legionary distance-slabs from a Roman wall; but what makes the gospel-page experience so singular, and for me so thrilling, is the simultaneous glimpse through the "gate" into the "garden" beyond. The scribe who lovingly painted this page was the keeper of the gate. He wrote in words which the whole of Christendom could understand, words which speak to us today; but the beauties of the garden with which he embellished his message represent his prehistoric, his pagan heritage, whether he fully understood it or no. It is a break-through to another epoch recalling the discovery of the Rosetta Stone, except that the two messages are entirely different. To my mind, they illustrate the essential dualism in the beliefs of Columban monks.

The dawn of this golden age of what is usually termed Hiberno-Saxon art did not break until about two centuries after the death of Columba, but this art was generated in the church which he did so much to promote, and I do not think an understanding of the saint and his brethren can be achieved without careful study of its masterpieces.

The first hints of what was to come are in the *Cathach*, described at the beginning of Chapter V: a book which, if it is not by the hand of Columba himself, must have been done within a few years of his death. But the climax comes with the great gospel-books of the late seventh and the eighth centuries, a fulfilment of that marriage of pagandom and Christendom which may be seen in its tentative early stages in the pages of the *Cathach*. As stressed in the first paragraph, the gospel message is transmitted formally in the language of the Roman world. For the Roman, as for the Greek before him, writing was the visual medium by which ideas were conveyed, and so absolute clarity governed the design and execution of lettering. Ornament, far less distortion, would be repugnant to the classical eye, conditioned by a code of aesthetics founded on function, symmetry and balance, and attention to proportion and to details such as serifs was justified only because it promoted easier reading.

Such an apparently prosaic attitude to the written word must have distressed Irishmen among whom eloquence had been a traditional cult from time immemorial. For them, the written word itself was an alien concept. It was impersonal, artificial, at first sight incapable of being bent to fit all the fine nuances of meaning which a skilled orator could employ. They were not so simple as to think the Romans incapable of rhetoric. They knew their Cicero and could admire resounding passages, perhaps could roll off "*Tantae molis erat Romanam condere gentem*" to better effect than most Romans had been able to do; but if the emotional Celt were involved to the very core of his being, as when he copied the gospels, it is evident he found Roman characters too rigid a medium for his feelings.

The codices in which the Irish scribes received the gospels were not, of course, written in classical block-lettering, but in a half-uncial Latin script not unlike modern "lower-case" type, and it is this script which the monks modified to the Irish or "Insular" script which we find in their gospel-books; yet even this less formal sort of writing was too regular a medium to satisfy their longing for spiritual expression, and as early as the *Cathach* something can be seen happening to the Roman script. Characters are becoming personalised. Suddenly they are coming alive, or as perhaps we should say, organic. The initial letters are stirring into movement, with a sort of life of their own like plants, sprouting tendrils apparently unnecessary but which suggest pirouettes of delight. Only a very unimpressionable reader could be unaware of the scribe's emotional involvement. And the main body of the script also is affected by this living quality, as though the initials were stones dropped in a pond, setting the surface a-quiver, a new effect which has been called the "diminuendo".

The earliest examples of books, such as the *Cathach*, show no inclination to borrow actual motifs or symbols from the pre-historic past. Nevertheless this living quality which has been described is a re-birth. There is an unmistakable link with pagan tradition in its restlessness: what Dr Carl Nordenfalk, writing of the initials, refers to as "the kinetic energy of their contours". This seems to me to be of considerable significance for anyone trying to probe the spirit of the Celtic church and its "saints". It is an indication that the Irish monks, much as they revered the orthodox faith, did not think the forms in which they received it adequate to their needs, that the new wine of their personal belief could not be contained in the rigid vessels of classical tradition. It might even be called a spontaneous rejection of the takeover of the revolutionary Christian movement by the monumental, unbending, outward religious forms of Imperial Rome, where after Constantine the temple evolved into the basilica, the idol became an ikon, and the gospel that God is love was expressed in the calligraphy once used by the officials of the Senate. The Irish monks meant no conscious, positive rejection of such things. But they found them alien to their simple natures, and also their faith had come to them by way of the Desert Fathers and so had derived from Judaistic rather than Hellenistic tradition, as we saw Wilfrid had been swift to point out at Whitby. They had in fact received their faith with a minimum of earthly trappings, and if their piety stirred them to look for ways of expressing itself it is hardly surprising if they turned instinctively to the art and lore of Celtic symbolism which came naturally to them. Almost at once the gospel-book became more than a mere book, however holy and precious. It became in itself a symbol, an object of magical power. It had to be seen to be such, and in a relatively short time a large part of the vocabulary of pagan symbolism had been dedicated to the service of Christ.

No one with any experience of the history of art would believe for a moment that the ornament of those early manuscripts is mere embellishment. For one thing, motifs merely borrowed from an older source to beautify the gospel-books would have lost something in the process of transference. They would seem wooden and would lack conviction because, symbolic in origin, they had been repeated by a scribe who no longer believed in the power of the symbol as his pagan forebear had done. There is no such weakening of conviction.

A page of the Book of Durrow, perhaps the earliest of the greater gospel-books and only perhaps a half-century later than the *Cathach*, is full of invention and every detail of it is vigorously alive. It is not difficult to find prototypes of its spirals on bronze bowls wrought somewhat earlier, or to trace those back to the spirals of the pagan Celtic art of La Tène; but there is every bit as much creative excitement and indeed eloquence in the initial letters of the gospel-book as in the devices on the Battersea shield or the pony-cap from Torrs. No doubt the sensitive, prepared surface of the calf-skin and the availability of pigments provided a new, enthralling medium to challenge the urge to create. This in itself would not explain the triumphant spirit in which the work is executed. The linked spirals are as restless, as "kinetic", as anything in La Tène art yet, like the engraved mirror-backs of the first century BC, which in another book I have described as swirling "with the anchored freedom of an aquatic plant dancing in the current", their movement is as controlled and disciplined as any form in nature.

The interlace patterns which are such a prominent feature of the Book of Durrow and of all the gospel-books are perhaps more strictly decorative. They are derived not from pagan Celtic originals, but come from the same source as Irish monasticism

Stone capital, Kasr Ibrim

itself, the Middle East. They may be found in Coptic manuscripts, even on stone sculptures, whence they spread to other Mediterranean lands and then to the West. But in the hands of Celtic scribes the interlace attains heights of elegance never touched in countries nearer to its source, and accommodates itself to the restless movement of the Celtic motifs. Interlace as carried through by the Hiberno-Saxon school is not only elaborate but very complex, demanding mathematical precision and the use of instruments; yet this seems to put no restraint on its living quality, and on many pages of the gospel-books, notably perhaps in the Book of Kells, it too seems imbued with symbolism.

That the scribe was reaching back into the race-memories of his people is never more obvious than when he makes use of stylised animals. Sometimes, as in the Durrow initial page of St Mark, terminal whorls sprout into birds' heads like buds unfolding; exactly what happens on the Torrs pony-cap and the

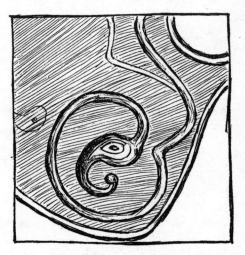

Bird-head terminal on Torrs pony-cap. National Museum of Antiquities of Scotland. 2nd cent. BC

Wandsworth shield-boss of nearly a thousand years before. The preoccupation with birds of the community on Iona has been mentioned repeatedly. I have insisted that the bird-lore of pagan Ireland survived into Columba's time as much more than a mere literary tradition, and it is too much to believe the scribe of Durrow introduced his bird-head finials without thought of their superstitious significance. In the animal carpet-page (Fol. 192v) of the same gospel-book the interlaced monsters come not from Celtic mythology but from equally pagan sources in Scandinavia, whose Viking raiders were just beginning to threaten Ireland. The only hint of Christian symbolism on this page is a tiny Maltese-type cross in the centre. It might well be asked, why this

Bird-head terminal in MS possibly from Lindisfarne, now in Vatican Library. 9th cent.

lovingly-executed introduction of the culture of a people then threatening Christendom with fire and sword? It is hard to say. In the middle ages, sculptors in churches introduced subjects which had nothing to do with worship and which they were certainly not commissioned to carry out, but those were not in prominent places, and this, after all, was a book which would lie on the high altar. Surely a scribe in his scriptorium within sight of a sea-horizon which any day might show the dark outlines of long-ships had some very good reason for introducing his Norse dragons. This is not a case of a double insurance-policy. With its little cross in the centre, the page might be symbolic of the plight of the faith in a pagan world.

Of course, again, the Celt was an insatiable eclectic. But we have to distinguish between this sort of borrowing and the spontaneous upsurge of his own past, as with the bird-finials. This latter is the more interesting. It stems from what Jung calls the "collective unconscious". Those birds reach back not merely to the first century BC but into the Bronze Age. Here indeed I think we do have the double insurance-policy, not perhaps deliberately introduced or seriously relied upon but executed more in the spirit of throwing spilt salt over the left shoulder, although in the seventh century it would mean much more than that. Jung believed this "unconscious" is part of all our heritage and can predetermine behaviour. Birds flock on the carpet-pages of both the Lichfield and the Lindisfarne gospels, although they have emerged from enigmatic forms into something more like realistic representation, though still captives of the general pattern. When we remember that Columba and his brethren lived generations before the great gospel-books we may assume the collective unconscious loomed very large for them.

Purely Christian symbols do not marry easily with Celtic symbolism, and the process of merging them took time. The Codex Usserianus Primus in Trinity College Library, Dublin, dates from around the year of Columba's death, and it looks more Coptic than Celtic. Here the scribe makes use of the cross in the form of the *Chi-Rho* symbol as so widely used in stone carvings. In the Book of Durrow the cross appears dominantly on a carpet-page (Fol. 1v), but it is a double-armed cross, and at a casual glance the page looks more like a Persian carpet than a Celtic manuscript and contrasts markedly with another carpet-page (Fol. 3v) which is entirely Celtic (or Hiberno-Saxon) and carries no Christian symbolism whatever. In the Durrow manuscript the imported elements of Saxon and Coptic are not yet fused with the Celtic, and this is interesting since the book seems to have been executed just after the Synod of Whitby, usually looked on as the turning-point in the fortunes of the Celtic church. The book's likely place of origin has been much disputed, but there seems no good reason to think it was not done in one of the Columban foundations, if not Durrow then perhaps Derry. In the books of Lichfield, Lindisfarne and Kells the cross forms a kind of ghostly feature of the carpet-page, always fancifully contorted to fit into the pattern. Never is Christ shown on the cross.

Representational painting does of course feature in the gospel-books, the more so as time passes and knowledge of iconography in the orthodox western world spreads. The evangelist symbols probably gave the scribes fewest problems: the man could be represented by an animal. It is fairly obvious there is a link here with carved animal symbols in the Pictish territories, at least some parts of which were being evangelised by successors of Columba. The lion symbol of St Mark in the Book of Durrow,

Lion of St Mark, Book of Durrow. Late 7th cent.
Trinity College, Dublin

for example, although at first sight it has a Saxon look, as if the artist were familiar with East Anglian jewellery such as the treasure found at Sutton Hoo, but the Sutton Hoo "lion" ulti-mately appears to derive from Pictish outline-pictures such as the wolf found at Ardross in Easter Ross, now happily reunited with its hindquarters in the museum at Inverness. Yet the Celtic scribe's model is plainly the Saxon piece, not the Pictish, because his lion has the stiffness and formality of the Sutton Hoo enamels. This gives us a significant chain of evidence. The Sutton Hoo treasure dates from about 650. The Ardross wolf is rather earlier. The Book of Durrow is dated to about 680. It is extraordinary how rapidly influences spread, so that a Pictish original could be imitated in the south-east of England, and the Saxon version imitated again in the area served by the Columban church, all within perhaps half a century.

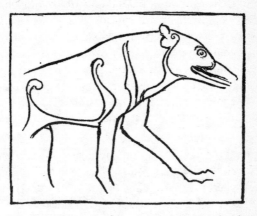

Wolf sculpture from Ardross. Pictish, 6th-7th cents. Inverness Museum

The most important evidence provided by this chain, however, is not of the speed of communications, but in its apparent corroboration of the view that the northern Picts at least had not been converted to the Christian faith even a century after Columba's mission. If the seventh-century Columban missionaries had been well established in the region around Brude's old capital, surely they would have been familiar with the marvellous animal carvings, and there would have been no need for the scribe of Durrow to have used as his model the rigid and very un-Celtic Saxon animal instead of a model much nearer home, and much nearer too to the traditional Celtic animal naturalism? If the sculptor could achieve such undulating, pulsating realism on stone, how much more easily could the scribe have done so with his sensitive brush on the sympathetic surface of smooth calf-skin? The swirling patterns on so many other pages of the gospel-book are proof that such a treatment came naturally to him. And likewise the superb eagle on the slab from the Knowe of Burrian in Orkney and the Burghead bulls from Morayshire find their way at second hand into other manuscripts. Orkney is supposed to have been evangelised; but as for northern Pictland in general, exchange of ideas with Iona and Ireland seems strangely poor if the Columban church were truly established there.

Much more at home with the animal symbols, scribes at first made few and tentative attempts to picture the evangelists themselves. Either the ancient aversion to anthropomorphism, the Celtic tradition of seeking for divinity in shapes other than human and reluctance to make gods resemble men except in vague and grotesque ways, or the awkwardness in depicting the human figure produced by this tradition, made the scribes shy of venturing to draw Christ or any man. It may even have embarrassed them to learn that man is made in the image of God, which is another way of saying that God is conceived in the shape of man. Man is the symbol of Matthew, so the Durrow scribe had to preface Matthew's gospel with a human figure, which is reduced to a flat area representing a mantle topped by a head and with two feeble feet attached to the hem. The fragment of a gospel-book dating from late in the seventh century preserved in the cathedral library at Durham (Fol. 38v) shows

Linch-pin, Wurttemberg. 4th-3rd cents. BC.
Landesmuseum, Stuttgart

that rare feature, a crucifixion scene, which the artist conceives not in realistic terms but as a piece of brooding symbolism, so that it seems to hark back to the fourth and third centuries BC, to Roquepertuse, even more to that sinister-looking metal linch-pin with its baleful eyes in the Landesmuseum at Stuttgart. The eyes of the Christ in the Durham manuscript stare at one with an almost hypnotic effect out of a foggy, yellow gloom not wholly, I am sure, the result of the ravages of time, and the undoubted power in this strange visage seems to me to be generated from the tradition of the Celtic head-cult images. The man-symbol of St Matthew in the gospel-book from Echternach in Luxembourg, now in Paris, has a body contrived entirely from decorative lobes—obligingly labelled *Imago Hominis*. The founder of Echternach was Willibrord, who came from Northumbria, but the book derives from the Irish school.

The supreme later manuscripts such as the Books of Lichfield, Lindisfarne and, above all, Kells, are not only artistic masterpieces but mirrors of their age, though we have to be cautious in interpreting what we see there. Doors are opening wide on the European scene, and the splendours of the court of Charlemagne have become both an inspiration and a challenge. The Kells "Christ attended by Angels" apparently fully reflects continental trends towards more realism: the scribe might well be observing the eleventh canon of the Council of Constantinople (692), which requires the painter of icons to show "the memory of Jesus living in the flesh". This group of manuscripts simply cannot be ignored by any historian attempting to assess the relations between the Roman and Columban churches.

However slow the effect of the Synod of Whitby on the church in Iona and Ireland, the impact of the Augustinian mission to Canterbury is marked in the manuscripts from outside this area. Eighth-century works like the Canterbury Psalter and the magnificent Codex Aureus reveal the lingering influence of the Irish school in some of their detail, but they are of continental inspiration, which is visible also in the Book of Lindisfarne, the Matthew figure of which seems totally alien to a Celtic scriptorium. Obviously there were radical changes on Lindisfarne after Whitby. It seems that Eadfrith wrote and decorated this great book before he became a bishop in 698, and although his training in the Columban school is manifest throughout, his familiarity with representational trends in the European schools is equally clear. This is in marked contrast to the Book of Kells.

Although beautifully done, the Kells Christ-figures are far away from the new continental realism, and pages like the great Incarnation Initial page are a triumphant reassertion of Irish devotion to the power of symbols. It is more or less contemporary with Lindisfarne, or at least it was in process of being done when the Vikings descended on Iona in 807, and features such as the canon-tables show the scribe was well aware of what was happening in Europe; but this book is the supreme example of the art of the Columban church and may well have been a conscious response and reaction to the advancing influence of Canterbury. It is a proud assertion of the Irish tradition by an artist who, in his field, has had no rivals. The artist is no longer bewildered by Mediterranean forms, and in the Christ-figures especially he has evolved a masterly compromise style of his own with finely executed head and stylised but credible draperies. But representation is subservient to symbolism in this dynamic visual poem witnessing to the faith of the man who created it. The strength of the all-embracing initial letter, boundless yet perfectly controlled, is central and majestic; and at the same time the jewelled imagery of the detail reflects the patient devotion of the artist and his simple delight in what he was doing. That pagan tradition is behind almost every square inch of the patterns matters nothing, for it is ceasing to be a backward glance and now involves a triumphant rededication to God.

If we were to assess the situation solely by the written chronicles, we might visualise the community of Iona at this time as the humbled, frightened remnant of a once-great church. We would be justified in thinking of the island as the refuge to which Colman and his followers had dejectedly retreated from Whitby, a refuge now threatened by the Northmen, terror of whom was driving the brethren back to Kells, there to complete their labours. But is there defeat or terror to be seen in those pages of "the Great Gospel of Columcille"? Columcille was dead two centuries before its completion, yet it is the fitting monument to his achievement.

No church is a spent force which can produce such a work of art.

Nor are manuscripts the only evidence in the field of the arts that the Celtic church did not go into decline after Whitby. The arts flourished too outside the scriptoria. Unhappily, on Iona the only stone monuments surviving from the time of the early church are two or three crosses, although it is believed many have perished. The finest is the St Martin's cross, although the Kildalton cross on neighbouring Islay might be reckoned even finer. Those crosses are just a little later than the Book of Kells, but they belong to the same epoch. In Columba's own lifetime the sculptors were far behind the scribes. Such monuments as there are in Ireland are rather rudely carved, and the influence of Whithorn is strong.

The first real sign of the development of a school of sculptors independent of the continental tradition, and reflecting the new monastic movement in Ireland, is the appearance of the interlaced ribbon pattern, deriving probably from Coptic Egypt, a good example of which is the Fahan Mura slab in Co. Donegal. Here the cross is entirely covered by interlace. Continental iconography makes itself felt, but the sculptors are ill-at-ease with it, and the figures flanking the Fahan Mura cross are crude in the extreme. There are some attempts to show the crucifixion, for example on a slab on Duvillaun island, Co. Mayo. In this case the Celtic element is limited to whorls outlining the body of Christ, but the artist is clearly unhappy with the rendering and probably also unhappy with the stone medium.

The scribes of the manuscripts were men like Columba himself, scholars, with a firm basis of foreign codices and psalters to build upon; whereas the sculptors were exploring a new dimension, with no guide-lines, and were faced with innumerable technical problems as well as the artistic problem of the human figure. The man who made the gilt-bronze Crucifixion plaque from Athlone, now in the National Museum in Dublin, employed a traditional medium and therefore had much more success. Here the head of Christ has unashamedly Celtic features, and the breast is covered with La Tène spirals executed with spirit and comparable with work on contemporary manuscripts. Where the real challenge to the sculptor lay was in how best to express the traditional restlessness, the dynamic sense of movement, in

Detail, bronze Crucifixion plaque from Athlone. 8th cent. National Museum of Ireland

a stubborn medium which gave no encouragement to fluid concepts to which bronze or ink on parchment lent themselves so readily. Not until he began to master three-dimensional designs in the eighth century did he learn how to translate his usual eloquence into stone. When this happens the foreign anthropomorphic challenge recedes, and he is able to marry Christian symbolism to pagan with powerful effect. The old lore creeps in too. Aquatic birds roost neatly on the arms of the cross, as they do on the slabs on Iniskeel, Co. Donegal, and on the Drumhallagh slab the flanking "angels" become, as Dr Henry has suggested, Finn-mac-Cool biting his "thumb of wisdom" in order to see hidden things.

The ultimate achievement in stone is the great high cross unique to the area under the influence of the Columban church. The high cross of Ireland is one of the most impressive monuments of Christendom, and this not only for its beauty but for it sheer symbolic power. In preferring the cross to the crucifix the Celt, to my mind, not only showed superior taste but also, as might be expected, a better understanding of the psychology of symbolism than his Mediterranean rival artists. The classical obsession with the human figure led to an emphasis on the countenance and body of Christ which produced insoluble problems for the artist. The Irish sculptor simplified the issue. He thought in terms of instant impact in wide-open spaces. Outline meant everything and iconography must be accommodated to it, and in itself was formal and symbolic. At Moone in Co. Kildare the Twelve Apostles become Celtic godlings who would not be out of place in pagan southern Gaul, and even those are reduced to a relief pattern. The crosses at Ahenny and Kilkenny are monuments of immense strength and must have struck awe into beholders when darkly silhouetted against dawn or dusk, and wonder when in the slanting rays of the summer sun their exquisite relief decoration comes alive. There is no Christ stretched on those crosses. Perhaps the huge ring, the "wheel", represents a halo, leaving the spectator to complete the agonised visage in his mind. The five bosses could stand for the body and limbs of Christ, as I am sure they do. Perhaps the most moving aspect of the raising of those great crosses is that they coincide with the first descents of the Northmen, with what the church called the "red martyrdom", so that they seem to be a rallying-call of the faith, and a rallying-call couched in the ancient language of symbols.

There has been reference (Chapter VII) to the appearance of the cross on Pictish sculptured slabs about the time of King Nechton's approach to Northumbria for instruction in Roman practices. Can we learn anything about what was happening by examining the form of cross adopted by the sculptors in Pictland? It is noticeable in the first place that the wheel-cross familiar to us as the Irish form is anticipated by the Picts in relief-carvings on the slabs. Plainly the idea came from southern sculptors and illuminators, although the Picts made it very much their own. Did the Picts, then, influence the Irish sculptors, perhaps through Iona? R. B. K. Stevenson believes they did, and it would be difficult not to accept this theory. The Pictish and Dalriadic kingdoms merged and their union was consolidated by the Viking threat, which made the island vulnerable, the heart of Pictland preferable as a refuge from the raiders. Pictland also provided an avenue to the south, and the Picts were much less averse to southern influence than the Irish. They came to enjoy illustrating Biblical themes as much as they did the hunting scenes traditional among them. Their supreme achievement is the St Andrews sarcophagus, virtually a classical piece executed by a man with a totally

XIV

The Coming of the Northmen

The longships of the Northmen faced the Columban church with a crisis far more shattering than its defeat at the Synod of Whitby 130 years earlier. The humiliation and retreat of Colman and his monks was not the end of Iona. The last chapter gave a brief outline of the Golden Age of Christian Celtic art, proof enough of spiritual and intellectual vigour generated by the church to challenge the view of so many historians that Whitby had been its death-blow. Eventually Iona conformed to the Roman Easter and the Roman tonsure, but it continued to preside over the main body of Irish Christians, and the saint venerated was Columba rather than Peter. I have dealt at some length with the art of the period because among the Celts the artist provides us with the main material evidence and insights about what was going on in his time. His work mirrors the spirit and temper of the people, for we cannot doubt it found eager response among them, and at the same time it is sensitive to the influence of the wider world, as Celtic art has always been. It may be objected the great gospel-books were luxury works, destined for the altar, but they are only the apex of a massive pyramid of achievement. Such a pyramid is unlikely to be reared by a society in decline, even if that society is rent by feuds and violence, a condition endemic with the Celts. Whitby made little apparent mark on that society. The coming of the Northmen was another matter.

The importance of the Irish Sea as a highway and as a link between Ireland, Scotland, Wales and western England has been mentioned. But it was also a seaway right into the heart of the Celtic west, exposing it to enemies who knew how to handle ships and fight them, which the Northmen certainly did. There is a common belief those marauders were mere pirates, that their main purpose was pillage and looting. If they had been no more than that they might have been contained, for the Celts were fierce fighters too, but those foraying longships were spearheads of a great expansionist movement. Their homelands were no

The Oseberg Ship, Oslo. From photo
by author

ruder than the lands they pillaged, as one may see in the Scandinavian museums. The Northmen were primarily a trading people, whose trade-routes ranged from Iceland to the Volga, and their ultimate aim in descending on Britain was colonisation and trade. Denmark in particular was under pressure from Charlemagne, whose armies had reached the Elbe and dominated the coasts of Frisia, and it is just possible their violence towards the monastic settlements of Northumbria, Scotland and Ireland may have been in part revenge for what their families had suffered at the hands of the mighty Christian King of the Franks.

The fact that the invaders wanted to found settlements made their descents systematic and therefore more dangerous, and they brought horses to enable them to drive deep inland. The two halves of Dalriada were thrown apart. Iona's hegemony over the church in the north of Ireland became precarious. Kells had to take over the responsibility, and the symbol of this transfer of power was the sending of the "Great Gospel of Columcille", the Book of Kells, from Iona to be completed in the scriptorium of the monastery ever after identified with it (814).

However high in honour and esteem Iona remained, it became for a time at least little more than a nominal holy place. The sacking of the island set the fates of Ireland and Scotland on separate paths.

Island monastic settlements were defenceless against the Vikings, even those in sheltered valleys inland were sacked. Authorities in Scandinavia, like Professor Almgren at Uppsala, have proved by actual experiments how open longships were capable of transporting a special small breed of horses as well as strong war-parties, so the striking power of the invaders was high. As to desecration, whether vengeful or mere savagery, the Vikings seem to have made a special point of this. It was more than a matter of destruction: the wife of Thorgeis, the sea-king, is said to have proclaimed spells at the high altar in Armagh. But loot provided a major objective too, and the museums of Scandinavia, particularly Norway, provide evidence of the rich store of metalwork, silver and bronze utensils, in the Celtic monasteries. Recovered from Viking graves, most of it has been broken up. This loot, together with surviving Norse names around the Irish Sea, points clearly to Norwegian Vikings, not Danes, as the earliest raiders. The fact that the Hebrides were formerly known as the Sudreys indicates they were colonised by people much further north. The Danes—the *Dubh-ghaill*, Black Strangers, as distinct from the *Finn-ghaill*, the fair ones—do not appear until they attack Dublin in 850, and Danes and Norwegians held one another in bitter hostility. The Irish *tuatha*, as always themselves divided, seem to have had an understanding for a time with the newcomers, as they got from them an offering of gold and silver for the church; but the two sorts of invader joined forces a year or two later.

Despite chronic strife among the Irish, the Norse were never to conquer the country as a whole. They were not able to do more than establish coastal settlements, which grew into towns. Most of Ireland's coastal towns today from Dublin to Limerick were Norse settlements and were probably used in the main as trading-posts, but also possibly as advance bases for attacks on the fringes of the Frankish empire, where rivers such as Seine and Loire rendered towns like Nantes and even Paris vulnerable. The impact on the church, however, was far more severe. Between them, the booty found in Norway together with the records of the time present a melancholy picture and indicate decimation of the great Columban foundations and of the cultural activity carried on by them.

How does one read the situation from the evidence of surviving art objects? It has been calculated that the metalwork from eight-century Ireland now in Norwegian museums comprises about half of what has survived, but the average quality of the work suggests the churches were quite handsomely provided. Raiders had no use for manuscripts, which were either destroyed or taken away by the monks and hidden. There is much less metalwork from the following century, the ninth. In part this may be due to the Vikings becoming established in their Irish bases, when they would not take the loot back to their homes in Norway. What they possessed in Dublin, Cork or Limerick, whether Irish work or rich merchandise from the continent or the East, would be less safe than if taken back to Norway and buried with their dead, because those towns were often sacked and burned by their enemies.

Ninth-century metalwork shows a slight falling-off in quality, though skilled craftsmen evidently were still available. What is of high significance is that as time passes traditional Celtic decoration and symbolism become more and more interwoven with Scandinavian styles. There are clear indications that the one-time "pirates" were being won over to the Christian faith, as it is impossible to believe the church would have sanctioned such wholesale dominance of Norwegian motifs if the Vikings were continuing to desecrate their holy places. The ancient genius of the Celt for absorbing material from other peoples and marrying it to his own traditions is clearly illustrated in this period; yet with the coming of the early middle ages metalwork reflects how completely the Norse incomers must have been absorbed by the Irish. Indeed the injection of foreign blood and ideas produced a renaissance out of which came such splendid things as the Clonmacnoise crozier, the cross of Cong, the shrine of St Patrick's bell. Not least among those late pieces influenced by the incomers is the *Cumdach* or shrine of the *Cathach* itself. This elaborate piece basically dates from the latter part of the eleventh century. It is metal-clad, the bronze at one time probably covered with gold foil. The upper portion was altered in the fourteenth century, but the panels on the sides are enmeshed in Scandinavian ornament, in a style transitional between the styles known as Ringerike and Urnes, the second marked by inter-coiling monsters, although these have not fully emerged on the *Cumdach* of the *Cathach*, nor yet on the shrine of the *Misach*, also associated with Columba. Both pieces could well have originated in the Columban monastery of Kells, where those Scandinavian modes seem to have been fostered. Foreign accent or no, this renaissance of the metalworkers' art appears to indicate a re-surgence in the Irish church.

The high crosses perhaps reflect the situation more clearly. They retain a certain amount of traditional decoration, but at least by the tenth century there is a new attitude to figure sculp-ture. At last the language of symbolism is seen to be yielding to the language of pictorial representation. The crucifixion is becoming established, although Christ is a tiny figure confined to the junction of shaft and cross-piece. Biblical scenes appear in panels on the shaft. High crosses like those of Muiredach at Monasterboice and that of the Scriptures at Clonmacnoise are monuments of great power; but just as the concession to realism weakens them aesthetically, by comparison for example with the North Cross at Ahenny, so also does it seem to imply a change of attitude in the community, both the priesthood and the general populace, which points to a weakening not perhaps of faith in Christianity but in their own native traditions. There is a vigour, a spontaneity at Ahenny not present in the figured crosses, at least to my mind, imitating as those do the iconography of far-off, alien peoples with whom the sculptor has no background in common. Has the language of the symbol lost its power? It may well be that, as Dr Henry has suggested, the Viking threat itself could be responsible: that it shows a cleaving to orthodox Christian practice under the desperate threat of pagan sacrilege, that the "pictures" are anguished borrowings from the Bible of examples of divine intervention in the face of danger, as the portrayal of Daniel in the lions' den. Those figure crosses leave us with the feeling the Celtic church no longer felt spiritually confident in itself, and that its artists were grasping at such straws as imported Carolingian ivories to help make their points. Some of the scenes shown can be interpreted as abject to the degree of betrayal. Dr Henry stresses the Fall of Simon Magus as illustrated on the Tall cross at Monasterboice and the Market cross at Kells as specially significant, because the tonsure of Simon is said to be the same as the tonsure of Columba himself, and St Peter is depicted aiding the downfall of Simon by jabbing him with his crozier.

The church did not change its organisation. It retained the old monastic pattern, monasteries ruled by *co-arbs*, who were successors of the founder, in certain cases such as Derry, Columba himself. The office of *co-arb* had a family or clan connotation. Each monastery still served the *tuath* by which its lands had been granted originally; but as it grew in wealth the spirit of it altered, and moreover, as the De Paors have noted, Norse Christians in the new townships were opposed to their church being dominated by the *co-arbs* with their tribal associations. In fact, those converts proved a Trojan horse to the Celtic faithful. By the eleventh century the towns were sending priests to Canterbury. The priests came back as bishops, and in no time Canterbury attempted to assert its superiority and pressed the King of Munster, Muircertach, to regularise the appointment of bishops and generally to reform the church. At the beginning of the twelfth century the church was put on a diocesan basis under bishops headed by two archbishops, a major blow at the hegemony of the monasteries, and soon continental orders, initially the Cistercians, were having abbeys built for them or were occupying the monasteries. Yet the old order offered stubborn resistance. The Columbans in particular clung to their ancient traditions, apparently even to preserving an oak grove at Derry which, some years after it had become an episcopal see, was devastated by a storm which must have disturbed deeply the faithful in the town. Flathbertach, head of the order and successor of Columcille, had immense support, and despite the changes was granted the right of being a non-territorial bishop of the traditional kind.

The arts of the time do seem to reflect this mood of opposition to change. Look again at the *Cumdach* (book-shrine) of the Stowe

Angel, *Cumdach* of the Stowe
Missal. 11th cent. National
Museum of Ireland

Missal, made at Clonmacnoise about the middle of the eleventh century, and now in the National Museum in Dublin. The craftsman, at this time a layman, has resorted to the ancient hunting scenes, with stag and hounds, and the animals have the haunch-whorls shown on Pictish carvings, while some figures of priests and bishops have heads which seem to have an even longer pagan ancestry behind them. Norse pagan tradition is also introduced, for the intertwined animal ornament on some metalwork and also in stone-carvings such as the sarcophagus at Cashel originates in this. To some extent those may be evidence merely of artistic conservatism and archaism. Yet late though they are I believe there is also an element of pagan superstition, to put it no higher, very much alive in the artist and in the community he served. After all, such feelings are not dead in Ireland or the western Highlands to this day.

The apparent dearth of fine manuscripts after the climax of the Book of Kells is not entirely due to losses by destruction or to their being hidden by the scribes. We have to look for them in the monasteries and libraries of Europe. Monks fleeing from the threatened monasteries of Ireland took with them as many of their books as they could carry to their places of refuge in Charlemagne's Frankish empire. Charlemagne was only too eager to welcome those holy men with their vast reputation for learning, and many went to the Irish foundations like St Gall and Bobbio. These later monks were not of course missionaries as their predecessors such as Columbanus had been. They were rather scholars, and they found at the Carolingian court the patronage they needed. Their presence on the continent re-dounded to the lasting fame of Ireland, but their learning turned away from the Celtic world of the islands and the northern valleys and glens, from Columba's world, and eagerly went to work to revive the world of Greece and Rome. Men such as Sedulius Scottus and Johannes Scottus Erigena were classical scholars unsurpassed in Europe, and the philosophy of the last put him far in advance of his age. A simple and uncomplicated faith no longer occupied their minds. Erigena's great work, *De Divisione Naturae*, is described by Pope Honorius III as "swarming with worms of heretical perversity". Those voluntary exiles looked back on Ireland as a place of fear where neither Christianity nor culture could survive.

However, as sometimes happens in places which exiles look back upon as lost, out of the chaos a new promise began to emerge.

It is surprising that the remaining high crosses of Dalriada, the St Martin's cross and the fragmented St John's cross on Iona, now replaced by a replica, and the beautiful Kildalton cross on Islay, belong to the Viking period. They are of the early ninth century, yet in 801 the Vikings burned down the monastery and a few years later, in 805, 68 monks died in "red martyrdom" on the sands of what is now known as Martyr's Bay. Stone-carving is a laborious art, and such prominent monuments could not be hastily hidden when the longships were sighted. Yet there were said to be many more crosses on Iona. It is the succession of raids which led to the transfer of the primacy to Kells, and with it the unfinished "Great Gospel of Columcille", which Dr Henry thinks may have been planned by the abbot himself, Connachtach, who died in 802. It is interesting that the St Martin's cross shows the Virgin and Child with angels, a motif unrepresented on Irish crosses but occurring in the Book of Kells, hinting at a common origin—perhaps a painting in the monastery's possession, as Dr Henry suggests.

Further murderous descents followed. The body of Columba was taken from its grave and carried over to Ireland, but Iona was not abandoned and in 818 the shrine of the saint returned to the island, to a new stone monastery on a site more secure than the previous one, brought by the abbot, Diarmaid. Skene surmises the relics would be placed on the south side of the altar. But in 825 the Vikings were back again. Blathmac, acting for the absent abbot Diarmaid, rallied his monks and tried to defend the altar, but all were slaughtered. It seems Blathmac knew the attack threatened and exhorted his people to "arm themselves with courage", as they were faced by certain death. First, however, he took the precaution of removing the shrine of Columba to a grave which he covered with sods. Some of the brethren, knowing it was the precious metalwork the Norsemen were looking for, begged Blathmac to give up the shrine, but he refused and was cut to pieces. In 831 Diarmaid took the relics to Ireland again, and they are believed to have been placed with the remains of St Patrick and St Brigid in a church at Down, by Strangford Lough.

Yet in a sense the mounting threat of the Northmen helped to bring about something which Columba had begun. Not Ireland and Dalriada only were in peril, but so also was Alba. The Norse grip on Ireland and the Hebrides prevented the Dalriad Scots from drawing strength from their motherland in the west, and at the same time their old enemy the Picts realised the danger threatened them also. The piratical raids were seen for what they were, the expansion of Scandinavian power, a power now extending as far as the Mediterranean. And hardened by the hammer-blows of Norse and Danes and Saxons, strong men were arising in what was to become England, men who themselves grew to threaten the divided peoples of Alba, which had become isolated. Picts and Scots could no longer afford to remain enemies. There had to be a union. This came about in 844, when Kenneth MacAlpine, his father a Scot of Dalriada, his mother a Pictish princess, claimed through his mother by the Pictish law of succession the throne of the Picts. So that in the moment of crisis, when Columba's ambition for his kindred in Dalriada seemed doomed, when the saint's own bones were being hid first here then there for fear of plundering pagans, a Scot of his race, of the blood of the Cinel Conaill Gulban, mounted the throne of a new Scoto-Pictish nation. At once this Kenneth made his power felt. Six times he led an army into Lothian and beyond, throwing back the Angles of Northumbria and the Britons of Strathclyde. He had begun to shape a nation and to give it some sort of identity.

Kenneth did not forget the debt of his nation to Columba. A Pictish king, Constantine, had built a church at Dunkeld in the heart of Fortrenn. Kenneth seems to have rebuilt it and brought there some, no doubt as many as he could find, of Columba's relics. This was an act of high significance. Where the saint's relics lay, there was his church. Iona continued to be sacred ground, but the island had been ravaged so often it could exercise no function as a mother-church nor preside over the "family". Dunkeld itself was not beyond the reach of those highly mobile Vikings, but it offered much more security than an island virtually under Norse domination. In 850 Tuathal was installed as Abbot of Dunkeld and, presumably, *co-arb* or successor to Columba, but he also became territorial Bishop of Fortrenn and of the southern Picts. He was in effect primate of the Columban church in Scotland; and although the use of the word *primus* in the *Annals of Ulster* may simply mean he was first in the line rather than titular head, head of the church he was in fact. Such abbeys and monasteries from which Columban clergy had been driven were again given to Columban monks, among them Abernethy, a Columban foundation. Skene suggests it was at this time the round tower was built, an Irish type of building the only other Scottish example of which is at Brechin, but the Abernethy tower is probably tenth century. Such towers served as refuges from enemies, but as their Celtic name *cloictech* indicates they were primarily belltowers and a monk would rally the faithful by ringing his bronze hand-bell from the topmost window.

It is here in the "waist" of Scotland that the new nation was forged. Here is the territory Aidan had disputed with the Picts, now both temporal and spiritual heart of the combined kingdom. Not far to the east is the battlefield of Nechtonsmere, where the Picts had put an end to Anglian penetration, and it has been suggested Restennet Priory may have been built to commemorate the victory, ironically, by the Saxon builders sent from Northumbria at Nechton's invitation: in fact that Restennet is, or was, a battle-abbey. But from the ninth century on into the early middle ages the church of the emerging nation of Scotland was the church of Columba, the Celtic church, despite concessions to conformity such as Roman tonsure and diocesan bishops. The much-disputed Culdees appear to have been a dominant element in the clergy of the time. It was Boece at the Reformation, maintaining the Culdees were survivors of the "pure" Celtic church, who is probably primarily responsible for an attempt to graft the reformed church of Scotland on to the ancient Columban church, a contention not altogether abandoned even today although Bishop Reeves a century ago showed it to be untenable. The Culdees were a monastic order, both in Ireland and in Scotland, but especially important in Scotland, and they seem to have performed the duties of secular canons. Abernethy, Brechin and Dunkeld were among their centres; so also was Monymusk in Aberdeenshire, from which the reliquary takes its name.

Our picture of this last phase of the church of Columba is dim, and it is difficult to sharpen it much from the evidence of material remains. The same period in Ireland has left much more behind it, for the round towers alone there number several score and can be called a typical feature of the older landscape. Some of the ecclesiastical structures in Scotland must have been stone-built, but little has survived. The Brechin round tower gives us one of the few glimpses into the obscurity. In the first place, since the Picts did not build such towers, it points to a renewed thrust of Irish influence, as Abernethy does. This is emphasised by the stone-carving above the doorway at Brechin, which shows a crucifixion scene, by now common in Ireland yet absent from Pictish sculpture. It is flanked by two priests, one carrying the tau-headed pastoral staff used by the Copts in Egypt, the other a characteristic Celtic crozier, or *bachuil*.

Priests like those carved at Brechin must have possessed ritual objects other than the staffs the sculptor has given them. The richness of Irish ecclesiastical metalwork has been mentioned, and surviving examples such as the cross of Cong and the croziers and book-shrines and bell-shrines are too technically excellent not to have been matched by many other beautiful things of the kind. It is unlikely Scotland was as well-endowed, yet the few objects there are indicate the link with Irish tradition had not been entirely broken. The bronze crook of the St Fillan's crozier in the Scottish National Museum of Antiquities has rivet-holes which suggest it may have looked like the crozier of the Dysert O'Dea monastery. It belongs to the eleventh century. The rather splendid silver-gilt case made to contain it is as late as the four-teenth century, though rather Carolingian in style, yet betrays a lingering hint of Irish feeling; but more important is the strong Irish keepership tradition associated with it, for there is a record of 1428 stating that the office of custodian of the relic had been conferred by the saint himself *in perpetuo* on an ancestor of one Finlay Jore, later called Dewar, of Strathfillan in Fortrenn, and this office continued faithfully in the Dewar family until one of them emigrated to Canada. The crozier returned across the Atlantic to the National Museum in Edinburgh a century ago. Heritable custody of this sort, whether of a crozier or of an office such as *co-arb*, is wholly in the Irish and Columban tradition.

A very few hand-bells such as priests used in the bell-towers have survived, but they are beaten out of sheet-bronze and are undecorated, so it is difficult to date them. One is in what may be its original locality: the bell of St Eunan, in a little kirk perched on the hill of Tom Eunan by the village of Kincraig, where the Spey flows through Loch Inch. There is a legend that it was carried off, but in the Drumochter Pass a few miles south it is said to have called out its name and flown back to its church. Tom Eunan means Hill of Adomnán, so there may well have been a Columban oratory on the site of the present kirk. Many of those bells were later encased in bell-shrines, as happened to the bell known as St Patrick's in Ireland. Two such shrines survive in Scotland, both now in the National Museum. They are medieval, with crucifixion scenes, but they carry on the Celtic tradition of veneration for the bell of a saint, and one of them was found in 1814 buried in a heap of stones near Kilmichael-Glassary, right in the heart of what had been Dalriada. No part of Scotland has been so permeated by feeling for Columba, which indeed lives on to this day on the western seaboard.

The most remarkable visual evidence of the persistence of this feeling lies in the sculptured stones of the West Highlands, dating from the fourteenth and fifteenth centuries. As the authors of a recent authoritative book on the subject state (K. A. Steer and J. W. M. Bannerman: *Late Medieval Monumental Sculpture in the West Highlands*), the key to the distribution of those remarkable sculptures is to be found in the fact that this was the ancient Lordship of the Isles, rather than in any lingering influence of the Celtic church; but on the other hand the school or schools of sculptors sprang up in that part of Scotland where there were relics of Irish art, many more then than now, and the Lordship of the Isles had roots in Hiberno-Norse culture. The largest concentration of those monuments is on Iona. Obviously the reason for this is that Iona continued to be sacred ground, and that for centuries the rulers of Scotland and Ireland, even of Norway, were eager to be associated with it and were sometimes buried there. Steer and Bannerman argue this art is Celtic only in the sense it was done by Celtic craftsmen who showed certain inherited qualities, such as fondness for interlace ornament. They underline the Romanesque sources of the decoration. It is, of course, absolutely right to emphasise this. The sensitive, living qualities of the best Christian Celtic art, derived from a pagan heritage, are not really present in those West Highland stones. But the phrase "certain inherited qualities" must be understood as covering not merely motifs like interlace but, more importantly, certain more profound qualities such as unerring taste and, above all, the feeling for symbolism as medium of communication. The Iona stones, like those in Oronsay priory or the church at Kilmory in Knapdale, have their quota of warrior-effigies in

Grave-slab with claymore. Prob. 15th cent. Kilmory, Knapdale. After Drummond

the medieval manner, but the really memorable monuments rely on symbols to commemorate the dead. Can anything be more descriptive than the portrait of a fighting sword—sometimes the *claidheamhmor*, the true claymore itself—associated with a galley with furled sail? This, in its way, is the language of the Battersea shield, or of the carpet-pages of the gospel-books, a visual form of bardic poetry. When the sculptor departs from this and attempts a more realistic rendering, as on the slab commemorating Bricius MacKinnon on Iona, what he has to say loses in the telling even if we do learn more about the arms and armour of the period.

It seems appropriate to end this book by coming back full cycle to the little shrine with which it began: the Monymusk reliquary. Its history, so far as this is known, is well worth completing.

In the first chapter it is mentioned that the reliquary has another name, the Brecbennoch of Columba. *Brec* or *breac* means a shrine, and *bennoch* blessed, so that this reliquary's ancient title is the Blessed Shrine of Columba. It may have no more certain association with the saint than some of the churches named after him. The first four centuries of its story are lost, but it emerges from the long obscurity as an object of such sanctity and importance that it is difficult to avoid the conclusion that it had special meaning for the early Celtic church and probably was preserved and venerated in one of the Culdee centres, possibly Dunkeld, to which Columban relics are believed to have been taken for safety from Iona. It resembles so closely the other Irish shrines that it must have been brought from the west, and it is so richly wrought that it can only have contained something of the highest significance. The earliest known reference to it in the records occurs before the year 1211. King William the Lion built a monastery at Arbroath (Aberbrothock), the monastery where in fact he was to be buried, and he gave the monks there the custody of the Brecbennoch. With it he gave the lands of Forglen, "given to God and to St Columba and to the Brecbennoch", and this the king did in return for the duty of service in the army with the Brecbennoch. In short he perpetuated the ancient Celtic custom, requiring the druids to accompany the king to war, later the abbots of monasteries for which the king had granted land. It may have been in this capacity that Columba marched with the men of his clan, as I suggested in describing the battle of Cul Dreimne. Dr Joseph Anderson deduced from the charter of William the Lion that the lands of Forglen must have been granted to Columba, and he points out the church there is dedicated to Adomnán. He deems it "nowise improbable" the the reliquary therefore may already have been at Forglen. Now we know that Bernard, the Abbot of Arbroath a century later, was with King Robert the Bruce at the battle of Bannockburn. He must have been performing the service enjoined upon his monastery by William, and we can assume he stood on the fateful field carrying the Brecbennoch, the thong attached to its handles slung around his neck, thus invoking the blessing of Columba on the Scottish army. Did he carry it "thrice sunways" around that army, as tradition demanded the *Cathach*, the Battler, be carried around the army of Columba's clan? Probably not, for such a ritual could scarcely have escaped mention in the records. Abbot Bernard may have had less stomach for a fight than the redoubtable Columba, because a few months after the battle he relinquished his responsibility by giving the lands of Forglen to Malcolm of Monymusk, with them presumably the Brecbennoch on the understanding Malcolm and his heirs should perform the military service in the name of the abbot "as often as occasion shall arise". Thus the Grants of Monymusk—itself, it will be remembered a one-time Culdee settlement—became hereditary keepers of the Brecbennoch. It remained at Monymusk, though the lands associated with it were disposed of to other families, and it was still at Monymusk when Dr Anderson read his paper on Celtic reliquaries to the Society of Antiquaries of Scotland in 1910.

We can never know what the reliquary contained. The book-shrines and the bell-shrines take the shape of the relic itself, and so does the shrine of St Lachlan's arm in Dublin, but the Brecbennoch is just a tiny oratory—if the artist of the Book of Kells pictured the Temple at Jerusalem in precisely the same form. It could have contained anything. Might it have been a fragment of the saint's own oratory on Iona? Was it a handful of dust from the floor of his cell where his holy feet had trodden? We may conclude that whatever it contained was something very personal to Columba, or was believed to be.

Bibliography

This list is selected for the general reader and includes no references to papers in learned journals or proceedings of societies

Allen, J. Romilly: *The Early Christian Monuments of Scotland.* Edinburgh, 1903

Almgren, Bertil: *The Viking.* Gothenburg, 1966

Anderson, A. O. and M. O.: *Adomnán's Life of Columba.* London, 1961

Anderson, Joseph: *Scotland in Early Christian Times.* Edinburgh, 1881

Anson, Peter F.: *The Call of the Desert.* London, 1964

Argyll, 8th Duke of: *Iona.* 1884

Bannerman, J. W. M.: *Studies in the History of Dalriada.* Edinburgh, 1974

Bede, The Venerable: *The Ecclesiastical History of the English Nation.* Var. editions

Bulloch, J.: *The Life of the Celtic Church.* Edinburgh, 1903

Brøndsted, Johannes: *The Vikings.* London, 1960

Byrne, Francis J.: *Irish Kings and High Kings.* London, 1973

Chadwick, H. M.: *Early Scotland.* Cambridge, 1949

Chadwick, Norah: *The Age of the Saints in the Early Christian Church.* London, 1961

— *Celtic Britain.* London, 1963

— *The Celts.* London, 1971

Cruden, Stuart: *The Early Christian and Pictish Monuments of Scotland.* HMSO official guide. Edinburgh, 1964

De Paor, Maire and Liam: *Early Christian Ireland.* London, 1958

Dillon, Myles, and Chadwick, Norah: *The Celtic Realms.* London, 1967

Drummond, James: *Sculptured Monuments of Iona and the West Highlands*. Edinburgh, 1881

Duke, John A.: *The Columban Church*. London, 1932, and Edinburgh, 1950

— *History of the Church of Scotland to the Reformation*. Edinburgh, 1937

Finlay, Ian: *Celtic Art: An Introduction*. London and New York, 1973

Henderson, Isabel: *The Picts*. London, 1967

Henry, Françoise: *Irish Art*. 3 vols. London, 1965, 1967 and 1970

Hughes, Kathleen: *Early Christian Ireland: Introduction to the Sources*. London, 1972.

Huyshe, Wentworth: *The Life of St Columba (Adomnán)*. London, 1905

Lethbridge, T. C.: *The Painted Men*. London, 1954

MacCana, Proinsias: *Celtic Mythology*. London, 1970

M'Lauchlan, Thomas: *The Early Scottish Church*. Edinburgh, 1865

McNaught, J. C.: *The Celtic Church and the See of Peter*. Oxford, 1927

McNeill, F. Marian: *Iona*. London and Glasgow, 1920

Mahr, Adolf: *Christian Art in Ancient Ireland*. Vol. I. Dublin, 1932

Menzies, Lucy: *Saint Columba of Iona*. London, 1920

Nordenfalk, Carl: *Celtic and Anglo-Saxon Painting*. London, 1977

Ó Ríordáin, Seán P.: *The Genesis of the Celtic Cross*. Cork, 1947

Piggott, Stuart: *The Druids*. London, 1968

Powell, T. G. E.: *The Celts*. London, 1958

Raftery, Joseph: *Christian Art in Ancient Ireland*. Vol. II. Dublin, 1941

Reeves, W.: *The Life of St Columba (Adomnán)*. Edinburgh, 1874

Ross, Anne: *Pagan Celtic Britain*. London, 1967

Ryan, J.: *Irish Monasticism*. Dublin and Cork, 1931

Simpson, W. Douglas: *The Historical St Columba*. Aberdeen, 1927

— *The Celtic Church in Scotland*. Aberdeen, 1935

Skene, W. F.: *Celtic Scotland*. 3 vols. Edinburgh, 1886

Steer, K. A., and Bannerman, J. W. M.: *Late Medieval Monumental Sculpture in the West Highlands*. Edinburgh, 1975

Stuart, John: *The Sculptured Stones of Scotland*. 2 vols. Aberdeen, 1856, and Edinburgh, 1867

Sullivan, Edward: *The Book of Kells*. London, 1914

Thomas, Charles: *The Early Christian Archaeology of North Britain*. Glasgow, 1971

Index

Authors of main early source material, such as Adomnán, Bede and Cuimine, are not indexed as such, as they are quoted repeatedly throughout. Saints are indexed as "Columba" or "Patrick". Numbers in brackets indicate the drawings in the text.

Other titles in the SCOTTISH COLLECTION

THE BRAVE WHITE FLAG *James Allan Ford*

THE LAST SUMMER *Iain Crichton Smith*

THE SCOTTISH COLLECTION OF VERSE
VOL 1 to 1800 *Ed Eileen Dunlop & Antony Kamm*

THE FIRST HUNDRED THOUSAND *Ian Hay*

DUST ON THE PAW *Robin Jenkins*

THE MERRY MUSE *Eric Linklater*

MAGNUS *George Mackay Brown*

THE BULL CALVES *Naomi Mitchison*

EARLY IN ORCADIA *Naomi Mitchison*

THE CHINA RUN *Neil Paterson*

WHERE THE SEA BREAKS *John Prebble*

A GREEN TREE IN GEDDE *Alan Sharp*

TIME WILL KNIT *Fred Urquhart*

WALK DON'T WALK *Gordon Williams*

SCOTTISH BIOGRAPHIES

BURRELL: PORTRAIT OF A COLLECTOR *Richard Marks*

AS IT WAS (Autobiography) *Naomi Mitchison*